Climate and Capital in the Age of Petroleum

Climate and Capital in the Age of Petroleum

Locating Terminal Landscapes

Jeff Diamanti

BLOOMSBURY ACADEMIC
LONDON • NEW YORK • OXFORD • NEW DELHI • SYDNEY

BLOOMSBURY ACADEMIC
Bloomsbury Publishing Plc
50 Bedford Square, London, WC1B 3DP, UK
1385 Broadway, New York, NY 10018, USA
29 Earlsfort Terrace, Dublin 2, Ireland

BLOOMSBURY, BLOOMSBURY ACADEMIC and the Diana logo are trademarks of
Bloomsbury Publishing Plc

First published in Great Britain 2021
This paperback edition published in 2023

Copyright © Jeff Diamanti, 2021

Jeff Diamanti has asserted his right under the Copyright, Designs and Patents Act, 1988, to
be identified as author of this work.

For legal purposes the Acknowledgments on p. ix constitute an extension
of this copyright page.

Cover design by Charlotte Daniels
Cover image © Natascha Libbert Fotografie

All rights reserved. No part of this publication may be reproduced or transmitted
in any form or by any means, electronic or mechanical, including photocopying,
recording, or any information storage or retrieval system, without prior
permission in writing from the publishers.

Bloomsbury Publishing Plc does not have any control over, or responsibility for, any
third-party websites referred to or in this book. All internet addresses given in
this book were correct at the time of going to press. The author and publisher
regret any inconvenience caused if addresses have changed or sites have
ceased to exist, but can accept no responsibility for any such changes.

A catalogue record for this book is available from the British Library.

Library of Congress Cataloging-in-Publication Data

Names: Diamanti, Jeff, editor.
Title: Climate and capital in the age of petroleum : locating terminal
landscapes / Jeff Diamanti [editor].
Description: New York, NY : Bloomsbury Academic, 2021. | Includes
bibliographical references and index. |
Identifiers: LCCN 2020055567 (print) | LCCN 2020055568 (ebook) |
ISBN 9781350191839 (hardback) | ISBN 9781350191846 (ebook) |
ISBN 9781350191853 (epub)
Subjects: LCSH: Petroleum industry and trade—Environmental aspects. |
Petroleum industry and trade—Social aspects. |
Capitalism—Environmental aspects. | Capitalism—Social aspects.
Classification: LCC HD9560.5 .C5677 2021 (print) | LCC HD9560.5 (ebook) |
DDC 338.2/728—dc23
LC record available at https://lccn.loc.gov/2020055567
LC ebook record available at https://lccn.loc.gov/2020055568

ISBN:	HB:	978-1-3501-9183-9
	PB:	978-1-4729-8492-0
	ePDF:	978-1-3501-9184-6
	eBook:	978-1-3501-9185-3

Typeset by RefineCatch Limited, Bungay, Suffolk

To find out more about our authors and books visit www.bloomsbury.com
and sign up for our newsletters.

To new friends. Old friends. Friends we'll never meet, and those we'll only ever know by brushing near in the streets. In the thick of a pandemic. When the tyranny of the biophysical and the closure of the domestic has settled into a bad mood. When the future tense cannot but be whispered, like the ways we hold one another.

Contents

List of Illustrations	viii
Acknowledgments	x
Third-party Material	xiii
Introduction: To the Terminal!	1

Part One From Coal Capital to Petroculture

1. Our Future is Still the Future of 1973: Shell's Foresight and the Petrocultural Penumbra — 21
2. The Cultural Work of Architecture: Fixed and Social Capital at Fiat — 43
3. Energyscapes, Architecture, and the Expanded Field of Postindustrial Philosophy — 61

Part Two From the Postindustrial Environment to the Concerns of Climate

4. Elemental Ethnography Between Hydrocarbons and Hydrology: Thinking with Greenland's Moraine — 83
5. Contrapuntal Ice — 99
6. Heliotropism at the Terminal Beach of Critique — 117

Conclusion: "Hail Horrors" — 133

Notes	143
References	149
Index	161

Illustrations

Figures

1.1 Pierre Wack, "Exhibit VIII, 1973 Scenarios." *Harvard Business Review* (September 1985).   35
3.1 Bernard Tschumi, Park de la Villette (1982–98). Bernard Tschumi Architects.   71
4.1 "Hydropower is a Major Clean Energy Source" research notes. Author research notes and photo.   93
5.1 My being with the tree and the tree's being with me. Tim Ingold, *The Life of Lines* (London: Routledge, 2015), 86.   108

Plates

1 Moraine in Kangerlussuaq, Greenland (September 2018). Photo by author.
2 Hemweg 8 Coal Plant, Amsterdam (November 2018). Photo by author.
3 Fujairah, UAE. Photo by author.
4 Greenlandic rare-earth elements. © Kiliii Yuyan. Reproduced with permission of the photographer.
5 Sermeq Avannarleq, Greenland. Photo by author.
6 Glacial rock flour, Sermeq Avannarleq, Greenland. Photo by author.
7 Poodles in the Luxembourg Gardens from Mel Chin's *The Arctic is Paris* (2015).
8 *Arkhticós Doloros* by Jessie Kleeman 2019. Photo by author.
9 Jessie Kleeman as *Qivittoq*. © Allard Willemse.
10 *Leviathan*, "Ben." Shezad Dawood. Video installation 2016.
11 *Leviathan*, "Ben." Shezad Dawood. Video installation 2016.
12 *Leviathan*, "Ben." Shezad Dawood. Video installation 2016.
13 *Leviathan*, "Jamila." Shezad Dawood. Video installation 2018.
14 Chris McCaw, *Sunburn* Gsp #428 (Sunset, Sunrise, Arctic Circle, Alaska). © Chris McCaw. Reproduced with permission.

15 Olafur Eliasson, *The Weather Project*, 2003. Monofrequency lights, projection foil, haze machines, mirror foil, aluminum, and scaffolding, 26.7 m × 22.3 m × 155.4 m. Installation in Turbine Hall, Tate Modern, London. © Olafur Eliasson 2003.

Acknowledgments

This is an existential crisis waiting to happen. Let me start from the end. I'm especially grateful for the expert editorial assistance from Calum McLean and, at Bloomsbury, Jade Grogan. In addition to others named below, I was lucky enough to have Cymene Howe and Allan Stoekl as reviewers and interlocutors as the manuscript came together. Thank you for your generosity and exacting eye. And Nicole Starosielski, whose intellect I fear and whose insights I inhale: the book would not have come together in the way it did were it not for your generosity and lightning-fast instincts. And for all you have done to help figure an elemental analytic for uncertain futures.

My colleagues and students at the University of Amsterdam have been a lifeline. Niall Martin and Joost de Bloois, in particular, for thinking through key sections of this book over beers, bikes, and seminars, but the LCA team more generally: thank you for friendship, mentorship, and inspiration—and for time. Time to let ideas shift; time for fieldwork to upend the character of my object; and time for reciprocal pedagogy. Thank you, Jan Overwijk and Daniel de Zeeuw, for clandestine walks through the emergency and for a constant reminder that the profane is funny as hell. Natascha Libbert for your book and the risks you take to get miles beyond the threshold of what it is we are technically and legally allowed to see, think, and feel. The Amsterdam School for Cultural Analysis strikes me in the same way that the work of art struck Lukács: an impossible thing that exists against its own impossibility. But the students that think a degree in cultural analysis is a good idea are the real impossibility. What a frightful and gentle force. This book found its footing during a particular graduate seminar in the thick of winter in 2019 around the theme of "Materiality between Planet and Globe." Megan Hayes, Alice Rougeaux, Lu Klassen, Renée Hoogland, Max Bouwhuis, Laura Pannekoek, and Stefan Govaart: what the hell is concrescence, again? Aster Hoving's research master's thesis showed me what an elemental ethnography could do in the right hands. Wait, Aster: do you know what concrescence means?

And friends who find common cause from across continents, demanding (always) better, more careful, and more precise accounts of extraction and its critiques. Jordan Kinder, Hannah Tollefson, Burç Kostem, Janna Frenzel, Jacob Goessling, and more. I love learning from you and this book has been shaped internally by our currents.

This book would have never found its ground, so to speak, without the care and confidence of Amanda Boetzkes. The At the Moraine project is like nothing I've ever been a part of. Greenland and its abundance of affective warmth and conceptual complexity has spun me around and altered my thinking for good. Learning from you on irresponsibly long hikes on "rough ground," amidst years of companionship, and startingly seamless bouts of co-writing is more than one can pay back in a single life. And to Lene Kielsen Holm at the Greenland Climate Research Centre, for invaluable direction, as well as the late Arnannguaq Hoegh, who remains larger than life. To our lovely collaborators in Ilulissat during an uncomfortably warm June in 2019: Mark Nuttall, Jessie Kleemann, Brice Noël, Mel Chin, Shezad Dawood, Chelsea Reid, Marija Cetinic, and Ben Premeaux—the moraine came into focus because of your precision and willingness to play. And to a young man named "Cadillac" who will one day be the Prime Minister of Greenland (for real). For songs and wisdom and for showing me (after 34 years) how to open a beer without bleeding.

I've had the honor to present many of these chapters as invited talks at KU Leuven, the University of Giessen, Dartmouth College, the American Comparative Literature Association's Washington DC convention, FIBER Amsterdam, The Sandberg Critical Studies Program in Amsterdam, The Marxist Literary Group's annual Institute on Culture and Society, and at the Glasgow gathering of the bi-annual Petrocultures Conference.

I had the privilege of spending a year thinking with the inimitable Darin Barney at McGill before taking up the post in Amsterdam. It was there that I learned so much about life after the PhD. Like how to order dumplings. But also how to sustain a critical analysis of media technologies and infrastructures and to read Heidegger without throwing things (that's a joke about *Das Ding*). Maybe more importantly, I also learned from Darin how to become an academic without succumbing to total and irreversible narcissism. Well. At least I learned what that might look like. My exam results are still pending.

It was Mark Simpson and Catherine Kellogg, Michael Watts and Sara Dorow who showed me how to rework the early chapters that whispered their way into this book. Comrades and companions who are now scattered all over, but whose thoughts form something like the content to my own sense of cartography: I'm very lucky to have had the chance to think, write, organize, and live near Brent Ryan Bellamy, David Janzen, Sean O'Brien, Norman Mack, Katie Lewandowski, Amy De'Ath, David Houseman, Andrew Pendakis, Kate Lawless, Justin Sully, Adam Carlson, Danijela Majstorović, Zoran Vučkovać, and Rob Jackson. And so many academic, political, and personal mentors: Jennifer Wenzel, whose intellectual precision and political care with words are humbling, scary, and endlessly motivating. Graeme Macdonald (please answer my emails), a basin of left-leaning gravity and a beautiful soul.

I mean, how are you all possible? How are such comrades and intellectual intimacies possible?

At the Banff Research in Culture Residency 2016 I had the pleasure to think about energy for a month in dialogue with a collection of companions including Jenni Matchett, Chris Malcolm, Heather Ackroyd, Dan Harvey, David Thomas, Jayne Wilkinson, M.E. Luka, Marissa Benedict, Cameron Hu, David Reuter, Maria Michails, Am Johal, Hannah Imlach, Thomas Butler, Matt Huber, Jacquelene Drinkall, and Mél Hogan. And at the first and second After Oil Schools too, where dozens and dozens of petroculturalists gathered and thought and wrote and verified that it was possible for a bunch of humanists and social scientists to gather around a common cause and to make things. With the same urgency and care demanded by the thematic occasion.

I started researching parts of this book about ten years ago at the University of Alberta, half a day's drive from the largest industrial project on earth, immersed in the still nascent but rapidly growing community of energy humanities scholars that would eventually go by the name of the Petrocultures Research Group. Sheena. Imre. Thank you for inventing a family. A field. And a *very* good reason to no longer limit my focus to literary history. But I only got there in the first place because Imre Szeman gave me a job before I finished my undergrad, in no small part because Mathias Nilges asked him for a favor. I needed the favor because I was broke and in a bit of trouble out east, and the only thing keeping me from finishing one degree and starting the next was six thousand kilometers and about the same in cash. Jason Potts gave me work to pay for grad applications after a good two years of critique, advice, and direction. So thank you Mathias, for bailing me out (and teaching me Marxism), Jason for seeing something in me, and Imre for literally every good thing that has happened to me since. I think I did good on most of the luck that came my way, but I'm not at all confused about the source of that luck.

Marcel and Lorenzo, for dance parties, fascination, and a steady supply of adventures. I hope one day you can read this and forgive me for all the mornings and evenings distracted by my screen. I really did my best. You will do better.

Mom, Dad, Katelynn, you continue to show me hard work, and you continue to confirm how hard we need to work for a world where hard work leads not to more inequality, but to its overcoming.

And Marija. Our comrade. For putting abolition in the active voice. Not in spite of, but because of the risks and the promise.

Third-party Material

Chapter 2 previously appeared as "The Cultural Work of Architecture: Fixed and Social Capital at FIAT," *Mediations* 28.1 (2014).

Chapter 3 previously appeared as "Energyscapes, Architecture, and the Expanded Field of Postindustrial Philosophy," *Postmodern Culture* 26.2 (January 2016).

Chapter 6 previously appeared as "Heliotropism at the Terminal Beach of Critique," *The Large Glass Journal* 27/28 (2019).

Introduction: To the Terminal!

Like a water mill turns wheat into flour, Greenland's receding glacier ice grinds geological debris into a fine powder called *glacial rock flour* (see Plate 1). This substance collects at the bottom of moraines, the unwieldy rubble found along the perimeter of the Greenland Ice Sheet. Moraines imprint the Greenlandic landscape with a dramatic time signature. They also demarcate a primary juncture between planetary transformation and global industrial development, for at the very same time that the earth's glaciers are reshaping the land with the crushing force of their melt, geologists are projecting an agricultural use for the by-products of this process: glacier rock flour from Greenland is being mobilized as a natural resource, a mineral compound that can be used to regenerate exhausted soil in tropical regions of South America.[1] It's more than a little curious: how the terminal decline marked by the Holocene's cryosphere is contemporaneous with the unleashing of ground for new economic exploitation in one of the planet's largest zones of industrialized agriculture. Worlds apart, South American agribusiness and Greenland's rheology are materially knotted in the vicissitudes of climate and the world-building drives of capital. Tipping points and feedbacks converge in strange ways at the moraine.

What else thrums in the rubble? In Kangerlussuaq, a former US military base 100 kilometers north of the Arctic Circle built in the 1940s to support Danish efforts against Nazi Germany in the North Atlantic, the moraine doubles as a site for twentieth- and twenty-first-century geopolitics. In the first two decades of the twenty-first century, it has remained the only airport in Greenland with the capacity to receive transatlantic flights from Copenhagen. The Americans sold the Sondrestrom Air Base, as it was called at the time, to Greenland's Home Rule government in 1992 for a symbolic $1. In 2018, China's largest transportation infrastructure company made a bid to buy the airport, triggering more than a little anxiety and fiscal generosity from Danish prime minister Lars Løkke Rasmussen (Lanteigne 2018).

The landscape of Kangerlussuaq stands at the terminus of the melting Greenland Ice Sheet—a major event in the planetary history of Earth—and at the same time it records the unfolding politics of infrastructure for a resource-intensive globe. Multiple concerns, logics, and drives meet here, drawing out various geophysical processes into multiple worlds that remain potentialities until different modal postures (including climate and capital) concretize that potential. In this book I refer to scenes of collision between these two axes—the planetary and the global, climate and capital—as terminal landscapes. A terminal marks the physical and logical end of one thing and the initiation of another, and the abstraction connecting the two sides of the terminal (what it ends and what it sources) is politically and ecologically significant because it both insinuates new worlds and also marks the end(s) of others. In this way I deliberately blur the line between a geophysical terminal like a beach, moraine, or ice sheet and an oil terminal holding crude in suspension between its concrete materiality and its abstract life as a commodity. So, the terminal is not the same as a border if by border we mean the line demarcating space, culture, and worlds, because while borders *can* and *do* change all the time, stabilization instead of flux is the border's primary property. Terminals, on the other hand, do not stabilize: they scramble categories and create indeterminate zones across political ecologies and economies. And in a discursive environment like our own when geo- and biophysical ecologies register as eschatologically pressed—mass species extinction, expanding zones of uninhabitability, compromised futures—my insistence on the *processual* character of the terminal stems from a commitment to situating and siting those ends. What this means affectively for the case studies that follow is that I avoid the catastrophism of eschatology latent in so many discourses on climate change and ideology critiques of the fossil-fuel industry. Instead, I locate the junctures at which material entanglements come together and fall apart, at the end of the world and the horizon of the planetary. To situate material entanglements in this way is to make them available for a future thinking of theory and politics in a world that is currently buckling under the weight of climate change, even while capital lumbers on.

This book is interested in two oppositions that seem to me important for how the humanities and social sciences have developed accounts of energy and environment and the ecological vagaries that entangle them: new and historical materialism, on the one hand; planetarity and globality, on the other. My conviction is that these oppositions are not binaries but analytic postures, and I take up these postures as necessary moments of social and ecological critique for the twenty-first century. Planetarity and globality name modes of attention to the dynamics that give form and content to the present from two different standpoints. In the case of globality, it is the scopic regime of capital providing the modal logic through which the earth is represented and known (Gabrys 2018), while planetarity names the elemental alterity of earth systems and hence a fundamentally different ontology (Spivak 2004). We do not really get to choose which one works best for us though, writing the other off as bad philosophy or Marxist hubris. For the time being, capital and climate are interactive ontologies. As for historical and new materialism, I treat them here as complementary modes of noting how matter comes to matter: for the former, it is the value form that ultimately organizes and animates the physical stuff of the planet into an exchangeable (and value-bearing) commodity, while for the latter, matter's autonomy from form as such is a consequence of its own animate and agential capacities. These oppositions bear on the process, concept, and politics of the terminal today in important ways, not just because capital's modal logic and the elemental alterity of the earth *coincide* and *intersect* all the time, but because the very category of modality implied by all manner of terminals, from ecological tipping points to the terminal decline and crisis of capital, impinges on any self-certain concept of *the world* that is under erasure.

The sites I track across this book reveal the ways that capital and animate materiality make and end worlds through unique modalities. Climate change (a kind of terminal point in social and natural history writ large) is a *necessary* feature of the historical logic of fossil-fueled capitalism (Malm 2016), while capital's constitution through the surplus value actualized in the realm of exchange depends on modal *abstractions* of a number of concrete histories, relations, and futures. The earth systems swelling and swirling into so many tipping points are no less abstract for their physicality, but the modality through which the world is drawn into and then seeded through global warming unfolds through an *eco*logical sense. Capital, meanwhile, *abstracts* concrete forms of labor (actual people doing things); the materials used up in the labor process (minerals, fuels, and so on); past labors congealed into the fixed capital of machines and buildings and servers; *and* the futures brokered both by financial speculation and the metaphysical drive of capital to grow at ever greater magnitudes on and on into a future it increasingly makes (and destroys) for itself (Daggett 2019, 102). That's what I mean by the different modalities named by climate and capital—one is a necessary ecological process, while the other is a *creation of worlds through the logic of abstraction*, and it is in their interactive determinations through the terminals I track here that I see a new political ecology insinuated at the moraine.

If we are indeed at the terminal point of capital's facility with cheap energy, entering into the uncharted waters of global warming's multiple tipping points, then we need a stronger account of where and how the terminal happens. This is because the terminal is both a state of things and a condition in which things relate. The argument of this book is that the concept and logistical infrastructures of the terminal focalize these oppositions between globe and planet, form and formlessness, *in medias res*—that, in other words, worlds are made and unmade at the terminal. The melting ice sheet in Greenland, on the one hand, and the handful of energy terminals that prepare fuels for financial measure across the globe, on the other—these are two poles of the terminal. One is in terminal decline, losing cryospheric form as it melts into the hydrosphere. The other is an unassuming mediation of raw materiality into the commodity form of energy, an abstraction of energy's crude form into its market and social forms. These two valences of the terminal solicit a kind of ecumenical materialism alert to the very different ways that fossil-fueled modernity cascades into what Deborah Danowski and Eduardo Viveiros de Castro call the *katechon* or time of the irreparable, the irreversible (2016, 19). The Greenland Ice Sheet is the site at which planetarity becomes globalization, in part because the ice sheet is already abstracted at the energy terminal. This sublation happens not just through human labor, as one might expect, but also through geosurveying and harvesting of vital energies surging as a cascade of tipping points (Arboleda 2020). The poles of the terminal contract; its noun and adjective coalesce *in situ*: planetary expression gets knotted to the hunt for cheap nature.

The ice sheet retreats; it withdraws from view. At the same time, it comes to dominate the imaginary and imagery of anthropogenic climate change, figured in equal measure by satellite technologies, ice core samples, docudramas, and political discourse (Grusin 2010). If the Greenland Ice Sheet—this impossibly large object weighing down on the largest island on earth—has become the greatest object of concern across the globe, then the moraine is the remainder by which we can reflect on its transformation. A terminal moraine is the outermost edge of glacial advance. It is marked by geological debris hoisted out by glacial dynamics. It is stratigraphically visible as a heap, as time accelerated by the dynamism of ice. As a text, the terminal moraine is marginalia, but its looseness draws attention to itself. Over the past three decades, the mass loss of Greenland's glacier ice has increased sixfold (Mouginot et al. 2019, 9239). Thanks to the conjoining efforts of nationally funded geologists, meteorologists, climatologists, and indigenous knowledge creators over that same period, Greenland has been held in the crosshairs of three competing forces: liberal reason, capitalism's energy culture, and indigenous sovereignty in a postcolonial nation-state with an uneasy orientation toward the parameters of its national development. Liberal reason, because the terminal decline of the cryosphere shifts the ground from which the God-given subject of modernity stands to reason. Capitalism's energy culture, because the US Geological Survey (USGS) has since the mid-2000s gawked curiously at the nearly 32 billion barrels of oil equivalent locked under the ice off the east coast of Greenland alone, while Chinese and Australian mining companies earn licenses for rare earth and uranium mining in South Greenland—the second largest deposit of rare-earth elements on the planet. And indigenous sovereignty, because the Inuit majority of Greenland are obliged by Danish accord to feed resource revenues (and hence self-exploit what the USGS offers up as hydrocarbon potential) into the last remaining tendril that binds Greenlandic nation building to the Danish state. The terminal moraine is a geophysical expression of the knotted chronotopes of industrial, colonial, and indigenous history. If the ends of the Holocene unfold most geophysically at the moraine of the Greenland Ice Sheet, it is not because the modalities by which land and labor get abstracted into capital's ongoing drives to make worlds are ending with it. The key opposition (and entanglement) this book lays out is the modal logics of climate and capital, and it is here *in the thick of the terminal* that we can see those modal logics interacting.

Tracking the flows of materials, modalities, and concepts through the terminal requires a situated and errant voice, but by early November 2018, I am only beginning to understand this. I am preparing to facilitate a public discussion in Amsterdam on the discourse of "tipping points," following the Intergovernmental Panel on Climate Change (IPCC) special report on "Global Warming of 1.5 °C" (2018). The report shifts attention from the atmosphere to the world ocean, but it doesn't make reference to the shipping industry saturating the ocean with cargo, diesel, and displacement. Around the same time, my friend Natascha Libbert—a photographer commissioned to document the expansion of the sealocks at IJmuiden at the interface of the North Sea and the River IJ—comes back from the sea, and her book, *I Went Looking for a Ship*, goes to press. The book takes its narrative structure from the flows both animating and concealed by the transformations of the terminal, and its text and image track the mediation of political histories, working bodies, materials, fuels, and futures. The exercise she sets for herself cannot resolve into either image or text, prose or poetry, much less policy, because the terminal puts pressure on aesthetic form. Natascha's book lingers in the terminal, tracking the materials that come in and out of these largely invisible (or at least unseen) spaces that line continental nodes of what

Laleh Khalili calls the "maritime transport enterprise" (2020, 3). I have been teaching Allan Sekula's *The Forgotten Space* to graduate students for a few years, but it only occurred to me after reading Natascha's book that the figure of the maritime vessel in Sekula's work, and the shipping industry more generally, appears to actively background the hydrosphere on which it floats—all the more striking as contemporary climate science shifts its gaze from the skies to the oceans.[2]

The IPCC report is more assured in its delivery, churning up a torrent of phrases about the reality check its authors have provided politicians and industry leaders given our shared proximity to a world cascading into ecological catastrophe is roughly a decade away. But I am distracted by a feeling my body remembers as soreness and ache, still lingering a month after walking at the edge of the Ilulissat ice fjord on the west coast of Greenland with my friend and colleague Amanda Boetzkes. It is a feeling that Lorraine Code, author of *Ecological Thinking*, might call sedimented experience, blending ethos and habitus (2006, 28). The embodied memory colors what I can see from my office window in the center of Amsterdam, as if the terminal moraine and the terminal infrastructure presuppose one another (see Plate 2). The terminal vibrates quietly. Receding into the background thrum of the city's lifeworld and the multiple channels that connect it to other places, like the base of a mountain in Norway, fiber-optic cables connecting Bloemendaal aan Zee to the shores of Dover or pipelines running between the port and Rotterdam—and from there Hamburg, Gent, and the rest of Europe. Natascha's book holds the elements of the terminal to a provisional form: photograph, travel log, poetry, and glossary, because those elements extend as infrastructures, political ecologies, planetary dynamics, rising seas, melting ice. Taking up the IPCC report means putting its concept of the terminal tipping point in tension with the contrapuntal ecology of the Greenland Ice Sheet and the energy terminal preparing hydrocarbons for the European market. To treat these as heterogeneous would be to repeat the kind of category error that got us in this mess in the first place. But the various representations of the terminal conceal, and therefore demand, embodied experience of the ecosystems and integrated landscapes they describe. Natascha's book provides as much in the title (*I Went Looking for a Ship*). But how do we go looking for the interface of climate and capital? Where exactly does that happen *in situ*?

In this book I read a wide range of representations in search for terminal landscapes: futures scenarios developed by Shell in the 1970s; architectural retrofits of Fordist factories at the brink of the postindustrial turn in Turin;

landscape architecture and sculpture in Paris and New York as the concept of energy begins to overtake the idiom of postmodernism; geological surveys of Greenland's subsurface mineral reserves; experimental film, photography, and installation art concerned with the elemental force of the sun; ecotourism's cultural archive in Greenland against indigenous performance art *on* the Greenland Ice Sheet; and my own field notes between the shores of the North Sea, Greenland, and the terminal infrastructure of Fujairah in the eastern Emirates—where petrochemicals and cargo from all five continents meet, store, exchange hands, and reroute. But I also read these representations with and sometimes against my own collaborative fieldwork in these same places, reading the ecological dynamics of terminal landscapes slowly, dialogically, and peripatetically. Sometimes there is resonance between the various objects of analysis, but more often there is a contrapuntal dissonance, and I made the decision to let that dissonance sustain my own thinking and writing instead of muting it in the service of an orthodox critique of this or that corporate or state actor. I learned from the feminist materialism of contemporary ecological thinkers like Anna Tsing, Elizabeth Povinelli, Cymene Howe, and Stacy Alaimo that things look different when you spend time thinking with the varied elements that situate relationality in place.

The thing about the terminal is that you do not have to look very hard to see it everywhere, but you do have to look. In my office in Amsterdam, for instance, I am seven stories high, so this scene is not typical for a cityscape that on average caps at four stories. I am neither above the city nor on its ground, but somewhere in between—a kind of oblique angle to topographical and peripatetic perspectives. What I see is a horizon not of sky but of wind turbines, coal stacks, and storage terminals. They line the banks of the River IJ, the major waterway that connects the center of Amsterdam to its Westpoort. From here, the turbines and smokestacks cluster and make visible the sea-locks under expansion at IJmuiden, where the landscape meets the North Sea. The wind turbines spin, generating up to 19 MW of power a day for Dutch consumers, and I watch not only the force of the wind figured in their revolutions but its velocity too, because the single smokestack that reaches into the sky blows its emissions directly towards my window. The smokestack is connected to the Hemweg 8 coal plant, which until the end of 2019 powered 750,000 homes a day at 650 MWe. The coal plant sits at the eastern edge of the port and is strategically placed next to *the largest gasoline and liquid bulk terminal in all of Europe*. The coal plant was there for everyone to see, though seldom could my students say what it was or did. But, then, it too met its end, decommissioned thanks to a class action lawsuit against the Dutch state for its deliberate contravention of its citizens' rights to avoid subjection to harm. The terminal is not static. Where energy, maritime trade, and the concerns of climate converge, potential worlds are always comingling—sometimes harmoniously, but mostly with grating dissonance.[3]

Annually, the port's eleven terminals handle upward of 40 million tons of liquid bulk—including gasoline, diesel, kerosene, LPG, chemicals, and biofuels—waiting for transport to market across the European Union. Unlike its larger sibling in Rotterdam, the Port of Amsterdam does not specialize in cargo but rather in what investors call *bulk cargo* or *wet trade*: not shoes and shirts but millions of cubic-meter storage. The volumes of storage provide the quantitative basis for estimates of future supply and demand—the practice of futures trading—which turns energy flows into financial commodities. Futures traders in Rotterdam, London, and Chicago seek intel on current capacity in terminals like this one in order to determine if the futures market is going bullish or bearish. And the world's leading independent tank storage company, Royal Vopak, has something of a monopoly on that intel in Westpoort. Vopak began as a storage and handling contractor for the Dutch East India Company (VOC) in the seventeenth century when spices, sugar, coffee, silk, and other colonial commodities were imported from Indonesia, India, Japan, and China. Today, they store an equivalent of 14,724 Olympic swimming pools' worth of petroleum products, petrochemicals, gases, and palm oil in sixty-eight terminals across every continent of the globe. The space between the Port of Amsterdam and IJmuiden is coextensively geophysical and financial. It is a terminal landscape insofar as it serves as an energy stock of postindustrial petroculture across the European Union, translating the world of extractive industries into a market form of energy. It is a landscape of terminals, but also an infrastructural zone at the western edge of Europe where the crude forms of fossil fuels are physically and financially mediated into what Roland Barthes might today call "terminal form."

In *Mythologies*, Barthes turns to the ends of myth and finds plastic. With plastic comes a paradox we ought to recognize as persistent: though the object form of plastic is infinite, each instance—" suitcase, brush, car-body, toy, fabric, tube, basin, or paper"—is an expression of "terminal form" (Barthes [1957] 1972, 97). Each object assumed by the material is simultaneously unique and serialized, reproducible and astonishing. It is as if the plastic object reunites exchangeability and use, where the particular and the universal themselves become momentary features of plasticity writ large. But the paradox of the singular and the multiple doubles as both phenomenological and material: " the reverie" of the subject who witnesses "the proliferating forms of matter, and the connections [she] detects between the singular of the origin and the plural of the effects" is dizzying (97); a proliferation of objects and yet an infinite encounter not of them (of objects) but of it (of plastic). The object form of the plastic object gives way to the terminal form of objectivity. Hence, what for Barthes makes plastic objects so many expressions of terminal form is twofold: they resist their own pliability and so appear to terminate what materially they are inclined towards once fixed in object form, while at the same time marking the limits of phenomenological certainty as to *what this thing is exactly*. Hence, in plastics, "the hierarchy of substances is abolished: a single one replaces them all: the whole world *can* be plasticized, and even life itself since, we are told, they are beginning to make plastic aortas" (99). The punchline is grim. Plastics become *plasticity* as their terminal form begins to rearrange the very relations between material in the "hierarchy of substances." But from where does this *terminal form* get its inertia, and to where is its force as a *condition* of materiality headed? Thinking Barthes' terminal form means returning to the terminal landscape from which petrochemical worlds converge with petrocultural ends.

"In 2010," according to the United Nations Environmental Program (UNEP), "30 billion tonnes of materials extracted globally were required to produce 10 billion tonnes of directly traded goods " (2016, 15). The 3:1 ratio is grotesque. In gross terms, this discrepancy between traded goods and extracted materials figures quantitatively the intimacy of the planet and globe. More striking still is the paradox of what Elizabeth Povinelli calls late liberalism's geontopower- the unceasing exorcism that one way of life performs on what it insists is the inert, lifeless matter of a planet: paradoxical because the calculus of capital underwriting late liberalism's distinction between life and nonlife needs *more and more* of the lifeless stuff of the planet to maintain the smooth flow of quarterly return. In the UNEP's phrasing, "Growth in global material extraction was such that per capita global material use increased from 7 tonnes per capita in 1970 to 10 tonnes per capita in 2010" (14). The authors of the report call this upward curve—recognizable elsewhere as the hockey stick graph associated with the great acceleration—the "considerable inertia" built into the "global system of material use" (14). The subject of this average is of course an imaginary one—the per capita figures the favored middle of liberal reason—but the point holds: the functional threshold of animate life and inanimate matter presses down deeper into the earth every year, a pressing down that of course intensifies the increasingly ungraspable and incalculable animacy of a dynamic and expressive planet. We might think of the UNEP report as a kind of elemental distillation of what, as an object, constitutes and gets constituted by the Port of Amsterdam. Infrastructures such as the terminal in Amsterdam dredge along multiple axes, transforming and informing a range of materials both nearby and very far away.

This is another way of asking: where does most of this matter dug up from the earth go? And how much energy is required to move 30 billion tonnes of material out of and then around the globe? According to the UNEP, "A raw material trade balance based on the attribution of globally extracted materials to traded goods shows that only Europe and North America have remained net importers of materials" (15). This trade balance abstracts an enormous amount of cultural and regional specificity, but it is worth staying with the scale of reference for a moment: while the rest of the earth is dug up, extracted. and shoveled into the furnace of globalization, Europe and North America—where most of that matter ends up as fuel and in commodity form—are getting heavier, and exponentially more dependent on that heaviness getting heavier. This is the doubled valance of inertia put quantitatively. Capital's centers drive accumulation, even as accumulation begets sluggishness. I am reminded again of Sekula's polemic against the discourse of immaterial production in *Fish Story* and *The Forgotten Space*. Despite the shrinking of the globe through telecommunication and high-frequency trading, global capital has never needed more stuff and more energy to maintain its telos into futures few of us want anymore. The sea-locks at IJmuiden expand, storage capacity in the port of Amsterdam increases, the depths of the river IJ are dredged deeper. The terminal landscape is where the trade balance in raw materials *informs* matter and materializes form.

It is in this way that we can see the operation that I am identifying with the concept of the terminal landscape. A terminal landscape is an endpoint and a beginning. It is a circuit of infrastructure between land and economy; between object and condition, or commodity and its historicity; between a particular location and global abstraction; between lived environment and political distribution; between energy history and energy future. The terminal landscape is a mobile concept that captures both dystopian industrial history and utopian possibility. It points to the recalcitrance of land and the desiring nature of futurity. But it also names the recursion between geophysical and topographical schemas that implicate energy culture and climate change with one another. Barthe's plastic is lodged in the aortas of so many bodies, floating around as the afterlife of petrocultural modernity, but is also the physical correlative of hydrocarbons concentrating ever more in the atmosphere and hydrosphere. Terminal landscapes are the connective tissue holding together scenes that split along infrastructural and physical lines. They gather genres of landscape from ports to ice sheets and all the lives distributed across them.

In this sense, Amsterdam is a terminal landscape in more ways than one. The visual imprint of energy culture rises up to mix with the cartography of the land and its vanishing point with the sky, where windmills, coal stacks, and heaps of energy stock disclose the mediation of the European energy market with physical and financial flows. The energy infrastructure here is neither invisible nor out of sight: it is clustered and hyper-visible for all to see. It is clustered around the vanishing point of the scene I observe daily from the university with more and more density every day because, as I write, the sea-locks at IJmuiden are undergoing a seven-year expansion in order to become the largest in the world. Once the expansion is complete, the extended Port of Amsterdam will have a capacity of 125 million tons of storage space for energy commodities. Expansion in turn works to incentivize increased vessel handling and storage capacity up the river at the Port (Safety4Sea 2017). Above ground and in technical terms, this is a landscape of energy terminals and thus a primary node, or chokepoint, in what is otherwise a global and distributed energy system. The terminal is dangerously sensitive in a way that the object form of fossil fuels is not.

The terminal is the container that abstracts matter into exchangeable energy. As a landscape, it holds to a point three overlapping and entangled economies: the global energy industry, the shipping industry, and the financial system, each of which in turn embed the media expressive of climate change, which form the other pole of the terminal as typology, with the political ecology of capital. It contains the crude form of fossil fuel in volumetric form awaiting a destination. It is important to not just think of the terminal as a man-made storage technology, though, but also as a medium that extends across the ecological meshwork of the planet. Containment across these two poles of the terminal—the tank farm and the ice sheet—is provisional, driving anticipation and anxiety at the same time that it attracts multiple mediations to see futurity set loose by the verb tense of the terminal. As matter in waiting, it accumulates and pauses. Futures traders bid for readings on stock in order to estimate the character of supply and flow. Geologists see through ice and rock to await recession and return. In their bid for readings, they also collaborate on a distributed ecology that distributes terminalia into the world according to the logistics of postindustrial resource economy. As resource, the stuff of the terminal matters the feedbacks of climate in concrete location. Financial abstraction is here intertwined with the geophysical existence of carbon amidst a logistical infrastructure that is both massively distributed across the planet and also concentrated strategically in the terminal landscape.

But the IJ is a terminal landscape below the water's surface as well, in ways that have long mattered in the history of Dutch landscaping. In expanding the width and depth of the sea-locks, the Rijkswaterstaat (the Dutch Infrastructure and Waterways Agency) expect rising sea levels caused by global warming to increase the volume of sea water flowing through the River IJ, and into the hundreds of polders that connect with it. The contrapuntal ecology of global warming means that what happens above the surface of water must be read off what happens below it too. Market demand for energy requires infrastructural expansion, while infrastructural expansion increases market demand for the stuff held in ever-growing terminals. This dialectic is triangulated by a third determinant, though, which is the physical instability of the hydrosphere that both lubricates seaborne trade of fuels in tankers and barges and threatens its coastal infrastructure. The sea is rising, and things are poised to get very salty.[4] The sea-locks at IJmuiden help generate, and are a response to, the concerns of water, but salinization caused by rising sea levels across the region signals major transformations to the ecosystems of the river and canals between the North Sea and Amsterdam. It will pose new infrastructural pressures on horticulture, filtration, and drainage systems that combine (and have long combined) to saturate this landscape with the immanent presence of water. High-saline water is flowing into the landscape as the Port of Amsterdam finds itself caught between the demands of capital and the imperatives of climate. For while the EU leads the policy discourse in energy transition in the twenty-first century—and Dutch engineers become world leaders in coastal water management in some of the same colonial regions resourced for the Dutch Republic's economic and cultural boom in the seventeenth and eighteenth centuries—the political economy of its energy needs begins to mix and become the very waters of a political ecology it helped create. The Port lets in the salt, and rising seas promise much more where that came from.

But where does it come from? It goes without saying that the Rijkswaterstaat's inclusion of the discourse of climate change into its Port expansion is in part a matter of pride in its history: when it comes to water, this country knows how to manage. But the foreshadowing of a salty future that threatens to corrode the infrastructure of the past is also a way of anticipating the realities of a future without claiming responsibility for it. Rising sea levels come from such a distance anyways, and it is no single actor's—let alone nation's—fault.

Between one third and half of all water contributing to the projected 2.5-meter rise in sea levels in the twenty-first century will come from the Greenland Ice Sheet 3,000 km northwest of Amsterdam (Noël et al. 2017; European Environment

Agency 2017). Hence, Greenland's ice sheet and the elemental forces flowing through Amsterdam's energy terminal are geophysically contiguous. They are interactive sites that relate materially through their elemental flows above and below the water line. It might require a leap of imagination to figure these two landscapes in the same frame of thought—it is certainly very difficult to represent visually. But the geophysical, financial, and social relations that imbricate them in a recursive ecology continue to intensify independent of anybody's willingness or ability to think them. They make up two critical zones of concentration and acceleration in a common topography that wraps the earth in the entangled flows of climate and capital. Furthermore, both sites can be written in the language of the petrocultural present, a term that comes from scholars in the environmental and energy humanities. The petrocultural present refers to the material and cultural forms of being, belonging, attachment, and energic dependence underwritten by the quantitative and qualitative dominance of oil and oil-based products beginning in the early 1950s, and which show no signs of abating despite a surge in popular demand for energy transition. The ecological and historical relationship between physical environments like Greenland's ice sheet and the infrastructured spaces through which fossil fuels flow in primary scenes of storage and exchange like Amsterdam means that any one terminal landscape is part of an expanded media ecology that pulls together different temporalities and histories. Cryosphere and hydrosphere, the globe and the planet, upstream and downstream investments, rising sea levels and salty futures—these are contrapuntal alignments that intensify recursively to one another in the expanded political ecology of our shared, terminal landscape. And it is this doubled valence of the "terminal"—a conclusion to a sequence on the brink of another, on the one hand, and a chronic state of transformation, on the other—that *Climate and Capital in the Age of Petroleum* rethinks for twenty-first-century theory and politics.

Reading across climate and capital

Amsterdam's not-so-hidden energy terminal and the moraine of Kangerlussuaq, Greenland are both determinate and emblematic scenes where the political economy and political ecology of fossil-fueled energy culture unfold in both time and space. But the core claim of this book is that it will require a recursion back into the genealogy of the present in order to fully articulate the entangled futures these landscapes help us anticipate. The structure of this book is then informed by the analytic distinction between the critique of energy, on the one hand, and the elemental ethnography occasioned by situated knowledge of ecological dynamics, on the other. While Part 1 focuses on the abstract, crude, and social forms through which capital distributes oil's elemental force over financial, social, and ecological futures, Part 2 shifts to a wider elemental speculation from the shifting grounds of the melting cryosphere. I do this through an attention and concern for how water, ice, and solar demand unique methods for interpretive and embodied inquiry at the terminal, and it is speculative because it's through those elemental forces that Part 2 shifts to the multiple futures named and occasioned by climate change. The voice I take up in the second part is deliberately not eschatological or tempered by the discourse of crisis. Instead I am practicing what Anna Tsing calls the "arts of noticing" (2015) amidst the lively and damaged scenes of political ecology altering our sense of the world at the so-called ends of modernity. Moving across the historical determinations of capital's facility with energy in Part 1 requires disentangling postindustrial resource modalities from the geophysical *processes* that make up the data and discourse of climate change. Hence my case studies home in on conjunctural shifts where what I call *energy deepening*, or capital's ever-increasing need for more and more physical energy, results in the naturalization of fossil-fueled futures. Part 1 therefore involves a provisional bracketing of the leitmotif of the smokestack and the tailpipe, of tailings ponds and precarious life forms, so essential to detailing and politicizing atmospheric concentration of greenhouse gases and the planetary tipping points guaranteed by climate change.

But the critical analytic I develop in Part 1 is deliberately limited to a study of how capital morphs its world-building logics to the affordances of hydrocarbons when they underwrite the value form. Plainly, any theoretical framework that insists on such a distinction between capital and climate in the final instance is neither for nor of this world. And it is in concert with a swell of new research in anthropology, cultural analysis, media and communication studies, and the environmental and energy humanities that forward theory for a damaged world that this book makes its contribution. But it makes one important proviso: abandoning an anthropocentric concept of the social need not mean losing with it the will and promise of socialism. Capital is not just a state of mind and it cannot be located (or dismantled) on the basis of ideology alone. Capital is a material force in the world so startlingly extensive and disruptive that geologists are now considering the degree to which industrial civilization—a form of life formatted to the rhythms and drives of capital through and through—has become the determining agent in natural history. But it is a material force in the world most concretely in and through its infrastructures. A posthuman socialism, like a humanist socialism, coheres in its critique of, and redistribution of capacities through, infrastructures.

To this end, Part 1: From Coal Capital to Petroculture describes the recalibration of the global economy to the rhythms and scale of the petroleum industry in the late 1960s and early 1970s through three case studies that draw out the relationship between postindustrial economy and petrocultural production. In the wake of the 1970s energy crisis, the financial structure of energy trading was reconstituted. By the 1980s, futures trading of oil would effectively drive the transition to a postindustrial market setting. In order to isolate the financial force of energy on other spheres of cultural and economic production, I develop the concept of "market media," dominant sources of information that communicate within the language of speculation and temporality, such as interest rates and bond pricing. Building on key insights about the integration of energy across cultural and social spheres developed in the environmental and energy humanities (LeMenager 2015; Szeman and Boyer 2017a; 2017b), I show in Chapter 1 how the price of oil began to mediate the expanded field of economic, political, and natural environments—and in turn redefined what an "environment" meant in both management theory and visual culture.

By introducing the critical concept of "petrocultural mediation" in my close reading of Royal Dutch Shell's scenarios department, I then turn it into an analytic frame in Chapter 2 to examine the rapid deindustrialization of the Italian North in the years leading up to and following the 1973 oil crisis. At the heart of my case study is Renzo Piano's decades-long ambition to code a postindustrial architecture in the idiom of land, energy, and culture, beginning with his early work for mobile sulfur extraction in the 1960s, through to his landmark works retrofitting the Fiat factory in Lingotto, Turin, and the Schlumberger factory offices—the world's largest oilfield electronic service supplier—and the Centre Pompidou in Paris. Moving from the deindustrialization of a distinctly petrocultural suite of buildings, I then zoom out to reframe some of the preferred terms shared across landscape architecture and object-oriented philosophies in the postindustrial era.

My third chapter follows the media ecology of landscape architecture as it gets formulated by James Croner, Stan Allen, Jesse Reiser and Nanako Umemoto, and Mohsen Mostafavi in order to show that energy deepening establishes itself in spatial forms, or the physical setting, of a fully saturated fossil-fuel society. In reading major landscape and landform projects in Europe and North America, I situate economic planning, energy distribution, and terraforming within a matrix driving a petroeconomy otherwise imagined as unshackled from both physical constraints and planning. By moving through exemplary instances of postindustrial landscape architecture, and the philosophical tradition of its theorists, Chapter 3 shows that the political economy of postindustrial energy is premised on excavating a posthuman source of value, rather than a labor-oriented one; it also shows that that this development becomes an impasse for speculative theory premised on so many object-oriented ontologies and antihuman materialisms.

In Part 2: From the Postindustrial Environment to the Concerns of Climate, I turn to the media ecology of the present in order to glean an environmentally attuned concept of terminal landscapes from recent renditions of infrastructure at the scene of melting ice and rising seas. Where Part 1 foregrounded a historical materialist framework for periodizing the relationship between energy and capital, Part 2 transitions to a new materialist framework in order to discern an expanded concept of ecology for twenty-first-century theory and politics. In Chapter 4, I begin *in situ* at the moraine of the Greenland Ice Sheet, learning the language of melting ice and infrastructural promise at the crossroads of Inuit sovereignty, Danish colonialism, and global capital. There, I show that melting ice fuels Greenland's postcolonial condition along two axes: on the one hand, the nation-state developed during the transition between 1979 (Home Rule Act) and 2009 (Self-Government Act) powered itself domestically and commercially by building five hydroelectric dams, powered entirely by water flowing from the ice sheet that covers 80 percent of its surface. Today, over 60 percent of the nation's energy is renewable, distributing the energy of its terminal landscape through five independent grids. On the other hand, Greenland's sovereignty coincides with global concerns for its ice. The Greenland Ice Sheet is expected to contribute upwards of one third of all water responsible for rising sea levels in the next century—a planetary inheritance of hydrocarbons accumulating amidst colonialism's and industrialism's political ecologies.

In Chapter 5, "Contrapuntal Ice," I elaborate a mode of reading colonial and economic tension across disciplinary frameworks drawn to the Greenland Ice Sheet by updating Édouard Glissant's seminal theory of ecological relation and Edward Said's contrapuntal reading for a melting world. I do this through open-plan fieldwork conducted in 2018–19 in Nuuk and Ilulissat with visual and performance artists, anthropologists, and an atmospheric scientist. I narrate the experience of adjusting the theoretical terms by which climate works as a concern in my own discipline of cultural analysis as the community of researchers gathered at the moraine of the Ice Sheet co-create a perspective on ice *in situ*. The ice itself becomes an interpretant and an actant at the intersection of our disciplinary and experiential modes of engaging its recalcitrance, and in this way the contrapuntal becomes a process of sensing climate through embedded and interdisciplinary practices. Through readings of the climate models of Brice Noël from the Institute for Marine and Atmospheric Research Utrecht (IMAU), Mel Chin's *The Arctic Is*, and Greenland performance artist Jessie Kleemann's *Arkhticós Doloros*, I end this chapter by demonstrating what I mean by "letting climate change theory." Thinking with the animate planetarity expressed at the terminal moraine of the Greenland Ice Sheet means sensing the cryopolitical ends of the earth amidst the fault lines of the nation-state and Inuit sovereignty. It means, in other words, pulling into contrapuntal relief the knotted lives of colonialism, capitalism, and climate change where melting ice unlocks enough hydrocarbons to carry us through this century. The terminal lumbers on.

Chapter 6 explores recent aesthetic interventions by Shezad Dawood, Chris McCaw, and Olafur Eliasson which help focalize the present through the solar relations figured and landscape of the terminal beach—that originary landscape where sea and land mix matter, distributing solar and lunar energies in turn. These medium-specific "heliotropisms," as I refer to them, offer unique and plural forms of critical perception that help accelerate the process of letting climate change theory, each using a distinct mood, materiality, and temporality. If it was on a sunny day at the beach that critical theory (as it was enumerated by Horkheimer and Adorno) witnessed the absorption of the subject into the logic of capital, then it is to the terminal beach of critique that we return today now that this same subject appears to be under erasure. In my reading, the return to the beach is not an effort to save that subject, but to attune to an aesthetic apparatus of perception necessary for its redefinition.

In mid-May of 2019, four tankers awaiting refueling in a traffic jam of two hundred were sabotaged under cover of darkness outside of the Port of Fujairah in the Gulf of Oman. A few weeks earlier I found myself standing on the beach of Fujairah, immersed in the environing of the shore by washed-up coral, plastics, jellyfish, and white foam that glitters with petrochemicals (see Plate 3). Here is the second-largest terminal in the world for heavy diesel fuel powering the world's fleet of cargo ships and oil tankers, and a strategic chokepoint in the circulation of energy and commodities. If something goes wrong in this particular terminal, global trade grinds to a halt. The Port of Fujairah is far off from the free trade islands of Abu Dhabi and Dubai, and is staffed predominantly by migrant laborers from India, Pakistan, and Bangladesh, but the Emirati petrostate is almost entirely dependent on what goes in and out of this space, as are the Asian and European ports where most of these ships are bound. Across the Gulf of Oman is the Iranian peninsula, making the waters separating the two a tense and contested energyscape. The ecological and economic debris are co-expressive at the beach, as the details that make this terminal landscape prefigurative of the geophysical and geopolitical resolutions on the horizon for a global petroculture stuck in its own terminal condition. Stuck, because the US Energy Information Administration (EIA) has recently made a startling claim about the challenge of transitioning to a renewable future: by 2040, the globe will need 48 percent more energy than it did in 2012 to support continued economic development, three-quarters of which will come from fossil fuels (EIA 2016). Meanwhile, the IPCC (2018) warns of a global tipping point not much more than a decade away, at which time a two-degree increase in global temperature averages will mean the eradication of upwards of 13 percent of global ecosystems; total loss of entire species; complete devastation of coral reefs, of 18 percent of insects, 16 percent of plants, and 8 percent of vertebrates; massive rise in sea levels; cascading volatility in storm systems and the unpredictable feedback loops associated with complete melting of Arctic ice; and major water shortages and displacement for over 400 million people.

The twenty-first century promises to be a terminal landscape, an era when a great many things (species, ways of life, biomes, and cultural imaginaries) come to an end. But the temporality of this century also consists of a set of interconnected and asymmetrical landscapes through which postwar energy culture circulates as econometric, cultural, and geophysical form. What technologies, habits, and habitats will fold in on the ecological realities projected by the IPCC and this dramatic increase determined necessary by the EIA? How will the geophysical landscapes now fully animated by global warming come to matter to the built, economic, and cultural environment tasked with realizing the energy demands of an economy caught between the concerns of climate and capital? And what critical frames of analysis are required to remain responsible to and for the relationship between landscapes uniquely sensitive to the accelerating feedback loops of anthropogenic climate change? As the very ground of modernity is shaken loose from colonial, critical, and liberal epistemologies, in what directions are we mediating the climate condition? I suggest that we cannot know without a media history of environment at the very terminal point of oil and climate change, globality, and planetarity. And, finally, that the realization of the worlds we want solicits a blockage of the worlds we do not. *Sous les paves, la plage!* To the terminal!

Part One

From Coal Capital to Petroculture

1

Our Future is Still the Future of 1973: Shell's Foresight and the Petrocultural Penumbra

This chapter is about fossil-fueled futures, but not the kind of futures animating anxiety about our geo- and biophysical conditions. Instead, it is about how the future became an object of analysis for Royal Dutch Shell (hereafter Shell) in the 1970s and how the abstract force of oil over macroeconomic trends provided them with a novel narrative structure through which to both anticipate and emplot planetary and economic futures. This genealogy matters for how environmental futures comes into focus today. Because while the future arrives through concerns expressed in world outlooks, scenarios, and emissions pathways, their shared attunement to the crude materiality of capital's political ecology has done virtually nothing to unnerve the logic of its political economy. In the dominant genres through which the future is rendered political, writing a proleptic path to the future remains tethered to the prolonged accumulation of capital. Even in the most improbable example authored by the IPCC ('P1–4' in the 2018 "Global Warming of 1.5C" report), the news for capitalists is more than good. In scenarios P1 to P4, each of which projects a portfolio of innovation, energy efficiency, new technologies, increased living standards, carbon storage, and alternative fuels into a net-neutral 2050 reversing the CO_2 bill of a capitalism freed to grow long into the future, the globe remains seemingly flush with the promise of capital (IPCC 2018). Concerned with petro-based visions of futurity like what passes as the IPCC's most ambitious and sustainable, this chapter historicizes the moment in the 1970s when Shell turned the future into a cultural and discursive object of knowledge through which to see most clearly (and act upon) the intractable knotting of energy, capital, and the new scale of the so-called "business environment."

I insist on referring to the knotting of energy, capital, and the historically specific concept of the environment, rather than using an analytic or environmental ethic that treats them as separate areas of concern, in keeping with the world-systems ecology framework developed by Jason W. Moore in *Capitalism in the Web of Life* (2015) and Elizabeth Povinelli's treatment of the "carbon imaginary" grounding her indigenous and feminist epistemology in *Geontologies* (2016). The point is to foreground the material dynamics through which capital, energy and planetarity are co-produced internal to a singular and historically specific ecology, even while ecological dynamics exceed the calculus of capital. Instead of foregrounding progressive and environmental forms of normative critique—claims such as "we *ought not* to grow our global economy of fossil fuels"—my focus here is instead on the narrative techniques by which the future of the planet is wedded to a logic of the market configured to the structural determinations of fossil fuels. This co-production occurs for Moore and Povinelli through the unique ecologies actualized across technical, cultural, and material systems, so historicizing (and critiquing) the political ecologies of fossil-fueled capitalism of necessity requires attention to the interactive dynamics of capital and energy. My focus on the sector-specific genealogy of futures thinking at Shell in the moment of the twin turns to postindustrial economic forms and postmodern cultural imaginaries is meant as a contribution to ongoing debates about the material and historical force of oil in the energy and environmental humanities.

Today, there are two dominant genres through which the future of industrial energy systems is written into an object of knowledge about which we might do something. On the one hand, environmental and economic "scenarios" take what is latent in the macro-tendencies of the present and imagine paths that might emerge from those tendencies. Scenarios, according to McKinsey & Company consultant Charles Roxburgh, "enable the strategist to steer a course between the false certainty of a single forecast and the confused paralysis that often strike [*sic*] in troubled times " (Roxburgh 2009). Authors of these scenarios include corporate strategists, consultancy firms, economists, accountants, and political analysts at Shell, the United Nations, the World Bank, and the International Energy Agency (IEA), in addition to regional and national level governments.

On the other hand, the future is also written in the language of "exchange." In futures markets, the future price of all manner of commodities—including oil, steel, grain, weather events, and securitized debt—is determined through a future price that anticipates bullish or bearish tendencies. That future spot price is an anticipated value paid in the present. It is also the capital raised in the present that, at least since the 1980s, has generated the financial conditions for a future telegraphed by the assemblage of actors, drives, and instruments eager to profit from temporal difference. In Fredric Jameson's landmark essay "The End of

Temporality," this economic infrastructure, elsewhere described by Giovanni Arrighi as the late stage of capital's cycle of accumulation (1994), produces new regulative abstractions where the accumulation of money takes on a life of its own outside the circuit of commodity production and consumption. Financialization is important in this regard because it conditions the tyranny of space amidst the excessive flattening (or in Jameson's Hegelian story, end) of time. And while the energy market is not central to either Arrighi or Jameson's interpretation of post-1970s financialization, Jameson does provide a side-note in that same essay about what in 2003 was the still-fresh example of the Enron scandal, where gross misconduct in energy futures trading resulted in jail time and the false calm of an economic sector capable of being regulated (and punished) by law. Where most critics read the Enron scandal as evidence that the financial sector was still in the final instance tethered to the so-called "real economy"—meaning it could not go on for ever generating fictitious capital without some modicum of accountability—Jameson insists on the opposite: "that under conditions of finance capital stock value has a decidedly semiautonomous status with respect to its nominal company and that, in any case, postmodern 'profitability' is a new category, dependent on all kinds of conditions unrelated to the product itself" (Jameson 2003, 703). The point is as much political as it is cultural because the hegemony of finance capital brings with it a set of economic abstractions that delink material production from profit. Yet, my point in this chapter is going to be that the future orientation of finance and the fossil-fuel industry become recursive to one another gradually in the 1970s, and that this matters (or ought to matter) for critiques of capital and concerns for environment. My argument is that the economic abstraction of fossil fuels into the medium of the market after 1973 makes its force and function in the global economy difficult to see in the way that the source of a penumbra is obscured by the distribution of its effects over the visual field, but that Shell's invention of a unique (and now widely adopted) technique for scenarios thinking on the cusp of the 1970s oil crises helps us see the emergence of that recursive futurity *in medias res*. Hence, while the eventual dominance of energy futures trading would come by the end of the 1980s to hold the present and future of the global economy to the concrete and abstract materialism of fossil fuels, my focus in this chapter is on a novel form of writing that future strategically and analytically, moments before the energy market was restructured. The genealogy I offer of the so-called "decision scenario" invented by Shell is interesting today for its redefinition of oil from commodity to medium of the market as such, narrating an emergent concept of oil that would eventually become actualized and operationalized in the financial sector over a decade later (even as it would recede from view in discussions of neoliberalism, the postindustrial, and postmodern culture).

Today, the financial form and tense of energy commodities intermingle with the genres of narrating the future authored by both the private and public sectors alike so intimately that it is nearly impossible to imagine a capitalism fully freed from fossil fuels. My aim here is to historicize the moment around 1973 when that dialectical closure was made thinkable internal to a company with enough political and economic power to make the closure a reality.

If the genre of anticipation involved in scenarios planning imagines the potential consequences of the present out into a horizon in order to refine structural risks and opportunities, the genre of exchange writes the future by optimizing the value available in the lag between today and tomorrow. But although the two genres appear to have different if not opposing narrative structures (one is about disarticulating the given and the possible, while the other is about tying the possible to the given), what soaks through both, at least since sometime around 1973, is the abstract materiality of oil. The future, our collective future, is still stuck in 1973 because the mode of oil-based thinking and its limitations have been codified into the scenario genre as such. Indeed, the separation of oil's abstract form from its crude materiality as a fossil fuel, alongside the saturation of the future in the terminal landscape of oil's concrete and abstract properties, is getting in the way of a radical politics serious about writing its way out of the petrocultural penumbra of the present. So, while the emergence and then rapid domination of energy futures markets over the flow of both fossil fuels and capital is a primary site through which energy dependency is written well into the future, I am interested here in how oil in particular began to express itself as a substance that exceeded the terms of regular commodities in the forms of thinking making sense of the 1970s within the energy sector itself.

My object then is the narrative structure by which fossil fuels get focalized into a medium of the post-1973 global economy: the narrative apparatus of 1970s scenarios planning baked into the forms of futures thinking animating environmental discourse today. An immanent reading of the apparatus for these initial scenarios helps us distill the distribution of fossil fuels across the penumbra that makes up our historical present and also the modality of anticipation with which the IPCC turns climate into concern. Fossil fuels in the post-1973 era begin to underpin the world market and are financialized amidst accelerated neoliberalization. This matters in the genealogy of the present because the political economy of fossil fuels remains secondary to the ways in which the terminal conditions nominated in so much political and cultural theory have been figured, even if their physical impacts on the planet have emerged as a primary environmental concern.[1] In this process of post-1973 saturation and synchronization that I track here, ideas of time, futurity, and world-making get altered and pegged to fossil fuels in newly significant ways. To detail the structural shifts into a world market soaked in fossil fuels, I first situate the turn to postindustrial petroculture in the larger political economy of twentieth-century fossil fuels by building on the critical turn to energy's market form in the energy and environmental humanities. In the second section, I move the analysis into the boardrooms of Shell in the moments leading up to the first oil crash in 1973. By reading pioneer scenarios planner Pierre Wack as a troubling but unique source for theoretical thinking on the material links between postindustrial economy, neoliberal imaginaries, and petroculture, I then suggest that reading Shell's reconceptualization of oil as the very medium of postindustrial historicity provides petrocultural criticism with a unique analytic with which to frame the economic and ecological contest over the future today. I demonstrate this by turning briefly in the concluding section to the generic conventions hardening the intractability of energy and capital in recent scenarios thinking ostensibly concerned with economic prosperity and environmental sustainability. I argue that the genealogy of futures thinking today is provided its narrative structure by the abstract materialism of an economy synchronized to oil's environment, and that the ostensible impossibility of imaging a future without oil (even when, as was true on April 20, 2020, oil becomes cheaper than free) is a signal crisis of the petrocultural penumbra.

Energy futures in the present tense

In a little over a year after the price of oil began its nosedive from $125 to $30 by January 2016, nearly $1.3 trillion had evaporated from the pockets of investors in the United States energy sector—a net loss representing roughly the entire GDP of Mexico (Loder 2015). The news did not seem so bad to consumers who, thanks to the then 76 percent drop in the price of oil, were effectively handed fuel rebates in an economy otherwise inflated by oil's effect on the supply curve. Yet, for the very same reason, the price drop caused by the intentional oversupply, and the unexpected success of "unconventionals" (such as fracked oil and natural gas in the US Midwest and the Dutch North), generated elastic effects across virtually all other sectors. This is because coal, natural gas, and oil prices are now so deeply integrated into pension funds, state and provincial revenues, public sector budgets, interest rates, and foreign investment strategies that price volatility now ripples across the economy like a change in climate. We are all, to use Stephanie LeMenager's wonderful phrase, "living oil," or at the very least overexposed to it in financial terms (LeMenager 2014).

Overexposure to the market rhythms (not to mention the cascading biophysical consequences) of fossil fuels is, at least in financial terms, a recent feature of life on Earth. According to Michael Watts, the US Commodity Futures Modernization Act in 2000 helped expose the energy industry to the speculative drives of international derivates trading at the same time that it protected traders from oversight and regulation. It is in the wake of this financialization of oil through energy futures trading that 70 percent of all oil is now traded on futures markets: in a typical day, Watts contends, "paper oil" exceeds trading of "wet oil" by fifteen to twenty times (Watts 2015). Until 2017, half of all global oil futures—including WTI and Brent Crude futures, UK natural gas, baseload and peakload electricity, and carbon emission allowances—were traded on the Intercontinental Exchange (ICE) in London (Meyer 2017). Oil is not the first commodity to feature in futures trading—most famously, tulips were in 1630s Amsterdam, while livestock, wheat, and other agricultural goods have all been packaged as futures contracts since the early twentieth century, not to mention that the more recent economic dominance (and cultural infamy) of mortgage-backed derivatives still textures global markets with the ebbs and flows of what Leigh Claire La Berge calls cultures of arbitrage (La Berge 2015). Financialization was a primary means by which neoliberalization restructured the global economy beginning in the 1970s, but the restructuring of the energy sector was a necessary precondition of that process. More to my point, oil became what both Timothy Mitchell (2011) and Daniel Yergin (1990) term the new gold standard for international exchange, becoming a distinctive force over the economy as a whole and thus also a unique historical object of study and critique.

To delineate the economic, political, and cultural forms of dependency that telegraph our entanglement with fossil fuels well into the twenty-first century requires isolating the transition from the era of posted energy prices to our current spot (or futures) markets that began in the wake of the 1970s oil crises. The emergence of futures trading in the energy sector—representing roughly 5 percent of energy traded in the 1970s and rising to a staggering 85 percent by 1989—is key to unpacking our dependence on fossil fuels because it marks a qualitative shift in oil's market form, contemporaneous as it was with the post-Bretton Woods currency contest and the postindustrial turn that followed.

Writing about the energy future means writing about the problem of writing about the future and futures of energy—wanting to, looking for ways to, but always running up against a problem of the genre of the writing itself: speculation on and interpretation of the present forms of thinking and modeling *that write* the future pre-emptively are not qualitatively of the same order of determination. Methodologically, this raises a key question emerging from petrocultural criticism over the past decade: Which genre of writing helps us historicize the future before it happens, in turn helping us conceive of contradictions and critiques adequate to the capitalist materialism that largely determines the shape of things to come? As Karen Pinkus (2013) shows us about carbon futures, when it comes to energy, the future is something that has already happened, but asymmetrically to the narrative structures that we bring to the game of recognition, so you have to bring more than one narrative structure to see it at all (a symptom, I would suggest, that we see playing out in the hermeneutics of periodization otherwise known as the Anthropocene debates).

As Melinda Cooper (2016) reminds us, Larry Summers, former Director of the National Economic Council under Barack Obama, thinks we have reached the age of "secular stagnation"—an impasse where capital neither has reason nor opportunity to invest at scales adequate to sustain macroeconomic growth (see also O'Brien 2018). Even the former editor of *The Economist* Marc Levinson (2016) insists that 1973 marks the beginning of a moment in the protracted wake of which we are still floating. In his account, the "Golden Age" of capitalist growth was underwritten by massive increases in labor productivity, capital investment, and cheap energy. However, by the time the oil crisis of 1973 hit, the base line of the economy had stagnated in the form of a "productivity bust" bringing "the long run of global prosperity to an end" (Levinson 2016, 79). When the Organization of Arab Petroleum Exporting Countries (OAPEC, now OPEC) embargo began on October 16, 1973, the US economy had already hit the dreaded impasse of "stagflation," where stagnant productivity levels comingled with an already hyperinflated dollar following Nixon's recession from the Bretton Woods agreements. Cheap and readily available oil surged through the technical composition of postwar growth, both accelerating labor productivity and signaling an energic limit to the organic composition of variable and fixed capital in the manufacturing sector. The enormous wealth created in the postwar period was now fixed either in long-term capital investments or in reserves accumulating at levels in excess of the opportunities needed to turn money into capital. By most accounts, the shock rise in oil prices did not cause the terminal crisis in 1973 because stagflation was already plaguing the capitalist core by the late

1960s.² But the reverberations of the price hike down into the depths of an economy already saturated in the energic capacities afforded by cheap oil meant that the post-1973 world would need to free up both the flow of energy and the flow of capital.

Looking for the real abstractions that oil makes possible for capitalism is a primary ambition of the cultural critique of oil developing in the humanities and social sciences over the past decade. Petrocultural criticism is a methodology—used in this chapter—for reading, historicizing, and politicizing the ubiquitous but avisual force of fossil fuels across social, economic and physical environments.³ In Jennifer Wenzel's terms, "this is the great paradox of fossil-fuel imaginaries: in literature as in life, oil in particular is at once everywhere and nowhere, indispensable yet largely unapprehended, not so much invisible as unseen" (Wenzel 2017, 11). By tracking the material and symbolic force of fossil fuels through the cultural forms codified across the industrial and postindustrial eras, scholars in the energy humanities have helped provide the critical mediations necessary to annul the dangerous conceit that energy systems and the resources that fuel them are technocratic and ahistorical features independent from culture.⁴ Yet, by reframing the problem of energy in terms of all manner of social and cultural forms, new perspectives have also emerged in the humanities and social sciences on the materialities that help animate long waves of economic history.

In this context, Imre Szeman's crucial intervention in "System Failure: Oil, Futurity, and the Anticipation of Disaster" (2007) did much to both introduce and rethink energy into the historical materialist frameworks of capitalism's *longue durée*. Put simply, there is no physical basis upon which to imagine the conditions for either British or US hegemony in the nineteenth or twentieth centuries without the political and productive capacity afforded by cheap coal and oil. The claim that capitalism is at base an economic formation built on a foundation of fossil fuels is almost too crude to sustain, but part of Szeman's point is that the environmental and economic pressures that come with the pending disasters of anthropogenic climate change on the one hand, and the terminal crisis of capitalism delineated by Moishe Postone on the other, only make sense when understood as twin expressions of capitalism's internalization of fossil fuels. Hence capitalism is not somehow determined by the concrete materiality of fossil fuels (critical though this materiality has been); rather, capitalism's production of distinctive genres of futurity are mediated by the social, economic, and regulative abstractions that fossil fuels make available. Seeing oil's persistence as an absent cause of these genres—Szeman calls them "strategic realism," "techno-utopianism," and "eco-apocalypse"—is an indispensable component of denaturalizing a future made in the (increasingly scorching) image of fossil-fueled capitalism. The closure formed between scenarios planning and futures exchange, however, underwrite the more speculative genres named in Szeman's map of the petrocultural imaginary.

In this way, petrocultural criticism is different from critiques of fossil-fuel companies, consumerism, or even the cultural ignorance of either supply- or demand-side emissions because the many objects and concepts that make up its archive spill out across the many axes of mediation that grid our critical compass: from geologic strata and atmospheric zones, forms of sociality and modes of governance, deep time and fast history, the political and the economic, to pipelines and productivity rates. When it comes to mediation, petrocultural criticism has its work cut out for itself. The expanded field of mediation involves not just hydrocarbons but also the historicity of their ecology. That is, petrocultural criticism takes as primary that there is no shortage of knowledge about the stuff itself—what it smells and looks like, how much we use, and so on, though any geologist would tell you that we actually know very little about its genealogies, and that our knowledge of its current state in the earth is mostly speculative—so that what is required instead is a larger view of how oil matters in social, political, and economic—as well as in geological—terms.

By looking for oil between the ubiquity of its presence in the lifeworld of contemporary culture and the avisual force it exerts over the *longue durée* of capitalism, the petrocultural "penumbra" begins to emerge as an important space in need of critical mediation where capitalism reproduces itself materially, discursively, and culturally.[5] The penumbra is what is both shaded out and created by a light source, or, to put it a little differently, the shadowy part of the picture you get when looking not right at the thing but at its distribution. The physical energy from fossil fuels is constantly distributed into the world not just as kilojoules and watts, much less liters or tonnage, but as a medium of the expanded reproduction of capital.[6]

Important for establishing the historical materialism of oil has been the work of Timothy Mitchell, who has helped unpack the discursive structures through which "the economy" emerged as a unique object of knowledge in the late nineteenth and early twentieth centuries. As Mitchell outlines in *Carbon Democracy* (2011), oil was initially imagined during the 1940s Bretton Woods meetings as a viable replacement for gold as an international commodity suitable to fix exchange rates. Following the Second World War, John Maynard Keynes and Harry Dexter White had proposed the creation of a third institution called the International Petroleum Council, alongside the International Monetary

Fund (IMF) and what would become the World Bank, whose jurisdiction was to be the regulation of key global commodities. Even Friedrich Hayek (1943), who spearheaded the intellectual opposition to Keynes, was arguing for a "commodity reserve currency" as oil was quickly becoming the most sought-after energy stock. Oil was then already very near its mid-century dominance over other energy sources internationally. Its mobile properties and superiority over coal as a fuel source (its elasticity) and its importance as industrial material in petrochemicals, industrial fertilizer, and mass-commodity production (its plasticity) made its regulative function over various economic spheres all too clear to those tasked with building a postwar path to prosperity.

However, it wasn't just the modern financial system that oil made possible, in Mitchell's account, but also that peculiar thing called "the economy" itself, which emerges discursively on the scene as an object of knowledge right at the moment that oil's elastic and plastic character sets the stage for the golden era of capitalist growth. The economy "was an object that no economist or planner prior to the 1930s spoke of or knew to exist"; economic analysis until then applied to "government, or the proper management of people and resources, as in the phrase 'political economy'" (Mitchell 2011, 124). By 1946, Edwin Nourse, Chairmen of the Council of Economic Advisors in the US, began asking for a policy environment in which decisions were conducted not in terms of the "the economy of the firm," but "the economy of the economy" (1953, 15–16). Economic abstraction, in other words, was nominalized as an object requiring a new science of national accounts as the energy source increasingly giving it shape became oil.

If the rise of oil is bound up with the emergence of twentieth-century economic discourse about itself, what does it mean to engage in cultural criticism of fossil fuels today on the other side of this recursive entanglement? Mazen Labban argues:

> Introducing financial logic to the study of oil engenders a space–time parallax between oil's representation as a physical commodity circulating in physical (and financial) markets and its representation as a financial asset circulating in financial (and physical) markets ... Both are real enough and have their own materiality, but each alone is an abstraction incapable of standing in for the oil market, whose objectivity is produced from the incessant displacement between two space–times of circulation.
>
> Labban 2010, 542

Labban's concern is primarily with the financialization of oil in the lead-up to and aftermath of 2008, but it is the origins of this parallax that I am after here.

In Mitchell's landmark essay from 1998, "Fixing the Economy," he sets the stage for thinking oil's determinate character on the discursive structures through which the economy became an object of knowledge:

> The power of the economy as a discursive process lies exactly with fixing this effect of the real (economy) versus its representation. The proliferation of models, statistics, plans and programmes of economic discourse all claim to represent the different elements and relationships of a real object, the national economy. Yet this object, as one could show at length, is itself constituted as a discursive process, a phenomenon of values, representations, communications, meanings, goals and uses, none of which can be separated from or said to pre-exist their representation in economic discourse.
>
> Mitchell 1998, 86

In this first phase of the argument, Mitchell is decidedly constructivist in his account of "the economy." However, by the time he turns his attention to oil in what becomes, in 2011, *Carbon Democracy*, a new sense of "this object" begins to syncopate the "real (economy) [and] its representation." As Mitchell writes:

> The economy came into being as an object of calculation and a means of governing populations not with the political economy of the late eighteenth century or the new academic economics of the late nineteenth century, but only in the mid-twentieth century... Its appearance was made possible by oil, for the availability of abundant, low-cost energy allowed economists to abandon earlier concerns with the exhaustion of natural resources and represent material life instead as a system of monetary circulation—a circulation that could expand indefinitely without any problem of physical limits.
>
> Mitchell 2011, 234

This not quite natural, not quite unnatural thing called the economy, in other words, depends both on the physical and the conceptual character of oil's industrialization—its cheapness and its abundance—and yet it is the very structures of representation (the forms through which values, communications, meanings, goals, and uses, to use Mitchell's words from above) that determine the material reality of a world soaked in hydrocarbons. This double bind—oil as both condition of representation and its object—is already embedded in Shell's genre of writing the future in the 1970s, a point to which I turn next. But, importantly, the double bind remains an important though widely overlooked epistemological framework from which contemporary futures thinking plots our way forward, to which I turn briefly in the final section of this chapter.

"Shooting the rapids" and the metaphor of oil

Pierre Wack opens the first of his two-part essay on Shell's invention of scenarios planning in the years leading to the first oil crash in 1973 with a decidedly postmodern zinger: "The future," Wack insists, "is no longer stable. It has become a moving target" (Wack 1985a, 73). Wack was then the scenarios team leader, a position he had acquired following his tenure as chief economist for Shell Française in Paris, and what he saw was a qualitative shift on the horizon of this relationship between energy and capital, where the two would come to syncopate the global economy as such. Since 1965, Shell had already used a first-generation form of scenarios planning much closer to the computer-generated forecasts used by Herman Kahn at the RAND Corporation, but problems arose when the department was asked to extend its initial six-year horizon date all the way through 2000. Forecasting, in Wack's account, does not help managers who are spread out across the different branches of the company to make strategically complimentary decisions because all they are made to see is the range of uncertainty at a higher resolution. As a genre of writing the future, the forecast clarifies the future through a computer-generated prolepsis from the present, and so tends to comfort managers back to an outlook underwritten by predetermined, as opposed to uncertain, elements of the future. From the perspective of the new scenarios department, forecasts taught managers to think like computers, and this was a problem. What was needed was a "different image of reality" to see what oil did to the future tense of the market, in turn redefining what oil had meant to the postwar economy (Wack 1985a, 84). Computer forecasts could not tell that story.

Anticipating this qualitative shift, as well as the quantitative effects for the industry, Shell therefore famously saw a way to hedge against the 1973 energy crisis, months before it happened. In later years, Wack would become the new economy's poster boy for daring and innovative thinking, able uniquely to "shoot the rapids" of the future.[7] Peter Schwartz, author of *The Art of the Long View*—the veritable bible of the professional association of futurists trained in futures thinking programs across the US—in fact credits the eponymous art to Wack, with whom Schwartz worked at Shell before himself taking over the scenarios team in 1982. By the 1990s, when Schwartz was helping to translate scenarios planning into doxa for leading US management schools, futures thinking had become a hybrid discipline combining design thinking and business fundamentals for the new economy, applicable in principle to any firm needing a clearer read on the future rapids of commerce. In its initial development, however, the metaphor of "shooting the rapids" named not just a confidence in the face of economic uncertainty, but also the very substance that gave capital a topography and character in the future to come. In the metaphor, in other words, the rapids exist in a deluge not of water but of oil, and it is the force of oil on "the business environment" that needs to be interpreted, rather than the most probable (or risk-free) route through uncertainty (Wack 1985b). In Wack's analysis, the tide of postwar growth hit a "technological recession" when it became "cheaper to acquire existing capacity than it was to order new capacity" (Wack 1985b, 144). Discouraging "new investment in industries that had been the engine of postwar economic growth" and accentuating "inflationary pressure" (144), Wack began to consider the implications for the oil industry. In the early 1970s, Wack's team would see the lineaments of this "new world of internal contradictions" and reason that a sound corporate strategy needed to account for oil's regulative function across monetary markets, productivity levels, and the global distribution of value in a world about to hit a wall. In the metaphorical shift from water to oil is a condensation of how Shell scenarios would come to reimagine the life source of the economy.

In this schema of thinking futures, however, are the very seeds of a method for petrocultural mediation required to confront today's environmental and social crises. This is not because we ultimately need to "think like Shell" to get out of the catastrophes they helped create, nor because oil companies are going to save us from ourselves as techno-fetishists like Statoil, Shell, and BP executives would have it. Rather, it is because in Shell's archive of thought are critical concepts of energy, environment, and duration that have as yet not been fully developed in the disciplinary or political fields most concerned with the environment of critique. Mixed into the metaphor of the rapids is an implicit claim about the historical specificity of oil as it becomes a medium, rather than a mere object, of exchange—the sea-change on the horizon of 1973. In order to translate this shift in the medium specificity of oil amidst its saturation of the global economy, Shell executives elsewhere in the company would need to unlearn one concept of oil in order to see its unique (and emergent) resource aesthetic. To affect this shift in consciousness, Wack makes the distinction between geophysical analysis more typical of forecasting, on the one hand—a mode that read the future price of oil based on the current supply—and the genre of uncertainties mapped by scenarios, on the other.

In fact, it was predominantly still the reports from Shell's team of geologists that determined the numbers and narratives of internal forecasting in the late 1960s before Wack took the reins of scenarios, and for him this geophysical structure to Shell's mode of "perception" blinded managers to an *emergent* business environment (Wack 1985b, 140). The earlier reports were about a crude form of projection where the likelihood of development remains indexed to geophysical probabilities of given reserves—that is, an analysis inoculated against socio-historical and economic determination, or the present projected into a future of its own making. For Wack, what was required was not just a new form of diagrammatically representing variables, but also a narrative structure for deconstructing the imaginary or worldview extensive with postwar growth. Angela Wilkinson, a counselor for strategic foresight at the OECD and a former member of the Shell Corporate Scenarios Team, and Roland Kupers, a former senior executive at Shell, both argue that this shift in thinking underwrites the move from probability to plausibility in futures thinking. As they explain:

> probability is useful in situations where historical patterns are set to repeat. However, when structural shifts are in play, new and unfamiliar situations emerge that benefit from attention to problem framing instead of problem solving ... The Shell concept of plausibility is very different from the emphasis on the single and most probable forecast [because] forecasting assumes that trends will not bend and that the future is a continuation of the past.
>
> Wilkinson and Kupers 2014, 82

Plausibilities is one of the key concepts around which Shell began in the 1970s to reimagine the world with oil not as a mere resource or commodity, but instead as both an object and subject of the business environment. To make the case using Shell's more recent, infamous 2050 scenario "Scramble" and "Blueprints" (Shell International BV 2008): "what happens at the end of the scenario, at the horizon date ... is not as important as the insights relating to the deeper, systemic dynamics revealed in the story."

The year 1973 was to mark the end of an era, the aftermath of which would involve new "systemic dynamics" requiring a new way of seeing not just the "rapids," but also the medium constitutive of its volatility. For Wack, the shift to plausibilities required a new theoretical framework able to delineate, position, and distill "predetermined elements" and thus a kind of cognitive map of energy's determinate structure in the historical present: "The point," Wack insists, "is not so much to have one scenario that 'gets it right' as to have a set of scenarios that illuminates the major forces driving the system, their interrelationships, and the critical uncertainties" (Wack 1985b, 146). Spread across Wack's archive are thus a set of procedures for "destroying [the manager's] view of the world" (1985a, 87). The manner in which scenarios "destroy" worldviews are not so much the forms

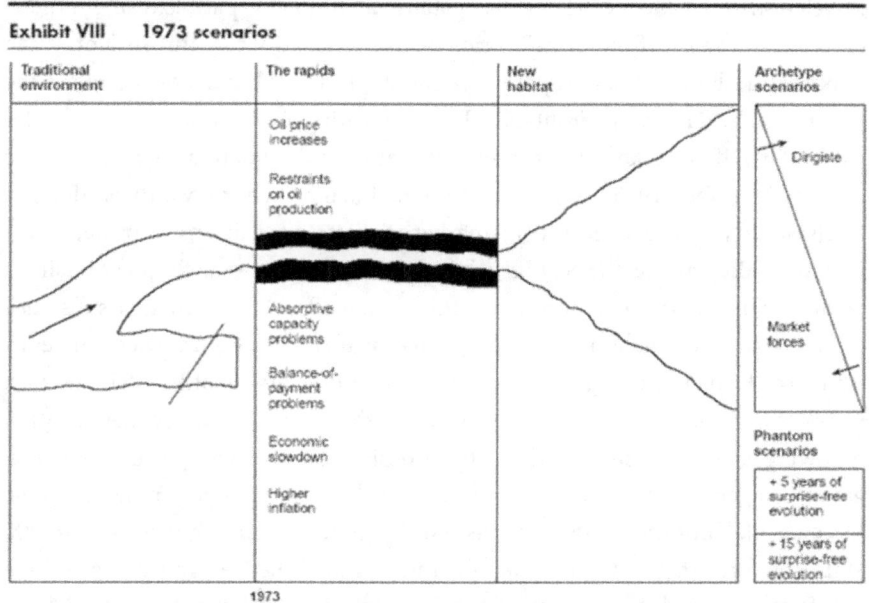

Figure 1.1 Pierre Wack, "Exhibit VIII, 1973 Scenarios". *Harvard Business Review* (September 1985).

of representing or diagramming trends, but the time and narrative structure required to do so. And because, on Wack's account, "a manager's inner model never mirrors reality, it is always a construct" (1985b 150), the scenario's team realized they couldn't simply memo out their diagrams to different branches of the company; they needed instead to turn planning sessions into three-hour-long re-education clinics. What we see here, then, is the first of many crucial differences between Shell's concept of the energy future and other methods vying for acceptance, notably those used at the RAND Corporation in the US: Shell's new concept of the business environment included a shift in the very narrative structure of past, present, and future—no longer geological or chronological, but a recursive ecology to postindustrial capital.

The major test case was a comprehensive scenarios package that Wack's team prepared in advance of what they prefiguratively saw as an invariable shock to oil prices in 1973 (see Figure 1.1). In the wake of the 1971 recession, as well as the Nixon administration's recess from the Bretton Woods Agreement (effectively turning the US dollar into the global de facto gold standard), the political and economic forces driving oil markets became uniquely sensitive to US inflation. In the Saudi context in particular, Wack's team anticipated a new behavioral pattern in relation to production levels—a pattern alert to the paradoxical synthesis between the value of oil and US price fluctuations. To verify this insight, Wack quotes a Saudi oil minister saying: "We should find that leaving our crude in the ground is by far more profitable than depositing our money in the banks, particularly if we take into account the periodic devaluation of many of the currencies" (Wack 1985a, 80). Though the national behavior towards production levels would vary widely from a pro-market orientation to a defensive, protectionist one as in the case of the Saudis, what was important about the new business environment was the macroeconomic function of oil, as both regulative substance of industrial output and monetary hedge against a US-dominated currency standard. Knowing that the Middle Eastern producers would widely adopt a restricted output schedule in response to their own currency depreciation following the Nixon shock, Wack's team designed a scenario presentation that gave managers upstream and downstream no choice but to relearn the economic force of oil. Until the 1970s, capitalist doxa dictated nothing but steady growth. With low growth on the horizon, Shell managed to hedge against the sudden shock experienced by the rest of the industry, first by beefing up short-term investments in coal, and second by cutting upstream investments in the Middle East and shifting its portfolio to North Sea oil.

In narrating the crucial shift in perspective that made Shell scenarios so different from other forms of projection and planning in the global economy, Wack mounts an unexpected critique of a cybernetic paradigm of futures thinking. Computer-based projections turned historical data into a form of pattern recognition that hit executives at the wrong discursive level, Wack argued. Economic growth in the postwar era was abnormally high—between 5 and 7 percent annually from 1950 until the end of the 1960s—and the historical data on inflation, growth, and oil prices from the so-called golden era of the western economy looked to executives like a solid baseline from which to imagine relative probabilities into the future. But they took an enigma for a paradigm. Incapable of seeing anything other than the present perfect tense of an economy that had normalized a false image of its own inertia during postwar prosperity, the US, French, and British governments famously all *raised* their predicted rates of growth for 1974 months after the OPEC embargo took hold in October 1973 (Levinson 2016, 76). The trouble, Wack reasoned, was that the US's recent delinking from the gold standard meant that the growing inflation crisis in the American economy would devalue the price of oil for Middle Eastern producers, since the barrel was now de facto priced in US dollars (and thus less valuable as inflation rapidly surged in the months leading to the OPEC embargo in 1973). Quite suddenly, the price of oil became recursive to the US dollar, so that the source of US inflation, namely a maturing of the industrial sector and the narrowing margin of profit for US businesses, would generate something of a macroeconomic problem in the form of stagflation: rising unemployment, low economic growth, and high inflation. For Wack, this meant that the 1970s were going to be unorthodox times, because no Middle Eastern oil producer would sit back passively as the US industrial sector dictated a crash in the relative value of a barrel from the other side of the world, bringing all boats crashing with the falling tides of profit.

The insight made available by the move away from a probabilistic approach permitted a shift in the problem of scenarios from data to theory, since only an expanded theory of the relationship between energy, capital, and global decision makers could begin to anticipate the kind of volatility that nobody else seemed capable of seeing. In short, Shell's new generation of scenario planners began working with a theory of political economy that put oil's simultaneously crude and abstract forms at the heart of the historical present. To *see* the macroeconomic and geopolitical saturation of oil, Shell abandoned a geological concept of oil's commodity form and developed a way of looking for its historical materiality across the markets it would come to synchronize. Shell long ago shifted their institutional understanding about the kind of thing oil is in the world: not a commodity among other commodities but a primary source of mediating the landscape of the postindustrial economy.

By 1973, oil had become the dominant medium of the market because of its multiple and contingent functions in industrial production, circulation, and financial speculation—what elsewhere I call "energy deepening," following Harvard economist Dale Jorgenson (Diamanti 2018). Consider, in other words, the event of 1973 as a unique moment in the history of energy when the socioeconomic structure of oil pricing became syncopated to the macroeconomic rhythms of global capital. This is reminiscent of Fredric Jameson's axiom in *The Political Unconscious* (composed in the thick of the 1970s energy crises) that history is not a text, but is nevertheless only available to us in textual form (1981, 102). That year is unique in that no imminent threat of natural scarcity or peak figured in Shell's map of the future. Instead, oil's quality as a macroeconomic and political form of regulation, emerging as it had been since its quantitative dominion over the economy, made available something like the lineaments of the whole—a vista onto the shape of things to come, paradoxical as that shape seemed to those seasoned managers who made up Wack's audience across Shell's international branches. To explain the turn to scenarios as an expression of exchange value's social construction is to lose the critical footing from which the historical specificity of energy and capital can be more fully understood, and hence (for our purposes) more fully critiqued. It is to lose the concept of structure and method alert to today's energy impasse. That concept of structure ought not to be so varied from the one Shell's planning department developed, where energy and capital were understood both normatively and functionally as recursive to one another.

Energy and climate

The success of the Shell scenarios department is not about their ability to predict the future exactly, but hinges rather on their ability to position themselves strategically amidst the "rapids" of the 1970s political economy. Wack's archive at the Oxford Futures Library is replete with warnings against the compulsion to develop and read scenarios as prophecies or forecasts on a future that is predetermined in the present. As a performative genre, scenarios at Shell are practically designed to immerse executives in ways of seeing the principal tensions and tendencies animating the business environment in order to unlearn firm-level habits of thought. At least in the first decade of the department, the scenario did not function as a macro-organizational mandate or branding platform as it has become more recently, but instead as a knot internal to the company deliberately designed to critically remake the concept of energy underwriting the different branches of Shell. Wack's own discourse on the origins and success of Shell scenarios focalizes its narrative on the company's ability to mitigate what elsewhere in the sector and larger economy were enormous financial losses in 1973, but the scenario as a genre of thinking the future has less to do with individual events than it does with the institutional shifts that help us refine our critical concepts of an energy system entangled with the earth's climatic condition. While the productive capacity afforded the manufacturing sector by coal in the early twentieth century had helped generate the conditions for "the economy" to serve as an object of knowledge, economists were nevertheless slow to reimagine the force of energy on the macrostructures animating the market. As much is clear from the rather late focus on energy's function in growth economics, which did not become a core concern until Sam Schurr—former advisor to the RAND Corporation, the Office of Strategic Services, and the US Bureau of Mines —began soliciting papers on energy resources and total factor productivity (TFP) in 1960 (Schurr 1960). Even then it would take another two decades before Dale W. Jorgenson began writing energy into the macroeconomics curriculum at Harvard (Jorgenson 1984). The case I have been making so far is that Shell makes available an immanent standpoint onto what happens when energy's market force starts to replace the crude concept of energy—as mere object of exchange, input cost, or environmental hazard. Gradually the future gets refocalized by a narrative structure that plots energy as a real abstraction, animating systemic dynamics far beyond the question of supply, demand, or emission.

An ideological critique of Shell's deployment of scenarios would miss the details around which oil itself began to unnerve the structures of thought organizing what was and continues to be one of the major oil producers on a global stage. While one way to read the pseudo-prophetic event of Shell's insight into the shape of things to come would be to say that it verifies the social construction of value in a sector of the economy already traditionally plagued by price fixing, monopoly advantage, and rentier capitalism, I am suggesting that what matters about oil's materiality in the postindustrial era exceeds the capture of any one firm or ideological structure.[8] In a social-constructivist account, Shell's uniquely generative role in the regulation of oil prices would get prioritized, and the conventional explanation—that the specter of scarcity drives managers to hedge against risk and to double down on short-term profit—would help explain the social perception motivating the agents responsible for Shell's scenario. I want to hold on to that thesis because it plainly matters that Shell both then and now help make a future to which they are subject, given the scale of consequence flowing from their own internal habits of thought. But another way to read the event of scenarios planning is as a temporary solution to the problem of representation plaguing capitalist modernity—the problem of rendering the real abstraction of value into a form of knowledge accurate enough to act upon—and the unique function of oil in generating that solution. What Wack's scenarios team make vivid for our critical standpoint on energy and environment today is that oil exerts an abstract force over the political ecology of postindustrial capitalism, and that mapping that force involves an analytic of its inertia into the forms of the future it helps write in excess of corporate or state authorship.

Certainly, the rollout of neoliberal policies in the west during the 1970s and 1980s helped create the agency we have come to associate with the financial sector through which 95 percent of energy is mediated before the point of consumption. The economic drives that continue to reproduce energy-intensive futures need to be consistently and thoroughly critiqued, demystified, and denaturalized. Where those drives get most clearly rendered into narrative form are in the scenarios published year by year across state and non-state organizations tasked with worrying about the often indistinguishable relationship between the business environment and the physical environment. In Shell's recent *Energy Scenarios to 2050*, for instance, anxiety about a socially and environmentally volatile horizon is imagined as part of the same path dependency telegraphed by "development," but with the proviso that "[o]rdinary rates of supply growth ... could naturally boost energy production by about 50%" by 2050 without a projected shortfall of "400 J/a—the size of the whole industry in 2000" (Shell International BV 2011, 10). The gap, or what Shell's vice-president business environment Jeremy Bentham terms the "Zone of Uncertainty" (10), is the space of economic and environmental collision, since without market-based CO_2 pricing and incentivized increases in natural gas-based industrial and domestic power in the developing world, the drives of capital expansion will crash through the sustainable horizon plotted by 2050. Capital expansion is here turned into an *effect* rather than the cause of what Shell are not alone in predicting will be a tripling of global energy demand by that year. The sleight of hand works to reproduce the future of the planet recursively to the resource naturalism of the neoliberal imaginary: growth becomes a naturalized structure for emplotting 2050, not only because it is impossible to imagine a world without it, but also because the so-called natural boost of energy production— emerging synergistically amidst "technological, geological, competitive, financial, and political realities"—will compel the concord between energy and capital indefinitely into the future (10). Put differently, growth gives shape to the narratives plotted across the Blueprints and Scramble scenarios, but it is the drives of energy deepening from which the concept of growth gets naturalized in the first place.

And Shell is not unique in its otherwise congenital claim that energy has become the agent of history. Nicholas Stern's now infamous *Review* on *The Economics of Climate Change* (2007), for instance, institutionalized a viewpoint foregrounding economic costs and benefits associated with "business as usual," concluding in no uncertain terms that "the overall costs and risks of climate change will be equivalent to losing at least 5% of global GDP each year, now and forever" (Sterne 2007, vi). Aggressively mitigating asset loss from climate change and increasing robust investment in carbon capture and renewable energy have become two leading policy points to turn climate change into what the New Climate Economy Commission regularly terms "an opportunity," but the inertia of capital's intimacy with an ever-expanding base energy is simply impossible to figure out from even the most eco-friendly scenarios of the future.

While it remains true that the current glut of oil on the market, beginning in 2014 and inflected uniquely by the COVID-19 health and economic crisis in

April 2020, as well as the rapid evaporation of speculative capital's ephemeral excess, exposes many of the mechanisms that *socially* construct the fiction of a spot price, we also remain no less exposed to the twisted dialectic that binds capital markets to energy markets. And we are exposed in more ways than one: so long as the future remains an object written in the medium of postindustrial petroculture, financial volatility will interweave with the unpredictable violence that comes with a world warmed past critical tipping points. With each passing year, our global economic system uses much more energy than it did the year before, and this—according to the IEA, the Energy Information Agency, the Organization for Economic Co-operation and Development, and the IPCC—is set to remain true for at least another half-century. The globe, put another way, has never used as much energy as it has today—a descriptive sentence that for the next fifty years is set to remain true each time it is uttered. This is another way of saying that no amount of debunking the socially constructed nature of speculation, much less the immaterial determinations of value, will help unnerve "the progress of this storm" (Malm 2018). Neither wet nor paper oil are fictitious in any useful sense, which is to say they are both materially bound to the energic demands of late fossil capital.

It is not just, in other words, that Shell's sheer force in the recent history of the world is so quantitatively large that we must crack open its ideological core in order to critique it. In fact, one thing I hope to have introduced is a non-ideological reading of the habits of thought at Shell—habits of thought that are able to both *represent* and *determine* the futurity of our shared energy system. And it matters for my argument that scenarios planning was first developed in relation to the specific structures of the oil industry—of energy commodities— and then extended by actors such as the IEA, the IPCC, and various national governments (most notably in Singapore and the UK) with the residue of this situated genealogy. It matters because the genealogy of scenarios planning that would come to dominate futures thinking across the private and public sector helps focalize the petrocultural penumbra: oil is more than one kind of thing in the figuration of the future. It is both an object of concern, tied as it is to emissions of CO_2 into the atmosphere and hydrosphere, and the primary medium in which the very thinkability of economic futurity is made possible. In the genre of scenarios now used annually to represent the proximity of the present to the future, oil is both the subject and object—a quantity that can be measured and anticipated, as well as a condition of capital's expanded reproduction. To say that capitalism remains dependent on oil well into the postindustrial era would seem like a violent understatement.

2

The Cultural Work of Architecture: Fixed and Social Capital at Fiat

This truth is, that just as there cannot exist a class political economy, so too there cannot be founded a class aesthetic, art, or architecture, but only class criticism of the aesthetic, of art, of architecture, of the city itself.

Tafuri 1976

Just under a decade after the two oil shocks of the 1970s, what was until then the single largest automobile manufacturing plant in Europe closed its doors. Only a few years later, the former Fiat factory in Lingotto, Turin reopened not as a manufacturer of commodities but as a cultural complex. Of course, Fiat's decision to reinvest a significant portion of its capital into an ostensibly unproductive capital asset—a building that on the face of things produced nothing, and instead housed cultural objects, leisure activities, education facilities. and entrepreneurial startup space—was anything but a free gift back to the economy of the Piedmontese, who fondly referred to the company as "La Mamma." Fiat Chairman Giovanni Agnelli reportedly owned nearly a quarter of the companies on the Milan stock exchange in the 1970s and with Fiat alone controlled 16.5 percent of Italy's industrial investment in research (Tagliabue 2003). Thus while the economic crisis in the 1970s ought to have gutted Fiat's industrial reliance on fossil fuels, the magnitude of their influence over macroeconomic trends and directions meant they, like Shell during the same time, could weather the storm and come out better positioned for the postindustrial society to come. In this chapter I argue that the postindustrialization of Fiat is a signal shift in the capacities of advanced capital to configure worlds proleptically: an important instance, in other words, of the terminal's logic playing out as a modal abstraction instead of a modal cliff.

The board's response to overaccumulation during the recession was a combination of outsourcing, property development, and what Josh Whitford calls "guided growth" (Whitford and Enrietti 2005). Understood as a historically specific economic strategy, Fiat's investment in culture—alongside the then-new research and development facility elsewhere in the city and manufacturing expansion into the Italian South, Brazil, and India—was a specific wager on how to extract future surplus value from a population that its own factories had until then organized as worker and non-worker alike. Now known simply as "Fiat Works," the complex's post-retrofit renaming was perhaps no accident, but instead an insistence on its postindustrial dynamism: Fiat Works.

Politically, this chapter's concern with Fiat's flagship factory will surely not strike most readers as incidental, given Fiat's role as both an antagonist in and a setting for what in the English-speaking world has come to be known as the birth of Italian Autonomous (and later Post-) Marxism. In fact, what strikes me as necessary to understand still, some fifty years on, is precisely the relationship between the political economy of architecture in places like the Italian North and the emergence of two competing though in a strong sense mirror positions on the nature of the new economy: on the one hand, a widespread enthusiasm at the level of macroeconomic policy in the cultural and creative content of what were then new ideas about the coming postindustrial society and, on the other, the political blowback against those same economic transformations—which in more recent debates has been dubbed, thanks to Silvia Federici's critique of it, immaterial labor theory (Federici 2006).[1] That is but one of the many theoretical positions that would emerge out of the heated years preceding the factory conversion at Lingotto. And while the explanatory and rhetorical power of these theses on affect and rent in what is called post-Fordism is not in question here, what strikes me as urgent is the need to consider earlier counter-tendencies in proletarian theory from which that more popular and influential one emerged: namely, the aesthetically attuned insights into economics made available by the criticism of Marxist architectural historian Manfredo Tafuri, on the one hand, and, on the other, the split precipitated between Mario Tronti and Antonio Negri with the publication of Tronti's 1966 *Operai e capitale* (*Workers and Capital*, much of which had already appeared in *Quaderni rossi* a few years earlier), in no small part because the recent shorthand "Italian theory" occludes the heterogeneity of what was arguably the most rigorous period of Marxist analysis in the postwar period. And the urgency of considering other directions in Italian Marxism in order to understand the kinds of cultural strategies developing at firms like Fiat is also not due to a nostalgia for a more militant period of struggle but is rather born out of a concern for a more politically attentive, and we might say older, materialism equipped with an analytic able to capture the interplay of the forces and relations of production (hence the interest in energic flows, architecture, buildings, urbanism, and the economics of fixed capital during the transition to intangible assets) than the one on offer by immaterial labor theory.

As a work of architecture, Renzo Piano's retrofit of the Lingotto factory makes murky the distinction between avant-garde architecture in Italy during the two decades leading up to the conversion's start in 1982—a period characterized by experiments and hypotheses largely concerned with typologies of collective living and megastructural interventions by Superstudio, Archizoom, and the group known now as La Tendenza—and the physical needs of big industry. A discipline imagined in the postwar period as uniquely political in its capacity to make concrete modes of socialist belonging through strikingly modernist forms, architecture, and architectural theory had by the 1970s reached a widely recognized terminus point.

Manfredo Tafuri in *Architecture and Utopia,* perhaps his most famous book in the English-speaking world, insisted that the professional impasse—a theoretical and political terminal, as it were—was written in the stars because "the fate of capitalist society is not at all extraneous to architectural design" (Tafuri 1976, 179). For Tafuri, what it meant for the two to share a fate was that architects had a defeated and yet critical "task" ahead of them: namely, the political function of architecture consisted in its capacity to put "the working class, as organized in its parties and unions, face to face with the highest levels achieved by the dynamics of capitalist development, and relating particular moments to general designs" (172). The "particular moments" of both the "working class" and "capitalist development" are here imagined at a much larger scale than their proximity in the factory, and so the modernist commitment to functional or figurative architectural forms of socialism, such as collective housing or even the *casa del popolo* (house of the people), is made—at least from a political perspective—obsolete. Though it was inconceivable for architecture to distribute or make space for socialism, Tafuri nonetheless saw in its specific material qualities the capacity to make available a version of totality, or "general designs," to a "working class" undergoing rapid transformation. Tafuri thus re-establishes the same critique of radical Viennese urbanism he had been developing in the radical journal *Contrapiano*— except that, in the case of the Italian postwar North, class composition and urban forms of economic planning make architectural *interventions* virtually impossible. For the same reason, however, Tafuri recognized the indispensability of architecture to a working-class standpoint because of its capacity to distribute both an aesthetic and economic materialism. The "search for architectural alternatives" to capitalism, his final provocation insists, "is a contradiction in terms" not because architecture was no match for capitalism, but because architecture at that moment had become a constitutive moment in the urban plan "of the technician, of the organizer of building activity, and of the planner, within the compass of the new forms of capitalist development" (182).

Though Tafuri's critique of what he calls an architectural ideology and its corresponding operative criticism is often understood as a dismissal of neo-rationalism or apolitical formalism in architecture, his argument through the 1960s and 1970s had far more to do with what I will here explain is the architectural logic of capitalism than with a capitalist logic of architecture. The former had always been at work through what Tafuri called "the utopia of form" and architecture's capacity to distribute both perspectives and people. But, with the rise of decision theory and the cybernetic revolution in economics, he imagined it had become a far more immediate impasse to something like a "radical antidesign" (179). In the cybernetic paradigm of economic development, Tafuri, wedding his criticism to that of leading design and planning theorist Horst Rittel, insisted that the old opposition between plan and value had fallen away, and in its wake was a model in which "the very structure of the plan ... generates its systems of evaluation" (175). The idea advanced by Rittel and taken seriously here by Tafuri was that growth in the new economy would consist of a version of surplus value planned in advance by state and private enterprise, and that the consequences for working-class composition (and the architecture that would distribute it) would be transformative in unpredictable ways. The integration of architecture into building cycles, economic zoning, and long-term regional plans signaled to Tafuri that the state and the private sector had signed a new accord putting architectural development at the core of its plans. Thus, in Tafuri's account, the postindustrial phase of capitalist development required architecture's capacity to rationalize the distribution of different kinds of value (geometric, social, functional, and property values, to name the most important).

This shift in how value is understood to grow in a contingent relation to the plan is worth underscoring: as we saw in the previous chapter, the financializaiton and neoliberalization of the western economy in the 1970s involved, among other things, a radically new concept of futurity. Both through the internalization of energy trading to futures markets, and the waning of productivity-driven growth, the coming postindustrial society (while no less saturated with oil's concrete and abstract properties) would begin to generalize the modal abstractions of the terminal out into the urban fabric writ large. In the next chapter I will call this generalization a form of *energy deepening*. Here I track the ways in which this process of deepening the distribution and breadth of energy is already under way through and as the architecture tasked with terminating the industrial world.

Without question the most material of all the classically aesthetic orders—which is to say the most voluminous, heavy, and static form of art according to both Kant and Hegel—architecture would turn out not accidentally to have accelerated a new phase of value-time necessary for postindustrialization. In Turin especially, Tafuri's particular attention to the overlap between urban planning and capitalist development takes the Fiat car company's economic and architectural activities as one and the same. Our purpose here is thus to reconsider Tafuri's claim that architecture sits at the core of postindustrial growth in relation to the other "Italian" position associated with immaterial labor theory, and to forward a modest hypothesis about what the capitalist world must look like for us to agree that there is something of an architectural logic to growth during the simultaneous dematerialization of the economy.

Fordism and Futurism, or, "architecture or revolution"

Fiat's wager on future economic development was an immediate response to a historic impasse in the Fordist paradigm of value creation. The board's decision to refunction its factory in Lingotto says as much about its own historical position within a politically hostile labor market—Fiat's other factories in Turin were of course key sites for labor struggles through the 1960s and 1970s and the historic center of Italian workerism called *operaismo*—as it does about what policy makers and industrial leaders imagined drove economic growth. Two such assumptions worth noting up front are first that intensifications of both the working day and the productive capacity of workers (relative surplus value by another name) are not the only means by which to valorize capital, and second that a capital asset geared for cultural production and circulation is a sound resolution to a liquidity trap. Neither assumption was entirely new in the 1970s. What was particular, however, was the emergence of a set of macroeconomic commitments within technical discourses on value that sought to generalize the kinds of bets unfolding at Fiat (more on this below).

Italian manufacturers' relationship to the question of technology and progress, when Fiat-Lingotto initially gained notoriety earlier in the century, was framed by at least two factors. On one side, an increasingly attractive Fordist mode of production appeared capable of transitioning continental Europe's agrarian economy, then still only sparsely punctuated by city states, to a national labor market needed for mass production. On the other, Futurism appeared as an avant-garde ideology adequate to aestheticizing and universalizing Fordism.

Taken as combatable modes of wedding material and labor together as an industrial force, Fordism and Futurism characterized the early stages of Fiat's dominance in the North and in the architectural imaginary of twentieth-century modernism.

F.T. Marinetti's "Futurist Manifesto" in 1909 was not a little certain about the source of their modernity, or what they modestly understood as "the very first sunrise on earth" (Marinetti 1909). Fueled on "machine gun fire," the "new beauty" of speed put the automobile at the core of their engineered future. Museums, libraries, and cemeteries marked and maintained the slowness of the past. Only with "factories suspended from the clouds by the thread of their smoke" would the "great crowds agitated by work," on Marinetti's account, bring modernity to a pace acceptable to its aesthetic, liberating them not from but to work. The romanticization of war and its aesthetic, which we tend to associate with Futurism today, only served half their project; the other took what would become the Fordist factory as the ground zero of a new society, of which war was only the loudest expression. Thirteen years later they would get Il Duce, the same year Giacomo Mattè-Trucco finalized Fiat's plans for its flagship factory of the future. Within the decade, Mussolini would use Fiat's heavenly fortress to stage Italy's own take on the fascist factory rally, filmed and distributed for all Europe's modernists to eat up.

Upon returning from a tour of Detroit and Chicago at the cusp of the First World War, Fiat owner and founder V.G. Agnelli commissioned company engineer Mattè-Trucco to design the largest and most efficient industrial complex in Europe. Indeed, for automobile manufacturing, Fiat-Lingotto came second only to Ford's River Rouge Complex in Michigan. The latter, finished in 1917 by Albert Kahn, translated Frederick Winslow Taylor's techniques for scientifically managing the division of manual labor into the assembly line for Ford's burgeoning empire. Each of the Lingotto's five floors was designated for a distinct phase of automobile manufacturing, with raw materials entering at ground level; assembly, motor calibration, upholstery, and finishing from floors one through five, all tied together by the first helicoidal ramp in the world made from reinforced concrete; and a full kilometer-long oval open-air test track on the roof. The Taylorist logic informing its layout was a direct response to a factory occupation of Fiat's older and more open plant in Turin by workers looking for syndicalist control of production in 1921. Sparked in no small part by Amadeo Bordiga and Antonio Gramsci's newly founded Italian Communist Party (PCI) in January of 1921, workers at the beginning of the decade, especially in the North, were encouraged as much from the left as from Mussolini's *Il*

Popolo d'Italia. Mussolini's newly minted fascists called for social and economic reform and a nationalization program nearly indistinguishable from the platform developed by the PCI in Livorno, though as two theoretical positions on value and distribution, the two could not have had less in common.

Internally, Fiat workers then as in the 1960s and 1970s made no mistake about which flag to fly. Theirs was red throughout, unduly flanked outside by the black shirts of Italy's other radical wing. Agnelli's appointment to Mussolini's senate in 1923 effectively sealed the company's political future, however, and with it the interim success of its ambitions for a monopoly in the region. Fiat's new factory, in other words, installed an organizational logic as much imported from Detroit as from the National Fascist Party's (PNF) Roman headquarters. Designed for an ideal division of optimized labor—a combination of cooperation for increased output and division for specialized assembly—Lingotto announced a future relation between labor and capital emblematic of advanced industrial production across the globe. And though the factory would outlive the PNF later in the century, one was unthinkable without the other in the 1920s.

That the Lingotto factory came to emblematize modernist architecture for both Reyner Banham and Le Corbusier, as well as a future coterminous with fascism for the Futurists at Capri and Mussolini himself, is because what makes it modern in both positions is a formalization of an economic promise in cultural terms. What for Banham is "the most nearly Futurist building ever built" arrives on the scene in the art world through Werner Graff 's visualization of De Stijl reloaded in a 1922 issue of *G* where the Turin factory brackets a more militant declaration of Bauhaus outlook: "Uninfluenced by the methods of mechanical technology, the new and greater technology begins—the technology of tensions, invisible motions, action-at-a-distance, and speeds unimaginable now in 1922' (Banham 1960, 193). The promise of a technological future for Graff, as for Marinetti and Mussolini, expressed itself in the new Fiat factory through a building and workforce understood not as complimentary but as singular. "Elementarism" (a term introduced and canonized in De Stijl by the Russian constructivist El Lissitzky) referred in the early modernist aesthetic as much to the rationalism of an architecture as to the technologization of the variable side of capital, which is to say human labor power itself. With newly available reinforced concrete and a technique of ribbing enabling a seamless spiral ramp to link floors one through five, Fiat-Lingotto materialized workflow not just through management but also in the building itself. The irony is that Mattè-Trucco's layout was actually more rigid than flexible as a result of its concrete flow. Resolving many of Lingotto's engineering flaws in 1937, the larger complex at Mirafiori (whose guest of honor during the opening ceremony was none other than Mussolini himself) separated workers into discrete buildings while maintaining flow with assembly belts and subcontracting. Still, the North's largest employer became so by understanding the project of mass production as an architectural one first, and a management one second. The postindustrial promise half a century later would be that technology had finally liberated mankind from heavy lifting; the claim in its Fordist mode is that workers, given the right buildings, have finally become technological.

No one took the singularization of worker and machine more seriously in the 1920s than Le Corbusier. That three aerial shots of Fiat's Lingotto factory line the final page of *Towards a New Architecture*, as the visual equivalent of "architecture or revolution," should come as no surprise given the book's core conviction in a machinic modernity (Le Corbusier [1923] 2008, 289). If the progress of enlightenment had stalled at some point in the nineteenth century for Le Corbusier, it wasn't because mechanization had come to organize most of social and political life, but rather that it hadn't organized it enough. Between the advancement of production and what were for him dead styles of an architectural prehistory lies the fundamental contradiction between the home and the factory, which his manifesto aimed to fix. His first order of business then was to make the house a "machine for living in" (107). Industrialization meant for Le Corbusier that "everywhere can be seen machines which serve to produce something and produce it admirably, in a clean sort of way" (277).

Le Corbusier's admiration for the "clean sort of way" that modern industry produced things found its most advanced expression in Fiat's factory at Lingotto. In Italy, Fiat's Fordism and Futurism looked to Le Corbusier like a prefiguration of the problem of "architecture or revolution" in no small part because of its maximization of the fixed part of capital in the production process and its mechanization of the variable part. Which is to say that Fiat's engineering feat at Lingotto supplied modernism, at least in Le Corbusier's parts of the world, with its aesthetic and economic synthesis. One could therefore say that in the 1920s, at least in the idiom of Le Corbusier's famous either/or, Italy didn't need a revolution: it just needed Fiat.

If what is made available in narrating Fordism and Futurism together, though, is a sense of the aesthetic (and in this case architectural) imaginary at the heart of the more technical qualities of that historically specific logic of production—which is to say in more simple terms that art history and economic history are best read not separately but rather as two sides of the same historical process—then Fiat's factory conversion would mark much more than a diversification of the company's assets. Fossil-fueled ideas of Futurist, Fordist, fascist, and modernist form alike congealed in the mechanization and optimization of labor through the Lingotto project. The automobile's hegemonic weight over the paradigm of production, both as a process and in terms of the products through which capital could capture surplus value, works as a kind of surrogate for the larger structures of petroculture it distributed into the world via infrastructures, habits, and a feeling of progress (LeMenager 2013, 4). It's for this reason that the aesthetic and economic shift prefigured in the factory's postindustrial retrofit are so important for catching the emergent force of oil over the new economy *in medias res*. Because the Lingotto factory works as a kind of synecdoche for the modal abstractions that would come to dominate the final decades of the Holocene, accelerating but also clouding our ability to recognize the age of petroleum *as an age*.

What I will suggest now, in other words, is that the conversion of what was once the largest car factory in the world into Europe's largest cultural factory, in an architectural idiom associated with craftsmanship and a sympathy for regionalism, is nothing short of a *material* blueprint for the postindustrial commitment to immaterialization, intangibility, and weightlessness.[2] Which is another way of putting Gail Day's recent claim that the architectural criticism Tafuri developed at the Istituto Universitario di Architettura di Venezia (IUAV) understood avant-garde negation in the postwar years "as wrapped up with capitalism's modern coming-to-being, its artistic innovations ultimately playing a role in social restructuring" (Day 2012, 80). Day's point, which is one she shares with Fredric Jameson in his earlier assessment of Tafuri's contribution to the history of dialectical criticism, is that Tafuri's patience in tracking the force of aesthetic negation in twentieth-century art tells us as much, if not more, about economic development and contradiction than economics itself. As I began to suggest above, this is due in no small part to Tafuri's intuition of a uniquely *architectural* logic of capitalist development—a distributive logic in which material and immaterial elements are brought to bear on the periodicity of space.

Piano's conversion of Fiat's Fordist factory is thus best understood up front as a conversion of its periodicity: a material reconfiguration of the aesthetics of Futurism in order to make space for an after to Fordism. In fact, Piano's earlier and still more famous Centre Pompidou in Paris, designed with Richard Rogers, paved the way for an expansion of the cultural sector into heavy industry (indeed, the façade of the Pompidou prefigures this expansion), a project whose mandate, Piano explains, "was to find a different tool for making culture and information" (Piano 1982, 23). The Pompidou thus gave an early indication of how architecture would give physical shape to a process of extraction invested in the immateriality of culture and information. The idea would be to externalize the infrastructure of the building: "utilities are positioned along the west façade and have been color-coded (blue for air, green for water, yellow for electricity, and red for the vertical air circulation systems)" and the "elevators and escalators have been placed upon the support structure, along the façade" in order to make the building's machinic qualities transparent. The Pompidou—and in a qualitatively new fashion at Fiat Works a few years later—began working out the aesthetic of a cultural economy in which architecture appeared to do a kind of work while the people inside engaged in activities until then thought of as outside the realm of economic growth.

The Pompidou's program to make the infrastructure of the building architectural, which effectively made the working elements of the structure transparent in order to thematize transparency more generally, was in fact the last (and not the first) in a sequence of Piano's work that began with his first three major projects from 1966 to 1970. The first was his earlier firm's initial results in experiments with polyester, plastics, and transportable structures. His Mobile Structure for Sulfur Extraction in 1966 consisted of a steel tension structure that could be erected in a variety of configurations *in situ*, reinforced by a polyester wrap that protected the sulfur mine and machinery from the environment (Buchanan 1993, 46). Studio Piano's 1967 Shell Structural System for the Fourteenth Milan Triennale used a similar steel infrastructure to support a transportable and multi-use glass fiber container that could house unlimited activities. And the third, the Italian Industry Pavilion at Expo 1970 in Osaka, Japan, used the principles invented in the first two projects and rendered the steel and polyester structural elements into a mobile square where Italy's newest industrial products could be framed by the most forward-looking product of them all: postindustrial architecture.

The Pompidou is the fourth in a sequence of projects interested in making interior space light and flexible (the two terms most immediately associated with Piano's career more generally), eliminating the gap between façade and structure. The Fiat conversion is thus part of a new sequence and is more accurately the sequel to what had then become the Building Workshop's first major retrofit at the Schlumberger factory in Paris, 1981–84. Schlumberger's specialization in electronic equipment was at the cutting edge of oil detection and extraction and had launched the company, by the end of the 1970s oil crisis, into what was quickly becoming the center of the economic universe: the energy sector. Schlumberger had, much like Fiat in Turin, rid itself of a significant portion of its workforce—indeed, on a macroeconomic scale, it was precisely the substitution of oil for coal that had dramatically increased productivity and thus decreased the relative size of the workforce to the rate of output in the manufacturing sector—and so its eight-hectare lot that once housed workers, industrial manufacturing, and management facilities needed to be reconfigured to accommodate the company's more capital-intensive future. This meant replacing the factory that sat in the center with a garden, and communal spaces for eating and meeting directly beneath and above it, housed in a Teflon awning. All the remaining structural elements were left intact, such as trusses and purlins, and the new infrastructural elements were again color-coded based on concrete, fenestration, circulation, and air conditioning. And while outside the building is a landscape architecture that anticipates much of the corporate campus architecture of the next fifty years, the idea at Schlumberger is to "invade" the factory's interior space with the natural elements that form the communal exterior through the planned continuity in color schemes based on botanical seasons. Work time inside the factory, which more concretely is based on the geopolitical and global economic thirst for, and the capital deepening implied by oil, is framed architecturally as the time of natural seasons.

Still owned by Fiat but financed jointly by Fiat's development company, SITECO, and the city of Turin, Piano's next factory conversion was carried out in four stages starting in 1984, coming in at just over $1 billion by the final stage in 2002. The division of labor at the new Fiat is no longer organized around the assembly of a material commodity but rather what is imagined to constitute the multifaceted activities of culture: an exhibition center, cinema, private gallery (funded and supplied by Agnelli's grandson), polytechnic university, concert halls, and a shopping center—all of which, according then to the *Architectural Review*, "constitute such a rich mix of enterprises for whom creativity is crucial that they should spark between them a lively and fertile entrepreneurial ecology" (Buchanan 1996). Of course, the fantasy here is that having space designated for social and cultural activities serves as a stimulus for innovation, and that innovation is a constitutive dimension of future economic development. However, that the husk of a Fordist factory can ground a value-creating set of activities, though not function as a site of production, is a wager on the logical relation between architecture as fixed capital and the accumulation of surplus value in whatever comes after Fordism.

At Fiat, in other words, it wouldn't be nature that drove the architectural imaginary of economic growth, but rather its cultural rhythms. And yet the distinction between the two, between an idea of economic time linked to nature and one linked to culture, would appear in Piano's architectural philosophy not as a contradiction at all, but rather as two sides of the same feature of architecture's unique facility with the "organic" (Buchanan 1995, 6). So while the heavy-handed landscaping seen at Schlumberger is more restrained at Lingotto, but nonetheless central to masking the new auxiliary spaces a multi-use cultural center requires, what instead gets naturalized is what architectural and environmental critic Peter Buchanan calls the building's "primitive consciousness": for the first time, Piano wired the entire structure with smart systems monitoring human movement, external climate, and supplies, all of which is communicated to a "central nervous system" (Buchanan 1995, 158). Only this way can the various exhibitions and open spaces on the first and second floors energize the entrepreneurial spirit of its other "incubator units" housing new and small businesses in need of Fiat's bump. As each venture grows, plenty of premium space is available for lease on floors two and three. Higher up is a four-star hotel and departments of the Faculty of Science at the University of Turin. In the middle of Fiat's famous rooftop racetrack sits the helipad and globular conference space, while the sixth floor of the private Agnelli art collection housed in the Pinacoteca Giovanni and Marella Agnelli Gallery emerges to tie the economic limbs of the building down to its cultural spine. Twenty-five pieces ranging from Manet, Renoir, and Matisse to Picasso and, with appropriate historical irony, Italian Futurists Giacomo Balla and Gino Severini, sit in the *Scrigno* (or treasure chest). The collection itself is part of the Agnelli family's estimated fortune of over $5 billion.

Thus what began on the concourse level as a "fertile entrepreneurial ecology" where startups rubbed shoulders with the creative class—which is to say where the intense capital deepening embodied in the building's conversion has provided the costly means for *cultural* and *creative* production—has upon ascending through to the sixth floor become the opposite. The means of more speculative, managerial, and intangible forms of production in the larger and more expensive spaces approaching roof level are the very cultural objects which the new factory has been designed to showcase. The fixed cultural assets emerge at the top of the factory where cars used to, in order to shore up the admittedly less valuable capital asset (the building itself) choreographing the Lingotto's workflow. The elasticity between the two forms of capital deepening—architectural on one end and art historical on the other—provides, to use the director's language, the organic composition of postindustrial production. What used to be the geographic center of class struggle in Italy had become by the mid-1980s the "nervous center" of Fiat's international division of labor.

It's also at about this time that Fiat began to diversify its investments and regional stronghold by becoming what we now know as the multi-sector behemoth Fiat Group. So far as workers in Turin were concerned, Fiat's expansion into property development and insurance meant the full-blown urban transformation of, and relation between, capital and labor. The closure of Lingotto, effectively Fiat's international headquarters for over half a century, came at the tail end, rather than at the beginning, of a twofold restructuring scheme. The first phase included breaking up the company effectively into a financial and property developer called Fiat Engineering and SITECO respectively, in addition to its more traditional role as automobile manufacturer. The second phase saw an internal reorganization of the production process itself: the new Melfi plant in the southern province of Potenza finished in 1993, surrounded by twenty-two subcontractor plants, is emblematic of the new just-in-time strategy we've come to associate with post-Fordist production and is one of many Fiat plants opened globally after the crisis of the 1970s. Phase two was a strategy as much about flexibility as it was about the maximization of fixed capital in the form of robotics in the place of variable capital—i.e., workers.

Layoffs reached 23,000 in 1980 in Turin with productive capacity slowing to 60 percent (Whitford and Enrietti 2005, 782). Meanwhile, Fiat Engineering opened Central Research Fiat (CRF), one of the most ambitious R&D centers in Italy since Olivetti's experiments in the 1950s and 1960s. Where the latter sought to formalize and facilitate an "anti-industrial" "republic of the intellect," Fiat instead committed itself to organizing both immaterial and material forms of production across the space of the city (Tafuri 1989, 37). Of course, the argument here is not that Fiat is exceptional in its deployment of a new logic of accumulation. Certainly, even in Italy its mobilization of capital away from the factory floor proper was facilitated and necessitated by the state through new taxation and financial laws, and the unfolding of a similar logic was visible elsewhere much earlier in the century.[3]

The introduction of a financial regulator, CONSOB, in the early 1970s is one such example, but perhaps more relevant to the transformation of Fiat-Lingotto is the aftermath of what came to be known as Progetto 80 in 1969–70. Championed by Giorgio Ruffalo at the Ministry of Finance and Economic Planning, Progetto 80 consisted of urban planners, economists, civil servants, and business leaders planning a three-tiered program for future economic and urban development in Italy. Aiming to grow the northern economy by 1980, the program cohered first in the construction of a system of accounting policy changes; second, program budgeting and integrated planning; and third, the regionalization of integrated planning. Unsurprisingly, its "long-term perspective" was one grounded not on an intensification of manufacturing exclusively, but instead a model of value creation choreographed by transformed urban relations (Planning Studies Centre 2012).

Perhaps most relevant for the discussion here, Progetto 80 laid the policy necessary to change valuation protocols in the Civil Code for property holdings in 1974. Instead of the "historical cost principle" determining the value of capital assets in which a building's initial cost and value trend attached to its land use determined its long-term value depreciation (and thus to what value it would contribute to the production process), new provisions were put in place to address events that change the asset's economic nature, such as the conversion of a prototypical Fordist factory into a hub for culture. Debates about which method best represented the value of an asset had been raging for decades in the US and UK in what is now known as the Cambridge Capital Controversy, or what Ian Steedman, Paul Sweezy, and others on the left called the "value controversy"— debates that if anything were about how fixed capital could be understood as value producing in the newly developed science of econometrics, once it was understood as a commodity just like labor. By the 1970s, however, the International Accounting Standards Committee (IASC) sought to globally abandon the historical cost principle on company ledgers and auditing reports. Market value came to replace the law of devaluation, and buildings that would have otherwise been depleted of their congealed value got a new lease on life. With new property law comes a new narrative of property, and instead of a graveyard of dead capital Fiat was able to expand the capacity of its capital assets to assume the uncanny appearance of workers themselves.

Social capital and its organic composition

A good part of the Italian left had already anticipated the kinds of transformations unfolding at Fiat at least a decade before the decision to close Lingotto. From the perspective of a Marxist analysis of the basic categories by which capitalism grows—namely the organic composition of capital in which the increase of constant capital (c), which is the capital invested in fixed assets like machinery and buildings, over variable capital (v) spent on labor power, or capital deepening in order to increase labor productivity, defines the general tendency of economic growth—the limit is a natural one, which is to say that it will develop internal to capitalist development, rather than external to it. At a certain point so little labor time is required to produce the same output that the class antagonism between proletariat and bourgeoisie becomes instead an antagonism between those with and those without employment. The organic composition of capital, in other words, has as much to do with economic growth as it does with the sustainability of social relations over economic time. The question then is not whether or not the logical limit to the Fordist value form had been reached by the 1970s (it had) but rather how best to characterize the strategic reactions that were swiftly remaking the shape of economic relations.

Clear already in 1963 to Mario Tronti was that while the traditional site of production in its factory form remained the dominant expression of working-class struggle, surplus value as the *sine qua non* of capitalist accumulation could not be explained or critiqued from the factory floor exclusively. That all of society had become a factory was actually, at least in Tronti's early analysis, a claim not just about the privatization of the city but about the socialization of capital and labor at a definite point of development in the organic composition of capital. On the question of whether or not the composition of capital over time takes more variable or fixed capital (or value from labor as opposed to machines), Tronti adds that an increase in the fixed component always means a simultaneous increase in the "non-paid part of the social working day."[4] Tronti does not mean simply that unemployment rises as machines do more work, but rather that the work done outside of the factory—namely, cultural, intellectual, and creative work, or social reproduction more broadly, including what by the end of the decade would be the most important oversight of all: gendered work—comes to constitute more and more of the variable side of capital once those lucky few with jobs show up to work.

Instead of an intensification of the paid part of the working day, which in Marx's terms would constitute an increase in relative surplus value, or what we can call the Direct Sphere of Variable Capital (DSVC), Tronti's thesis about the social factory is premised on a claim about the intensification of human labor before it arrives on the labor market, or what we could call here the Indirect Sphere of Variable Capital (ISVC). Tronti's hypothesis that more and more surplus value comes from the reorganization of the ISVC, or "the social factory," is another way of highlighting the social and energic history contained in the organic composition of capital, which is to say that both v and c and the ratio between the two are results of infrastructurally mediated conditions external to the factory at any given moment.

But the intensification of the ISVC brings with it immediate consequences too for the process by which the value embedded in fixed capital is produced, consumed, and valorized over the course of the total workday, in addition to the variable side of capital. "[W]ithin this process of production," Tronti maintains, social capital "produces, reproduces, and accumulates new capital; it produces, reproduces and accumulates new labor-power" because "at this level the division between necessary labor and surplus-labor does not disappear at all: it is simply generalized, i.e., socialized in the total process of capitalist production" (Tronti [1963] 1973). So, while one side of the organic composition of capital is intensified, the other follows suit by virtue of the social organization *outside* the factory required and implied by a high degree of capital deepening *inside* it. And the final twist to what appears first as a tautology is that the increased value produced in the ISVC is itself the result of a form of capital deepening outside the factory in which large-scale capitalists begin investing in the infrastructural means of social reproduction, about which Fiat knew plenty by the time they hired Piano to update their flagship factory.

Thus, the transformations that would become both architecturally and politically explicit at Fiat in the following decade, and more generally associated with post-Fordism during the 1970s through the 1990s—that is, postindustrialization and with it immaterial forms of production—had in Tronti's early estimation little to do with a return to rent or a fundamental breach in the capitalist value form. Rather, the economic and social transformations increasingly becoming paradigmatic during the most intense years of Italian ultra-leftist struggle were logical extensions of tendencies embedded in the most fundamental laws of capitalist accumulation, however misleading their initial appearances were for the traditional left. "Capitalists," Tronti continues, "know this well: the real generalization of the workers' conditions can introduce the appearance of its formal extinction" (Tronti [1963] 1973). Its formal extinction, however, only appears as a negative image in its organizational forms, which by 1966 across Europe was already breaking apart at the seams. Trade unions, parliamentary parties, and the like continued to take as the beginning and end of socialism the identity of the working class, but its function in the production and valorization of capital had shifted from beneath its feet. "Because of this," Tronti concludes, "when the working class politically refuses to become people, it does not close, but opens the most direct way to the socialist revolution," in no small part due to the emergence of a new phase of value where the ISVC began making up for the shortfall in the DSVC (Tronti [1963] 1973). As we have already seen, however, the capitalist concern with the working class as such was both the cause and result of capital deepening inside the factory and a form of what I'll call, in the next chapter, energy deepening external to it.

This is another way of saying that what Piano's factory conversion made material was the particular architectural relay that would mediate direct and indirect spheres of variable capital in relation to a postindustrial materialism deeply concerned about the nature of value. The idea here, though, has been to read the architectural and aesthetic history of Fiat's economic transformations in order to distinguish between the types of radical materialisms that would take shape around its factories. Piano's cultural conversion didn't merely figure a future growth model as a set of immaterial forms of labor, but instead materialized the architectural side of postindustrial work as the setting in which increasingly indistinguishable spheres of variable capital would get mediated into value. The so-called shift into cognitive, creative, affective, or, broadly named, immaterial forms of labor, in other words, seems to address only half the picture of postwar political economy. As capital assets, the architecture of Fiat not only coordinates and leverages, but also assumes an active role in the transformation of cultural activities into value, just like its shored-up value in urban fixed capital has as its aim the coordination of the unpaid part of the workday. Thus, to the extent that any viable movement of proletariat force is finally able to abolish "the present state of things," the *state of things* in the age of immaterial assets will remain a very material concern, which is to say that the so-called immaterial, financial, or creative economy never eliminated, but rather intensified, the capacity of architecture to work, and for work to congeal in architecture (Marx 1845). Piano's most recent commission for the Stavros Niarchos Cultural Center, touted as the "'rebirth" of Athens (Ragazzola n.d.)—i.e., the ground zero of late capitalist austerity and ultra-leftist confrontation—should therefore surprise no one when it imagines culture as the bailout package for which we have all been waiting.

3

Energyscapes, Architecture, and the Expanded Field of Postindustrial Philosophy

In a special report to the *New York Times* entitled "Power, Pollution, and the Internet," tech reporter James Glanz made public what was until then a bit of an industry secret: digital forms of information were not only environmentally unfriendly compared even to the thick and heavy forms they replaced; more surprising still, the so-called immateriality of information, the internet, and our everyday engagement with it had produced a worldwide Leviathan hungry for quantities of energy "sharply at odds with its image of sleek efficiency and environmental friendliness" (Glanz 2012). Digital farms or warehouses require the energy output of thirty nuclear power plants because, whether in use or not, the information housed in these warehouses remains online. Inside each warehouse are enormous complexes of servers, wires, and electrical circuitry (the heat from which can be visualized from space) that need constant cooling. According to Pierre Delforge of the Natural Resources Defence Council, "Data center electricity consumption is projected to increase to roughly 140 billion kilowatt-hours annually by 2020, the equivalent annual output of fifty power plants, costing American businesses $13 billion annually in electricity bills and emitting nearly 100 million metric tons of carbon pollution per year" (Delforge 2015). And because most electricity comes from coal, diesel, and petroleum products, the so-called immaterial economy is not only premised on, but actively motivates, the rapid expansion of an energy infrastructure now indisputably responsible for significant contributions to climate change.

Glanz's report and many others like it, including Ingrid Burrington's for *The Atlantic* (2015), foreground the infrastructural and environmental costs of the internet in order to temper the association of digital culture with weightlessness and green immateriality. My claim in this chapter, however, is that the infrastructural truth of the postindustrial economy involves an equally troubling if not coterminous feature of the postindustrial: the inseparability of constant increases in global energy wealth since the 1970s (today's climate crisis) and the simultaneous decrease in labor requirements across the global economy (today's unemployment crisis). The aesthetic misrecognition of digital culture and communication as immaterial takes place in a larger context that includes the disfiguration of labor from its social ground, which I refer to as energy's "economic elasticity," and the emergence of fossil fuels as a form of social regulation, which I call the "social plasticity" of oil.

This chapter will clarify the aesthetic economy of postindustrialization by establishing that, while development in the Fordist era was primarily designed to standardize and increase labor productivity in and around the factory, *the postindustrial economy is instead premised on redefining and reshaping all landscapes as energyscapes, and all energy as economic elasticity.*

In the critical theory that has grown up alongside landscape architecture and ecological urbanism, intensive and extensive growth in flows of energy and information across landscapes gets recognized as an opportunity to endorse and experiment with speculative philosophies and so-called object-oriented ontologies. By moving through exemplary instances of postindustrial landscape architecture and the philosophical tradition its theorists mobilize, this chapter claims that the political economy of postindustrial energy already implies an object-oriented ontology rather than a labor-oriented one, and that this (along with the intellectual position that celebrates it) amounts to political disaster.

Energyscapes and the infrastructures of accumulation

"Energyscape," in the account that follows, names the expanded field—the historical and physical settings—in which capital accumulation is provided its energy infrastructure, which is to say where energy is optimized aesthetically and socially for the sustained growth of capital.[1] By combining energy with landscape in the settings I nominate here, I am not just referring to what Alberto Toscano and Jeff Kinkle call "logistical landscapes" (Toscano and Kinkle 2015, 205), such as the ports, oil patches, pipelines, and freeways captured by photographers Allan Sekula and Edward Burtynsky. Certainly, logistical or infrastructural landscapes are critical to the smooth operation of everyday life. What I am more interested in here is the aesthetic and economic saturation of postindustrial landscapes with energy-intensive infrastructures, so that logistical landscapes, sites of resource extraction, industrial factories, and postindustrial cities are sewn together in an expanded field of what this book calls terminal landscapes.[2] In order to calibrate what I have elsewhere called the peculiar carbon-capital complex, or what Andreas Malm (2013) has called "fossil capital," the postindustrial economy makes seamless the circuit of energy extraction, circulation, and consumption. Specially planned economic zones provide the economic and logistical infrastructure required to keep postindustrial growth apace, while energyscapes—which is to say the infrastructural and technological base of the fossil-fueled fantasies driving the immaterial, the digital, and the fluid—normalize particularly troubling features of what we might term the aesthetics of a vanishing labor force at odds with the carbon-capital complex. The expanded field that makes logistical infrastructures and energyscapes recursive to one another is the terminal landscape of postindustrial capital, a material and historical relation that as we will see in my conclusion can already be anticipated (as both Isabelle Stengers and Marx do) from the coterminous birth of thermodynamic reason and the industrial mode of production.

At the level of cultural theory and philosophy, this aesthetic economy is expressed as a set of conceptual preferences shorn off of a form of materialism that triangulates labor, capital, and energy. These features include the liquid, plastic, and elastic preferences of political economy and political philosophy in the postindustrial era, both of which have, consciously or not, driven the concept and standpoint of human labor power into the ground and excavated an accelerated, albeit accidental and depoliticized, unity between capital and energy in the meantime.

There is no shortage of committed attempts to expose the true environmental costs of energy-hungry infrastructures. The trouble with exposition, however, is that one can no more see a pipeline through a computer screen than one can see the caloric and affective output of a Chinese worker in a smartphone. Part of this is a problem of scale, no doubt. In the words of Peter Gross, who helped design the data warehouses that anchor the internet, "it's staggering for most people, even people in the industry, to understand the numbers, the sheer size of these systems' (quoted in Glanz 2012). Infrastructure more generally, of course, remains for the most part hidden from view, except when its contents are exposed, distributed, spilled, or sabotaged. This is why the struggle to visualize infrastructure is central to any environmentalist politics, as Nicole Starosielski explains (2015), both because ecological devastation is a logical outcome (rather than an accident) of our global energy system and because state security blocks easy knowledge of it. When it comes to infrastructure of any kind, talk of state security and terrorism is never far away.

Environmental risk, however, is logically tied to the specifically economic function of energy infrastructures. Globally, the IEA predicts that, in order to maintain growth, energy supply will need to grow by 45 percent between 2006 and 2030 to more than 17 billion tons of oil equivalent annually, 73 percent of which will be consumed by cities (International Energy Agency 2008). A significant portion of that energy will be tied to the production, distribution, and consumption of digital information. Already in 2013, the Information and Communication Technology (ICT) ecosystem used 50 percent more energy per year than the aviation industry (Mills 2013). This accelerated correlation between economic growth and energy consumption has been steadily climbing since the Industrial Revolution. The World Bank's estimated sixteenfold increase in economic output in the twentieth century ("from about $2 to $32 trillion in constant 1990 dollars") indexes a seventeenfold increase in annual commercial energy consumption (from "22 to approximately 380 EJ") during the same period (Smil 2010, 14). This, in a nutshell, is a statistical picture of the saturation I have in mind when I refer to the energyscapes that provide economic growth with its infrastructural fix. For while a good deal of the energy consumption that has made capital accumulation possible has been at the site of production—what World Bank experts term "commercial energy"—we are increasingly unable to imagine either public or private activities that do not require an enormous amount of energy mediated by an impossibly complex system of automation, logistics, and infrastructure. This colloquial fact of energy, however—that we not only use a lot of it, but are hard pressed to find spaces, activities, or ideas about the future that do not—obscures an equally implicit but perhaps more politically volatile fact about the historical shape of the capitalist exploitation of labor.

Metaphors and lexical fields that clothe so-called "immaterial culture" have gone a long way to occlude digital culture's spatial and historical contours. As Allison Carruth has recently suggested, most of our ecological metaphors for digital technologies, such as the "cloud" and "streaming," mask, "willfully in some cases, what is an energy-intensive and massively industrial infrastructure" (Carruth 2014, 342). The coincidence of the infrastructure of digital culture with our postindustrial energy system recedes both phenomenologically and logistically to the level of setting, rather than occupying what in literary studies gets called "content." The experiences of daily life depend on an ecological characterization of infrastructure, not because some hidden truth about the internet lurks beneath the surface of its presentation, but rather because economic growth, state security, and postindustrial culture are all contingencies of a political economy that weds the growth in value to the increase in the total energy circulating through the spaces we inhabit. Digital culture is an expression of a resource aesthetic whose ecological reality runs deep, but whose economic logic is hidden in plain sight.

Making visible the economic and ecological contents of infrastructure, however indispensable a practice, does not of necessity generate a political counterforce, precisely because the economic and ecological contradictions of a world formed by fossil fuels are intimately bound together. Energy's economic elasticity comes in the form of the logistics revolution in shipping and manufacturing, as well as the productivity gains made through automated and energy-intensive technologies, while oil's plasticity—which is to say its capacity not only to fuel daily life, but to give it a material shape as well—regulates and modulates the economic value of postindustrial society. Elasticity portends the world-making force of capital out into various realms of abstraction that are no less real for their modal force on the rhythm and density of historicity as so many market metrics. And plasticity puts our bodies and the environments that situate us ecologically in touch, as it were, with the texture and toxicity of capital as it internalizes hydrocarbons into its diegesis. These two poles of fossil capital are both intimate with one another and critical antinomies—in an older language, the concrete and the abstract—and I have been making an argument in this book for why the terminal names the place where they are most proximate.

It is clear now, following WikiLeaks, the BP oil spill, and other daily manifestations of what is an otherwise deep and hidden infrastructure, that knowledge of infrastructural content does not lead to its politicization (Szeman 2013, 147). This is because, to use Amanda Boetzkes and Andrew Pendakis's useful phrasing, the fossil fuels on which life today depends provide us with not just plastic products but also plasticity as a historical "paradigm" (Boetzkes and Pendakis 2013). From the now inseparability of exchange rates and oil prices to the plastic materials of everyday life, or what Boetzkes and Pendakis call "contemporary neoliberal fantasies about the capacity of individuals to endlessly make and re-make themselves," the world since the second half of the twentieth century is fundamentally saturated with and mediated by social, economic, and psychological plasticity (Boetzkes and Pendakis 2013). Digital culture is the example *par excellence* of plasticity's two sides: on the back of enormously complicated and expensive infrastructures, as well as a multitude of electronic materials made from oil, comes an experience of immateriality, lightness, and global communication emancipated from the weighty limits of matter. Plastic's materiality is world shaping, just as its immateriality—or the experience of speed, freedom, and deracinated communication—contours the social. The energy system we find ourselves in depends on this dialectic between oil's universality, its conditioning of the possible, and oil's material or infrastructural realism—the weighty anchor for postindustrial life as we know it. Hydrocarbons give the postindustrial world a sense of a *world* by unhinging it from geographical limits—a freedom expressed through the postindustrial immediacy with both itself and more industrial parts of the world that is made possible by digital communications and logistics.[3] The spatial and temporal aspects of oil's dialectic generate a setting unique to its plastic qualities, which is what in my title I term "energyscapes": a concept that, like the land- and mediascapes it refigures, names both the form and historical specificity of the setting in which we find ourselves.

Catherine Malabou's 1996 book on Hegel and plasticity made clear the problems and possibilities of the plastic dialectic in the age of oil, while her recent turn to cognitive plasticity has redefined the concepts of the cerebral and the imagination. For her, plasticity involves itself in our thinking about it, since at base it is "a capacity to receive form and a capacity to produce form" (Malabou [1996] 2005, 9). Like many of the contributors to the collection on *Plastic Materialities*, Alberto Toscano (2015) turns plasticity into the concept that captures both the materiality and epistemological condition of a critique of capital today, insisting that capital accumulation depends on a constant making and remaking of locales and regions in its own image. Through *Climate and Capital* I have been thinking about capital's plastic relation to setting through the category of "modal abstraction." My contribution here is to double the dialectical sense in which capital depends on plasticity, since plasticity itself is tied not just to the abstract capacity to give form, but also to the historical specificity of the energy system from which its material expression (plastics) comes. If capital remakes the world in its image, its global success in the twentieth and twenty-first centuries has been wholly contingent on its ability to turn fossil fuels into both its essence, by achieving growth gains through energy deepening, and its appearance, through the plasticity of postindustrial social relations and the objects that surround us. What I mean to draw out from the philosophy of plasticity and the energy infrastructure that gives form to the digital, "immaterial," and postindustrial forms of work and communication is the context in which to critique the explicitly political ambitions of postindustrial philosophy.

Following Levi Bryant, who coined the term "object-oriented ontology" (OOO), I understand speculative realism, actor network theory (ANT), and OOO as speculative positions connected at multiple axes (Bryant 2011). My claim here, however, is that each articulates a shared fantasy of the world in the measure that they are constitutive of a postindustrial philosophy that imagines capital as a form of energy, but not energy (and its infrastructure) as a property of capitalist exploitation.[4] I counter this shared fantasy by establishing the indispensability of dialectical thinking in a plastic world, which is a consequence of the energy regime I am trying to foreground, since the postindustrial dialectic between energy and capital (in my account) is what cuts across the philosophical hubris of speculative philosophy. Bryant's own attempt at providing speculative philosophy with a politics importantly grounds itself in what he calls "thermopolitics" (Bryant 2014), where he turns energy into a fact of nature that cuts across so-called critical theory and its obsession with discourse, rather than treat it as a concept tied to capital, capitalism, or the historicity of its ecology. Energy stands in as the interruption of "second nature" by "first nature" in speculative realism, ANT, and OOO because these positions abandon dialectical thinking and thus any chance of mediating the historicity of energy and its relation to capital. In order to think about the historical specificity of concepts, especially ones that seem to refer to matter itself, Bryant and others would need a specifically *historical* materialism (Galloway 2013). In a sustained retort to Bataille's theory of energetic expenditure—a philosophy of energetics suspiciously omitted from Bryant's own account—Michael Marder insists, "spliced into the exorbitant circulation of biochemical and solar energies, economic structures present themselves in the guise of natural givens, whether or not nature is assumed to be in a state of equilibrium or disequilibrium, energetic balance or over-abundance" (Marder 2017, 77). The point here is that the very appearance and conceptual emplotment of energy across its relatively short history in the natural and humanistic sciences is both bound up with and (naturally) irreducible to capital's modal abstractions. And the name we have for that sort of problem is a dialectical problem. Capital no doubt expresses itself as energy all the time, but only because of its unique capacity to combine what Marx in the "Critique of the Gotha Program" called *natural* sources of use value and *human* labor into a force severed, and therefore ostensibly autonomous, from its origin (Marx 1951, 19).

Postindustrial landscapes

Articulating the setting of the infrastructural base of postindustrial society is a means towards historicizing the relationship between energy, capital, and labor. As I have suggested already, setting is neither the space nor time of a drama exclusively, but rather the texture, rhythm, and environment in which it takes place. Isolating the force that both capital and energy exert on a setting can only occur in what Rosalind Krauss (1979) famously called an "expanded field," because energy and capital are not things in and of themselves. I am invoking Krauss's celebrated insights into the "rupture" in art history sometime around 1970 because the transformation that concerns Krauss (the elastic logic of sculpture amidst the turn to land art) is both contemporaneous with and constitutive of the one that concerns me. At the end of her essay (which is as much about the weird things going on in the sculpture of Robert Smithson, Robert Morris, Richard Serra, Sol LeWitt, Alice Aycock, and so on as it is about historicism in criticism), she asks her audience to consider a theory that addresses "the root causes—the conditions of possibility—that brought about the shift into postmodernism" (Krauss 1979, 44). Because she is troubled by historicism's "genealogical trees," Krauss wants to promote an approach that addresses "the cultural determinants of the opposition through which a given field is structured" (Krauss 1979, 44). In the vocabulary of the expanded field of sculpture, this means that the political economy of the 1970s is not autonomous from that decade's aesthetic economy. Krauss's role in formative debates about the role of artists in designing the postindustrial environment, as we see in a moment, is another indication that what she meant by the expanded field had everything to do with overlapping spheres of political and aesthetic economies, in addition to the historicity of medium. This at least is what lurks behind the notion of an expanded field in the first place, even if that essay means to stick to a specifically aesthetic reading of that field until its final page. Krauss's critique of historicism escapes medium specificity, which is why much of her work that follows the 1979 essay develops a theory of what she calls the "post-medium condition" (Krauss 2000, 32).

My own account concerns itself with putting "energy deepening" at the heart of the expanded field of the postindustrial, and thereby to identify such deepening as a crucial component of what Krauss called the "root cause" of postmodernism. Energy deepening is a root cause because it made possible not only the financialization of the global economy—which, erupting on the back of the energy futures market in the transition to a postindustrial economy, impacted currency delinking, rapid expansion in resource industries, and the artificially cheap energy for consumers and businesses available for a period—but also a whole host of digital technologies that enable and shore up the so-called immaterial, creative, and affective turns in the global economy. Energy deepening, then, provides the infrastructural link between what in an older vocabulary would have been the base (postindustrialism) and superstructure (postmodernism) of our current era. When directors of the then Organization of

Arab Petroleum Exporting Countries (OAPEC) began an embargo on oil shipments in 1973 in response to the US involvement in the Yom Kippur War, it exposed the increasing saturation of global markets in the geopolitical and material properties of fossil fuels, as I showed in Chapter 1. Only two years earlier, Nixon's recess from the Bretton Woods Agreement meant that a new standard of value was on the horizon, since the US dollar that was meant to replace gold was more vulnerable to market fluctuations than physical reserves of commodities like gold, sterling silver, or oil. In a handful of years, energy had become more than an intensive factor in the productive forces of society and had begun to contour the very substance and landscape of the market.

Contemporaneous with energy deepening at the market level, however, was an equally dramatic turn back to landscape in architecture and urban design at the cusp of postindustrialization. The precise moment when landscape became the general frame of reference for architects is still widely debated. For architecture theorist and historian Felicity D. Scott (2007), the ambition to "design the environment" was already made explicit during the Universitas Project hosted at MoMA in 1972. There, design curator at MoMA Emilio Ambasz invited participants as varied as Krauss, Joseph Rykwert, Peter Eisenman, Octavio Paz, Henri Lefebvre, Jean Baudrillard, Manuel Castells, and Hannah Arendt to collaborate on an interim report imagining "Institutions for a Post-Technological Society." Though the report reached only a limited audience, it nonetheless established a specifically "post-industrial conception of environment" that involved new scale, in Scott's words, "such as systems theory, cybernetics, information theory, and semiology' (Scott 2007, 89–90). The environmental impact of the world's being saturated with difficult-to-extract sources of energy had already begun to shape the world at a theoretical level even before the first major oil crisis, yet the spatial paradigm that emerged in response to it foreshadowed the oxymoron of postindustrialization: in order to temper the environmental costs of industrial cities, the postindustrial city would need a wholly new infrastructure hungry for energy.

In Grahame Shane's (2006) brief history of the discipline, Kevin Lynch's call for an "ecological approach to landscape" in his 1984 *Good City Form*—itself a response to Howard Odum's 1963 *Ecology*—paves the way. In Shane's genealogy, echoed by many of the key players in American landscape urbanism, the turn is expressed loudest somewhere between the Parc de la Villette competition in Paris (1984–89) and the International Building Exhibition for postindustrial renewal in Germany's Northern Ruhr region (1989–99)—where Leon Krier, Peter Eisenman, Elia Zenghelis, Rem Koolhaas, and Aldo Rossi submitted landmark proposals. The biggest names in the architecture world seemed, in both Shane and Richard Weller's (2006) accounts, to confirm that architecture had broadened its ambitions to include what the discipline's key theorist, James Corner, called "a truly ecological landscape architecture" for which architecture "might be less about the construction of finished and complete works, and more about the design of 'processes,' 'strategies,' 'agencies,' and 'scaffoldings'" (quoted in Weller 2006, 77). Art and architecture historian Kenneth Frampton's 1995 'Toward an Urban Landscape', in addition to Koolhaas's landmark essay "The Generic City" and Paola Viganò's *Territories of a New Modernity,* to name but a few examples, announced that the turn from architectural objects was complete, and that what now needed to be designed were landscaped settings.

Even in this origin story, what fueled the turn from objects to settings in architecture and design was not merely a raised environmental awareness, but also the site-specific demands of development initiatives explicit about the ambition to postindustrialize. In the case of Germany's Emscher Park (the historical center of coal and steel production), the aim was, as Kelly Shannon puts it, "simultaneously [to repair] environmental damage and [to project] economic renewal" (Shannon 2006, 148), while for Bernard Tschumi's Parc de la Villette—the former abattoir district of working class Paris first built in the 1860s—the aim was to turn the city's center of caloric production into a permanently unfolding "event" (see Figure 3.1). In Tschumi's sense of the word—a hybrid term mutated through conversations with Jacques Derrida, who collaborated and wrote extensively on the project, and Michel Foucault—"the event here is seen as a *turning point*—not an origin or an end—as opposed to such propositions as form follows function" (Tschumi 1994, 256). Modernism's commitment to the concrete contours of the architectural object no longer captured the ambitions or capacity of urban design, since for Tschumi the relationship between building and landscape was interactive, always "turning." Instead of objects in space, Tschumi sought to build an environment.

Tschumi was relatively clear about his discursive ambition at La Villette, which was to materialize a "deconstructive architecture" that would extend beyond the "drama" of object-functions (what users do in a building) to the coordinates of a "setting" (Tschumi 1994, 256). Hence, inside the park are individual *folies* or interactive sculptures in a variety of shapes and sizes—some look like excerpts from a children's playground, others half-finished scaffolding for a bank façade—while the total landscape of La Villette is the setting Tschumi set out to design. For Derrida, who took great pleasure in elaborating the meaning of La Villette, the *folies* were material equivalents to the ongoing

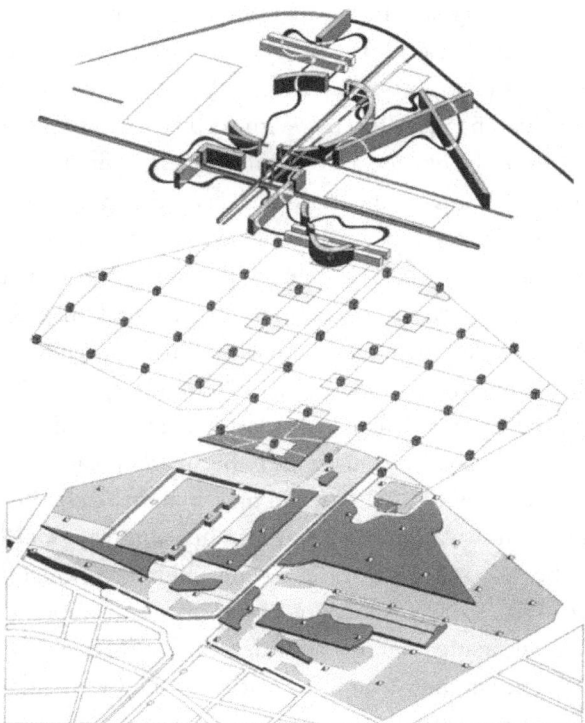

Figure 3.1 Bernard Tschumi, Park de la Villette (1982–98). Bernard Tschumi Architects.

"invention" necessary for the new economy, of which La Villette is a flag bearer (quoted in Tschumi 2006, 257). Thus, in both form and function, La Villette announced an ambition for the coming turn to landscape in architecture, which was to subtract spaces from the realm of the immediately productive (a coal mine, steel mill, or abattoir) in order to design an indeterminate setting where use, invention, and program are variable.

If what fueled Tschumi and Derrida was La Villette's deconstructive ethos, it was only due to the theoretical weight then attached to indeterminacy in general. However, those that would look to the project as a sign of things to come in landscape urbanism—the US's two leading figureheads, Charles Waldheim and James Corner, for instance—would see something much more interesting underway. Corner (2006) put it best (though many landscape theorists would echo him in order to distinguish their practice from classical landscape theory) when he named "terra fluxa" the new terrain of architecture and landscape. Liberated from the two axes of space characteristic of architecture's classical domain, terra fluxa "suggests shifting attention away from the object qualities of space (whether formal or scenic) to the systems that condition the distribution and density of urban form" (Corner 2006, 28). In Corner's eyes, architecture's move towards landscape was also a move from objecthood to systemhood. Thus, while it looked from the outside as if architects were invited into the garden at La Villette, major firms and theorists such as Corner, Waldheim, MVRDV, Koolhaas (whose own proposal for La Villette was most inspiring for Corner), and Foreign Office Architects (FOA) understood the project to have advanced the already growing turn to landscape in the architectural imaginary.

This also helps explain why, just as quickly as major architects turned their attention to landscape in the 1980s and 1990s, landscape architects redefined landscape as a form of infrastructure, or more generally as a design approach to infrastructure space. Corner himself did this in the major 1999 collection *Recovering Landscape*, but W.J.T. Mitchell had established the inseparability of landscape and the infrastructures of power in his *Landscape and Power* (1994). In addition to the early influence of Deleuze on architecture and urban theory in the 1980s and 1990s, the widespread redefinition of landscape to mean a place where information, matter, energy, and ideas flow was a consequence of the gradual obsolescence of industrial infrastructures—and ways of thinking about infrastructure—upon which the postindustrial was predicated.

Landscape infrastructures

In David Gissen's estimation, the architectural shifts toward "research," "organization," "landscape," and "infrastructure" are generally part of the same historical process:

> This involves not only a turn toward specific geographical concepts and theories, but toward material and representational transformations as well. We can see this in various contemporary works that advance the territory of maps over plans, the flow of matter over subjects, and the concept of environment over that of space–time.
>
> Gissen 2011, 42

Gissen charts the decline of design—a professional aesthetic practice tied to the modern movement, but also to the types of commodities that were necessary to generalize modernity—and the recent ascendency of the geographical as the disciplinary and political terrain of architecture. Design, in his account, was about accommodating a space–time of modern governance, whereas the geographical is about setting up the postindustrial matrix of "governance, production, and management" that are otherwise "everywhere and nowhere" (42). Even if this geographical ethos is not universal across building practices, for Gissen, Stan Allan, Jesse Reiser, and Nanako Umemoto of Reiser + Unemoto, among many others, it defines landscape architecture's material function in the postindustrial economy.

Several important figures in landscape urbanism have anchored their vision of the new economy to Aldo Rossi's canonical provocation in which architecture names the mediation of matter and energy. In their field manual, which doubles as a postindustrial manifesto for energy's material economy, Reiser and Umemoto go as far as to implicate architecture's "substance, its scale, its transitions and measurement" with "the dilations and contractions of the energy field" (Reiser and Umemoto 2006, 22). For Resier and Umemoto, whose built and theoretical ambition is self-purportedly to realize the full and determining potential of "material and formal specificity over myth and interpretation," this alliance between the spatial aesthetics of architecture and the fluid tectonics of "the energy field" is not novel, but restores an older idea (23). In Rossi's late modern version of landscape tectonics, architecture's principle sits between the two sides of *tempo* in Italian, namely "both atmosphere and chronology" (Rossi 1981, 1). Thus, what is *architectural*, as opposed to merely built, is the "fog" that "penetrate[s] the Galleria in Milan: it is the unforeseen element that modifies and alters, like light and shadow, like stones worn smooth by the feet and hands of generations of men [sic]" (2). Though Rossi's motivation in re-describing architecture as atmospheric in the 1980s was to design political spaces, the economic crisis that occasioned his investment in 1981 generated similar conclusions among other developers.

Architecture's landscape is here reimagined by Rossi and then Reiser and Umemoto as atmospheric space (like weather) and materialist time (the smooth stones after generations of pilgrims) in order to calibrate its forms to the "energy field" it mediates. We might expect the primacy of energy and "material logics" in architecture to result in a civil engineering approach to aesthetics—that is, optimized distribution of forces—but Reiser and Umemoto generate what in 2006 is in many ways a novel materialism much closer to speculative brands of contemporary philosophy than to Rossi's new rationalism (Reiser and Umemoto 2006, 27). Indeed, they most want to move past the rationalist approach to distribution of forces, which for them "precludes the productive and rich capacity of matter to define or influence geometry" (74). Using Manuel DeLanda's speculative philosophy as their cue—work that predates Quentin Meillassoux's veritable bible for speculative realism in 2006—their novel tectonics prioritize *intensive* properties of matter over *extensive* ones.

Diller, Scofidio + Renfro's Blur Building for the 2002 Swiss national exposition (Expo.02) has become notorious for its dramatization of intensity over extension. Blur, in their words, "is an architecture of atmosphere—a fog mass resulting from natural and man-made forces" (Diller, Scofidio and Renfro n.d.). Users cross a narrow bridge out into the middle of Lake Neuchâtel in Switzerland until they reach an enormous cloud that seems to hover autonomously between the lake and the bridge. The cloud itself is the lake vaporized through 35,000 high-pressure nozzles, guided by the building's "smart weather system." Though the cloud itself is supported by an intricate piping, plumbing, oil rig-like structure that extends into the lakebed, its architecture is properly landscaped since it both responds to, and produces, weather systems, and also reduces the visual field to a minimum in order to maximize the atmospheric. In this version of landscape architecture, figuration is abandoned in favor of a generalized and atmospheric ground.[5]

Both Reiser + Umemoto and Elizabeth Diller have tied the rise of intensive spatial properties to the dematerialized production sites central to the information economy. The new office space, in Reiser + Umemoto's theory of tectonics, and in their major Dubai office tower "O-14," is characterized by shrinking hardware, expanding "soft spaces" (Reiser and Umemoto 2006, 109), and a landscape designed to augment creative and non-programmed forms of work. "Against Program" is the way William J. Mitchell puts it when he describes the spatial paradigm required to settle the digital, postindustrial economy in cities not yet ready for it (Mitchell 2013). Program, in his criticism, implies a hardware priority that stunts creative use and co-opts communication between user and building, and between building and system. Hence, Corner's paradigm shift, where landscape urbanism moves from *"terra firma"* to *"terra fluxa"* (Waldheim 2006), is one that saturates the larger field of urbanism today, and is situated not just within the philosophical tradition of new materialism, but within the spatial coordinates of the energy-rich postindustrial economy too.

It should come as no surprise that the peculiar qualities of energy in its material form—namely, those intensive properties emblematic of design and the theoretical preference for flows—have come to dominate the way many people think about space and its organization today. My argument so far has been that the carbon-capital complex is built on optimizing the social and economic plasticity of oil through the elasticity of energyscapes. The replacement of human labor time with a combination of dead labor in the form of machines and nonhuman sources of power is a governing law of economic history. Thus, as human labor is freed from the factory floor and its static hardware, the absent cause of postindustrialization—namely, energy deepening at a most alarming rate—begins to saturate both theories and plans for the postindustrial setting. As global energy supply increases gradually, energy's economic elasticity is optimized through the specifically gradient qualities of oil, including its plasticity and elasticity at the sociocultural level and its intensity and extensity at the level of setting.

If energy has become the dominant point of reference for many designers and landscape urbanists, it would perhaps explain why landscape urbanism is at times as able to normalize the energy structures of a fossil-fueled postindustrial society as it is to arm that same society with an environmentalist countertendency. This at least is the line that Mohsen Mostafavi (2010) walks in his opening remarks to the mammoth *Ecological Urbanism* collection. Mostafavi, dean of the Harvard Graduate School of Design, promotes an ecological approach to urban design first defined by Félix Guattari. Initially developed in Guattari's *The Three Ecologies* in the 1980s, "ecosophy" read through the lens of landscape is a commitment to developing intensive capacities across the environment, social relations, and human subjectivity (the three ecologies) (Guattari 2000 [1989]). Here, energy is shed of its economic function, and instead promoted as an ecological force *counter* to capitalist modernity. Instead of programming energy-efficient spaces, Mostafavi insists that a design approach to the environmental crisis views the fragility of systems "as an opportunity for speculative design innovations rather than as a form of technical legitimation for promoting conventional solutions" (Mostafavi 2010, 17). The fragile relationship between human energy needs and environmental sustainability is "the essential basis for a new form of creative imagining" (26). And what finally proves illustrative for his vision of ecological urbanism is the informal markets of the lumpenproletariat in Lagos and Brazil, and the reclamation of abandoned brownfields for community gardens in Detroit and New Orleans. Thus, when Mostafavi insists that "ecological urbanism must provide the necessary and emancipatory infrastructures for an alternative form of urbanism" (40), he means infrastructure as a form of spatial product that enables stimulating forms of postindustrial interaction: the market and the farm are economically complementary, and offer an image of urban life with both manufacture and power generation cut out.

Pop-up factories, for instance, are not part of this picture, but are presupposed by it—like the coal plants and oil refineries currently fueling the global economy.

Externalizing production and hydrocarbon infrastructures at an aesthetic level is primary to ecological and landscape approaches to the problem of postindustrial energy. These "aesthetic" clues about an urban modality ecologically coded are meant, in Mostafavi's account, to offer a picture of a design ethic able to "counter the global dominance of capitalism" (Mostafavi 2010, 50), plausible in one obvious sense since carbon and capital appear to have been disarticulated in this view of the world. The transition out of capitalism, in ecological urbanism's most distinguished voice, is simultaneously a transition out of petromodernity.

Whether strategically excised from the picture or made the dominant variable in future projections, energy systems and the *energyscapes* they imply have become the primary concern in ecological urbanism and landscape architecture. What I have been arguing here is that this preoccupation gives a theoretical insight into the physical impact of hydrocarbon systems on the social and economic settings in which we live and on the design principles through which the carbon-capital complex establishes itself in the physical and social setting of the postindustrial. To the degree that energy in its most abstract definition is that which animates all matter, landscapes of any variety will thus also be *energyscapes*. What the postindustrial economy requires, however, are spatial modulations of energy deepening, since without energy deepening there is no economic growth, and without spatial modulations of energy there is no setting for expanded cycles of deepening. In addition to reimagining the spatial field of architecture as an energy field, the turn to landscape in architecture has brought with it a redefinition of architecture as a form of energy infrastructure for a new economy. From the trading floor of the energy futures markets in New York, Chicago, and London, to the ports, pipelines, and servers that facilitate the cultural conditions of late capitalism, energy deepening animates the expanded field of the global economy in a recursive ecology with the terminal landscapes it both draws forth and impacts in turn.[6]

Philosophy and the problem of energy

The aesthetic preference in landscape architecture and ecological urbanism for intensive properties, such as energy and information flows, and the infrastructure systems that maximize them were necessary features of the larger project to postindustrialize key economic spaces. This, I have been suggesting, is neither an accident nor a tendency separate from the philosophical disposition that has matured during the same postindustrial transformations at the global stage. It is not an accident because the philosophical turn to intensive properties in Deleuze, Laruelle, De Landa and Meillassoux is always a form of theoretical legitimation that gives license to the speculative characteristic of their philosophical tradition, a stance premised on a rejection of nearly all philosophies tied to industrial forms of measurement and thinking. Historically and theoretically, speculative realism and the object-oriented ontology it made possible depend on an insight into intensive properties of matter, of which energy is the most obvious, important, and economically valuable. Yet neither of these two positions, nor the political philosophy of accelerationism indebted to them, takes seriously the elasticity that energy deepening makes available for capital after oil reigns supreme—an economic elasticity so significant, in my account, because it is responsible for both the aesthetic and economic effacement of labor in the postindustrial economy.[7] Thus, while a reading of energy as cosmic force animates much of speculative philosophy, energy's dialectical imbrication with capitalist accumulation appears only at the register of climate change.

Here I want to be very careful not to misrecognize the political and philosophical motivation behind the conceptual preferences that animate speculative philosophies of the present, but instead to situate those preferences in an economic field equally, if not more, invested in them. Deleuze no doubt has the right idea when, in *Nietzsche and Philosophy* (2006), he distinguishes between energic force and force as will, and it is in this matrix of materialism that Peter Hallward convincingly characterizes Deleuze's philosophy as "an exercise in creative *indiscernment*, an effort to subtract the dynamics of creation from the mediation of the created" (Hallward 2006, 3). Certainly, the ambitions of Nietzsche, Whitehead, and Bergson reside in the former—in the philosophical optimization of creativity, instead of the rather more dialectical game of discerning "the mediation of the created" (Hallward 2006, 3)—and for this reason Nietzsche's fascination with the eternal return of energy leads Deleuze not to the critique of specific forms and uses of energy (industrialized coal, oil, fertilizers, and so on), but to the celebration of creativity as such. If for Nietzsche "the world" is "a monster of energy, without beginning, without end," and whose only will is 'the will to power', as it is famously described at the close of *The Will to Power* (Nietzsche 1968, fragment 1067), we might hazard to supply this picture of the world with what gives it its contemporaneity, to paraphrase Benjamin (1968 [1955], 261/thesis XIV). My intention here is to track the way the conceptual distinction between energy and intensity pans out when what is in need of conceptualization, critique, and politicization is very much the material history of energy's concept, including its philosophical, aesthetic, and political economy. What happens to philosophical disposition when it is confronted with the urgent need to historicize the smooth synthesis of industrial energy systems with social creativity, mass unemployment, and the epistemological impasse of a fossil-fueled modernity? My claim here is that it will have a very difficult time recognizing the normative versions of its ambitions without the capacity and motivation to discern forces that mediate the created, that give eternal return a sense of specificity, and so on.

What then mediates the created in a postindustrial landscape premised on untold quantities of energy, radically uneven concentrations of capital and rapid environmental destabilization? My claim in the opening section of this chapter was that capital has never before been as bound to its capacity to deepen and extend energy-intensive forms of production, circulation, and consumption as it is in the postindustrial era, a tendency largely responsible for the political and critical hostility to labor. But the expanded field of postindustrial economics that I have been posing to the tradition that celebrates the energic is not historically unique in its preference for energy in the abstract over labor as the mediation of energy and the value it helps expand.

An important predecessor to the postindustrial philosophy I have been shadowing here is Isabelle Stengers' critical realism. Stengers' speculative critique of empiricism and positivism makes space for, but is crucially distinct from, more ludic materialisms that today celebrate creative energy and energy in and of itself. What distinguishes the critical realism to which I wish to return from the more recent iterations that follow from the postindustrial philosophy I have named as such is its attention to conceptual conditions and its commitment to mediation in the face of radical uncertainty. On the other side of scientific and critical realism is a critique of energy that returns us to the thermodynamic reason of capital.

In the tradition continued by Isabelle Stengers—a tradition heavily indebted to the work of Michel Serres and Gaston Bachelard—the occasion for a speculative form of philosophical realism stretched back to the heart of industrialization, or more specifically to the irreconcilable rupture between mechanics and thermodynamics. Animating the gap between a thermodynamic faith and the rational observation of mechanical force in Stengers' account is the aesthetic economy of the former. The idea of "conversion between 'forces' was initially an aesthetic idea," she maintains, "which communicated with the presentation of an 'indestructible force' that gave nature its permanent unity" (Stengers 2010, 179). This "indestructible force" stretched back to Leibniz's "life force" and to the post-Kantian philosophy of nature, both of which cohered in an aesthetic irreducible to scientific reason. For Stengers, energy and its nineteenth-century theory requires an aesthetic understanding of universal convertibility—and this would matter later, once energy and human labor became ostensibly interchangeable in the postindustrial period—since for energy to make sense, it must be equally visible in the burning candle or the heat given off by a chemical reaction as it is in electrolysis, the electric battery, and the steam engine. Hence, what energy initially establishes is not just a theory of matter's behavior, but what Stengers calls "a 'way of seeing,' an aesthetic" that unified not just the rhythms and tendencies of the physical world, but the disciplines charged with studying them (192).

Lurking behind the metaphysics of energy and the theory of thermodynamics is, in Stengers' words, an energy "landscape" involving not just scientific inquiry but historically specific structures of thought (Stengers 2010, vii). And the implications for political economy—which in the 1860s was up against what would prove to be its most hostile opposition to date, namely Marxism in its most mature stage—are not difficult to grasp once Stengers extends her critique to the theory of entropy and its consequence for value standards of work. The leap of faith required for the theory of universal energy convertibility gave the industrial economy its economic doxa. At issue is the relationship between measurement and the object of measurement when energy is understood as a form of work. In the formative theses of Carnot and Clausius, *the measurement of energy necessarily creates* the object called energy. This is because "in the case of energy transformations ... measurability is in no way a 'given,' it must be created, fabricated from whole cloth" (Stengers 2010, 210). Motivating this scientific form of perlocution is a conundrum introduced by the theory of entropy: namely, that not all transformations are reversible. Though the first law of thermodynamics states that energy can be neither created nor destroyed, the second law eliminates any chance of equivocation between transformations since entropy names that portion of energy that permanently escapes transferability. Thus, one cannot measure energy like one can measure the extensive properties of matter (length, volume, weight, and so on) because at its heart—and this is why object-oriented ontologists and landscape architects are both blind to and stimulated by energy— *energy is pure intensity, with no inherent extensive properties, and thus not measurable from within a rationalism premised on extension.* Unlike mechanical force, which has a source and a result that on paper can be reversed, energy "obligated the physicist to be conscious that he was a manipulator, an active participant in the definition of equivalence" (Stengers 2010, 211).

The point here is twofold. Energy (in its two faces—one positive force, the other negative entropy) is in Stengers' words a "rather strange" object for science.

It is strange because it betrays the logical forms of measurement that had, until then, defined not just scientific systems of measurement but economic forms, too. And this is the second point. The labor theory of value emerged as a logical extension of the mechanical universe lock, stock, and barrel. Labor power, in its original formulation, was a measurable form of energy, the equivocation of which was supplied by the wage. Energy and its enigmatic theory made any measure of human energy (labor) more than a little odd, since the value of a commodity implied an economy of different states of accumulated and potential energy (labor, most obviously, but capital too). If labor is a form of energy, and energy is pure intensity evading rational measurement without the active intervention (and invention) of an observer, then the specifically economic form of rationality associated with classical political economy would require as much faith as the physicist measuring energy. Positivism, both in physics and in economics (and the money form of value is the greatest positivism of them all), was already a form of speculation, since what these fields took as their universal objects (one energy, the other labor time) troubled the very enterprise they supposedly verified.

On the cusp of the thermodynamics revolution in science, Marx was fast on the heels of the second enterprise. *Capital* is an enormous exercise in a type of materialist critique that intervenes, too, within the logical assumptions of the then-novel science of political economy in order both to expose its fallacies and to catch a vista from within its contradictions onto what might succeed it. We might then call Marx, like Roy Bhaskar does, the first realist in the modern era (Bhaskar 2009, 241). Stengers, too, comes close to recognizing the significance of energy's historical and complimentary coincidence with the political economy of capital in the nineteenth century. Her critique exposes the way that the political economist's aesthetic challenge of tracking the appearance of value back to its sources is the same challenge that sits at the heart of thermodynamic reason. From the perspective of Stengers' critical realism, the enigma of value is the enigma of energy, the historical unfolding of which provides fossil capital with its resource aesthetic.[8] Understood from within Stengers' critique of thermodynamic reason, the contemporaneous evisceration of labor as a critical standpoint and the ludic misrecognition of energy's inseparability from capital come as no surprise in an expanded economic field premised on both.

Part Two

From the Postindustrial Environment to the Concerns of Climate

4

Elemental Ethnography Between Hydrocarbons and Hydrology: Thinking with Greenland's Moraine

Part 2 of *Climate and Capital* shifts its analytic and geographical foci away from oil and instead thinks in relation to the elemental entanglements of water, ice, and thermal radiation unleashed by, but also semiautonomous from, the age of petroleum. My argument across the three chapters in Part 1 was that the terminal has become the site where concrete materialities are abstracted into a multiplicity of forms—financial commodities, emissions, and future ecologies—and that its understated status in contemporary environmental discourse is a problem in need of redress. Terminal landscapes such as the Port of Amsterdam, the virtual futures figured by Shell scenarios, the postindustrial zone of 1980s Turin, and the energyscapes surging amidst the architectural posture of creative cities, are all examples of capital's terminalia. Fossil fuels do more than provide raw force to a mode of production. They also restructure the rhythm, intensity, and texture of the social relations they fuel. But the point that I have been making so far is not that fossil fuels thus determine sociocultural relations through some alchemy they carry into the world via pipelines and coal plants. Something happens *in medias res*, between extraction and consumption: energy gets repackaged as commodity, and the metaphysics of capital comes to both abstract the fuels that circulate across the global market and in turn become materially wedded to the affordances of those fuels. This last point is easy enough to admit: a glut in oil proves horrendous for futures traders and commodity markets alike, and yet environmental discourse in the past decade has routinely insisted that the real problem keeping our global economy bound to fossil fuels is in the compulsion to extract (and so we should keep it in the ground) or in habits of consumption (and so we should abstain and deter). The terminal ought to convince us that the inertia of fossil-fueled modernity exceeds the metonymic clarity of extractive sins and consumptive addiction. Rather, that inertia of fossil-fueled modernity is compelled at ever greater magnitude through *abstraction*. And the terminal's conceptual, logistical, geophysical, and speculative landscape is where capital abstracts the crude materiality of the petrocultural into more than one kind of thing in the world, occasioning in turn more than one kind of analytic orientation.

Analytically, oil asks after a specific set of critical habits. With oil as my compass in Part 1, I offered three case studies modeled by the particular forms its elemental force takes once capital distributes its multiple formats into the world as so many values. To track these forces meant taking up a critical perspective able to disarticulate appearances—of progress, innovation, and growth—from historical and material determination. But while criticality is a necessary component of an elemental analytic, I will begin to suggest over the next three chapters that its hermeneutic (and often self-satisfying conclusions) cannot occlude the noticing of and caring for worlds unfolding into the planet's ecological near futures. An elemental analytic does not exclude hydrocarbons, but you cannot get very far down the road of historicity if your ethnography of oil is restricted to its viscosity, chemical composition, lithospheric genesis, or aroma. This is because fossil fuels are always already abstracted by the historicity of exchange—they do not stockpile, refine, and burn on their own—so an elemental fetishization of the concrete and the crude means losing how hydrocarbons bind to capital in addition to oxygen molecules in the air. Part 1 was an attempt to demonstrate how an elemental ethnography of oil might work in the postindustrial period.

But in jumping back across the diptych with which I began this book—from the oil terminal of the Port of Amsterdam to the terminal landscape of the Greenland Ice Sheet—a different elemental voice and posture is needed in order to hold the terminal in focus. In shifting the focus from oil to the elemental forces of water, thermal, and ice, however, I am also emphasizing how the terminal oscillates *with* what it leaves out materially from abstraction. The melting Greenland Ice Sheet, as we will see, is materially, historically, and economically bound up with what happens in the terminals lining industrial ports all over the world, but those same industrial terminals are also dwarfed in their spatiotemporal profile compared to the sheer size, force, and planetary consequence of the receding Arctic cryosphere. Industrial and geophysical (or better, cryophysical) terminals are recursive to one another asymmetrically. As a larger term that names the conditioning of future political ecologies, the terminal captures the interactive translation (and untranslatability) of these two cadences of abstraction and concretion—industrial infrastructure, postindustrial capital, and ecological dynamics—even as their interactive logics spin out of focus across different scales.

Centering the end(s) of the earth

I was not thinking too seriously about the place of Greenland in the post-1970s life of oil when I began researching for this book. Growing up as a working-class, white settler in the suburbs of Canada's most populous region, Greenland only ever figured as a frozen landmass expressive of the relative distance from Canada's mainland to Newfoundland, the easternmost province stretching out into its own time zone and sharing its "Iceberg Alley" with the southwestern edge of Greenland. I learned too that Greenland "belonged" to Denmark as a young student of geography—its name on maps always conjoined to the parenthetical (DK)—a simple enough concept implying that the giant island in the Arctic was uninhabited, dotted perhaps with a few Danish flags left over (anachronistically) from the time of Vikings. Despite the proximity of the country in which I grew up to Greenland, it remained at the very edge of my settler-colonial imaginary. I learned later that in fact Greenland was neither an empty place nor a Danish outpost, and that its official language, Kalaallisut, is a dialect of the same language that Inuit peoples in northern Canada speak (an important feature, too, of what was largely untaught in Canadian public schools). And like the violent history of colonialism in the place where I grew up that would come to be known as Canada between European settlers and First Nations peoples, forced settlements, religious conversion, and the "diplomatic" theft of wealth marked Greenland's history and present in ways that are still overlaid with colonial apologia. And of course I learned too, as I began to study the political ecology of climate change more seriously at various universities, that Greenland's ecology was central in the larger dynamics unfolding across the planet—that cartographies, in other words, are contiguous, constantly drawn into various currents, histories, and planetary dynamics.

The trope animating much ethnographic writing on the Arctic has long been that its ice, atmosphere, and peoples exist at the end of the earth. In his photo essay "End of the Earth," for instance, cinematographer Murray Fredericks goes to Greenland and asks *National Geographic* readers to consider what 'nothing look[s] like?' (Fredericks 2015). As a visual trope underwriting his film, *Nothing on Earth*, "nothing" is actually a reference to the opposite of human-made infrastructures, none of which are visible as arching time-lapse sequences of calving icebergs, northern lights displays, and whiteout storms mark the terminus, or ends, of the anthroposcape. Fredericks' discourse of emptiness and ends—"drawn" as he was to the 'polished white emptiness of the place'—refers back to a popular mode of imaging remoteness and scale as features of a frontier at the ends of a distinctly colonial concept of "world," and a frontier as a space to test the limits of the human where few or no others appear to exist. The polar sublime of Emanuel A. Petersen's romantic paintings between 1936 and 1946 continues to lurk in the ethnographic intrigue of the Western gaze. The terminal landscape this tradition translates is remote, far removed from the temperate geographies of colonial centers in Western Europe, North America, and Australia, even if a UNESCO-supported hike around the edge of the Sermeq Kujalleq glacier in Ilullissat is just shy of a five-hour flight from Copenhagen and a fifty-minute connection from Kangerlussuaq. Ecotourist expeditions, including a number sponsored by WWF and National Geographic, regularly boast of the opportunity to find yourself at the ends of the earth.

But the ends of the earth have more recently come to signal not just the edge of navigable space, but a temporal terminus too. There, resource-intensive forms of life over the long arc of industrial and colonial modernity come to roost, while animate and warming ecologies tip the surface-mass balance of Greenland's land-based ice—both in marine-terminating outlet glaciers and subglacial melt—into terminal decline. In the popular science writing of Jon Gretner, Greenland's ice is both at the vertical end of the map (seen from a Euro-American standpoint, at least) and, more profoundly, confirms the enormity of a tipping point *already* reached in the earth system, an event "immense and catastrophic that could not be easily stopped" (Gretner 2019, xv). For Gretner, melting ice observed by the NASA IceBridge program in the late 2010s turns the colonial convention of exoticizing the Arctic into a confirmation of ecological filiation: for the curious and concerned observer alike, the terminal condition of Greenland's ice is as much an ending to *our* historical epoch as it is a dynamic playing out at the so-called physical edge of the world. The tipping point observed by NASA and others since the early 1990s brings the temporal and spatial ends of the world crashing into one another: a landscape whose radical alterity from the cultural geographies of modernity now troubles the self-certainty of settler subjectivities for whom environmental stability has long been a prerequisite for knowledge and progress.

Greenland's ice sheet is a physical and continuous object measuring nearly 1.7 million square kilometers. At its ablation zone—the perimeter of the ice mass undergoing annual net loss—is what journalists now routinely call the "ground zero" of planetary global warming: the remote periphery suddenly internalized as the center of history in the popular and scientific imaginary. But Gretner is not alone in mixing cartography with chronology in his discursive translation of earth sciences into a cultural idiom of climate change. Indeed, this is precisely the historiographical twist compelling much recent critical work in the environmental humanities. In the first and cornerstone thesis of Dipesh Chakrabarty's landmark four theses on the "Climate of History," for instance, "anthropogenic explanations of climate change spell the collapse of the age-old humanist distinction between natural history and human history" (Chakrabarty 2009, 201). The western concept of progressive history around which the determinate will of political subjects coheres depends largely on the correlative agent responsible for the making of history: namely, a triumphalist notion of the human, against which thrums the relatively static background of the natural world. Part of Chakrabarty's point is that the moment we take anthropogenic climate change on as a dominant feature of contemporary historical thought and conflict, that formative opposition between the active and passive voice of history collapses. *Environmental* humanities, as opposed to a *liberal* humanities, admits this troubling collapse as an ongoing theoretical and ontological challenge. But the anthropogenesis of climate change names a premise equally troubling to contemporary history: the *anthropos* and its modern constitution is, at scale, able to move mountains, as it were, because its agential prowess is, among other things, "geological." This second (and oft-cited) premise is worth quoting at length:

> The mansion of modern freedoms stands on an ever-expanding base of fossil-fuel use. Most of our freedoms so far have been energy-intensive. The period of human history usually associated with what we today think of as the institutions of civilization—the beginnings of agriculture, the founding of cities, the rise of the religions we know, the invention of writing—began about ten thousand years ago, as the planet moved from one geological period, the last ice age or the Pleistocene, to the more recent and warmer Holocene. The Holocene is the period we are supposed to be in; but the possibility of anthropogenic climate change has raised the question of its termination. Now that humans—thanks to our numbers, the burning of fossil fuel, and other related activities—have become a geological agent on the planet, some scientists have proposed that we recognize the beginning of a new geological era, one in which humans act as a main determinant of the environment of the planet. The name they have coined for this new geological age is Anthropocene.
>
> Chakrabarty 2009, 208–209

I am not especially interested or concerned with the nomenclature of the Anthropocene, but the metaphor of geological agency and historical terminus stands out here as worth lingering on for its implicit periodization of ends. Note here that for Chakrabarty there is a dialectical back and forth between the animacy (or *non*human activity) named by climate change, and the anthropogenesis (and its material foundation in an "ever-expanding base of fossil-fuel use") of that same change in climate. As a "geological agent," the *anthropos* of contemporary, fossil-fueled reason is internally marked by what had been previously and necessarily excluded from the purview of History: the *geos* of the planet long thought by western historians to lack life, reason, and historical constitution. For Elizabeth Povinelli, this geological edge to life and nonlife (and all the legal and economic privileges that accrue based on how the distinction is figured) haunts the edge of what she terms "late liberalism"—a limit that is reified by sustainability and conservationist responses to ecological catastrophe (Povinelli, Coleman, and Yusoff 2017, 173). Nearly all of what folds into the archive of study for the discipline of History occurs during the geological epoch known as the Holocene—roughly the past 11,700 years. But that same archive is emplotted by the institutional impulse toward greater individual, social, and material freedoms for those to whom the *benefit* of History had been institutionally and legally ensured. Without the energic swell of work at the disposal of the subject of freedom—a swell fulfilled first by the institution of slavery amidst the initial uptick in capitalism and colonialism alike, and then by the industrialization of cheap fossil fuels in the nineteenth century—the very notion of a sovereign subject of liberal reason would have made no sense. For those to whom the *burden* of History accrues, however, this narrative was more of a fiction anyway, but one now inverted as the historicity of inequality and exploitation in former colonial geographies gets figured as so many apocalyptic futures for first world readers. In Jennifer Wenzel's account, "Europe's others were once seen as inhabiting a lesser past; here they are seen as inhabiting its projected future anterior" (2020, 37). The burden of fossil-fueled history is quickly becoming the burden of an ecological future already unfolding in the present, albeit unevenly. But Chakrabarty's point here is that the dirty secret of that "mansion of modern freedoms" is a material one, and it is that same plotline that gets exposed as a tragedy once the environmental background to History flares up (or melts) as so many tipping points, extinctions and eviscerated habitats. The "termination" of the Holocene, in Chakrabarty's formative theses, is also the termination of the classical concept of the human, entangled as it is with an ever-expanding and affordable resource base able to move and maintain freedom from necessity. The elemental force of hydrocarbons, in this story, is bound up with the capitalist modernity responsible for its unearthing.

But elements compound, bond, and repel in an expanded environment animated by their biogeochemistry. If the age of petroleum shares its terminus with the Holocene, then an unleashing of elemental contrarieties such as water, fire, and ice is in keeping with what in the environmental humanities *qualifies* our field's claim about the envelope in which the humanities does its work: an ecology that saturates, permeates, and challenges the human, or at least our inherited notions of its constitution. And that termination unfolds most immediately at the terminus of the Greenland Ice Sheet, where fossil-fueled modernity and the melting into focus of the "edge" of the planet converge in the globe's first independent Inuit state (Nuttall 2008, 64). An elemental shift in ecological theory that I am after here is one that blurs the causal and critical lines between the historicity of hydrocarbons and the animating force of planetary dynamics. Accordingly, this chapter seeks a situated perspective on the melting of ice and the futures premised on the terminalia of the Holocene, a perspective that brings together the history of hydrocarbon exploration and the fluid imaginaries of hydrological flow as it textures the struggle for indigenous sovereignty.

Even as the ecological drama of ice draws the globe's focus to the Arctic, it will turn out that petrocapital's abstractive gaze is always near to hand: the planetary dynamics unfolding at the threshold of cryosphere, hydrosphere, atmosphere, and lithosphere is both compounded by and in turn generative of fossil-fueled modernity. Indeed, at the end of the last decade, it looked very much to most observers both inside Greenland and abroad that the path to sovereignty would be paved in hydrocarbon revenues. The US Geological Survey (USGS), in partnership with the Geological Survey of Denmark and Greenland (GEUS), had just completed its geological survey of East Greenland's petroleum resources, estimating in 2007 that the largely unpopulated eastern coast had a startling 31 billion barrels of oil equivalent in oil, gas, and natural liquid gas (a significant portion of which was trapped by the Greenland Ice Sheet) (Gautier 2007). Meanwhile, the same survey team had already found over 100 billion barrels on and off the coast of West Greenland, where much of the infrastructure and population of the country is concentrated. To put things in perspective, the Permian Basin's Wolfcamp shale in West Texas, assessed by the USGS in 2016 (and announced the week of Donald Trump's inauguration as president) contains roughly 20 billion barrels of oil. According to Stephanie Gaswirth at the USGS, Wolfcamp was "the largest estimate of continuous oil that the USGS has ever assessed in the United States" (U.S. Geological Survey 2016). In December 2018, the discovery extended to include Bone Spring formations in West Texas and New Mexico, nearly doubling the estimated reserves (Blum 2018). In Greenland, the survey confirmed decades of suspicion: that, as the ice melted, Greenland would open for business, and on a scale enjoyed by only a handful of countries in the twentieth and twenty-first centuries. And the news did not go unnoticed in the energy industry. By 2014, twenty-four exploration licenses had been sold by the newly established Home Rule Government of Greenland. And the timing could not have complicated matters more. Greenland is in political transition following over 300 years of colonial rule by Denmark—a condition of postcoloniality that wraps the concerns of ice in a complex arena of politics and economic inertia toward resource-intensive development. The rapid exploitation of natural resources in order to facilitate economic and industrial modernization looked not just like an obvious choice; indeed, exactly because of the postcolonial terms set by the Danish government, Greenland had no choice at all. To pay down the block grant and sever the last legal bonds to its colonial past, Greenland would need first to generate 50 percent more revenue than the current value of its subsidy from Denmark, or roughly 1 billion euros (Danish Parliament 2009). The entire GDP of Greenland in 2016 was 2.3 billion euros, 90 percent of which came from fishing.

Thinking with the moraine

With my colleague Amanda Boetzkes, I went to Greenland first in the fall of 2018 to learn more about how ice and oil figure in the political discourse of Greenlandic sovereignty. The project we initiated during that first stay in Ilullissat and Nuuk would eventually culminate in a research and artist residency situated "At the Moraine' of the Greenland Ice Sheet."[1] The project involves an elemental ethnography of ice at the nexus of climate change, postcoloniality, indigenous knowledge, and the energyscape of late modern fossil capital. These four modalities on their own could be said to pre-exist the withdrawing of ice, but the moraine left in its immediate wake is a basin of attraction where the nexus itself gets written into by the animating force of ice as it grinds out new ground. It is hard to see or think this nexus from space or through any one disciplinary frame that gives formal definition to the ice sheet. Deliberately, then, the project begins by inviting those concerned with ice to speak about it and to compare concepts, instruments of measure, and the means by which the formless force of ice in Greenland provisionally and partially affords certain *forms* of behavior towards it. This is what we mean to suggest by elemental ethnography: a collaborative mode of open-plan fieldwork sensitive to how elements write themselves into human and nonhuman worlds, and how those same worlds write themselves into the elements they summon as means and meaning. But it is messy as a research practice, almost never confirming what one wants or expects to hear or see. Among the various theorizations that linger on the elemental from

Emmanuel Levinas and Luce Irigaray in continental philosophy, Jeffrey Jerome Cohen in ecocriticism, the Greenlandic anthropologist Lene Holm and her volume on *The Meaning of Ice* with Shari Fox Gearheard (2013) about the circumpolar, and Timothy Neale, Thao Phan, and Courtney Addison's introduction to the anthropogenic table of elements in *Cultural Anthropology* (2019), it is the emphasis on force over form that captures analytic attention. The elemental is what compounds, flames fires, or melts melt—the exception, it would seem, to Hegel's great chiasmus found at the heart of the philosophy of nature where matter is always *informed* and form always materialized: the elemental is what verbs the chiasmus, situating the object but not sticking around in the way that a particle does. And as earth systems' feedback loops distort the stability of any geophysical ground upon which to study the present, an elemental ethnography seems to us more necessary now than ever.

Bringing together indigenous and non-indigenous anthropologists, glaciologists, performance and video artists, and various humanities disciplines, the larger project aims to develop creative and immersive research practices able to read the elemental interplay of a recalcitrant cryosphere where it writes itself ethnographically precisely where it *was*—at the moraine. Our sense so far is that each of these categories of concern *see* and *read* ice in a discursive, aesthetic, and epistemological frame that, while never fully independent of the nexus, also always implies a politics of seeing that makes up the historical and geophysical specificity of ice at their convergence in place. These categories of concern are differentially recursive to the terminal landscape left in the wake of melting ice, both causes and effects of it. Geophysical dynamics converge to produce moraine, storying the elemental knots and currents that translate thermal energy into hydrological pressure and viscosity. But stories about the deep geological history and ecological near-future also accumulate as so many stories at the moraine. Sometimes they are written in the same idiom, taking up conventions of developmentalism, as happens when geologists contracted to the oil and gas industries deploy Landsat imaging to see the moraine as a natural infrastructure for extractive aspirations; sometimes through the interpretive frame of indigenous performance, as I introduce in the next chapter; sometimes through the complex drives of an emerging state invested in resourcing its sovereignty on the postcolonial terms set elsewhere, as I am detailing here.

During our interviews at the parliament offices, or Inatsisartut, in Nuuk, the story that began to emerge with seeing the elemental affordance of ice came with the four-year hydrological survey of the entire island that the Government of Greenland initiated later that year. The infrastructural promise of Greenland's hydrological potential positions the country's grid-to-come at a conflicted angle to renewables, extractive industries, Inuit sovereignty, and the largest landscape with which transnational discourse on climate change has concerned itself over the past two decades: the new center of the planet's ecological future. The survey focalizes melt through the framework of current, and the current is what lurches the nexus I mentioned above forward into an uncertain future.

Importantly, the USGS survey was the first to look *through* the ice, as it were—or to, in the survey's phrasing, "assum[e] the absence of sea ice," and in more ways than one (USGS 2016). Horizontally and vertically, to see the future of fossil fuels, geologists have to first imagine the ice out of the picture, and by imaging ice out of the picture, the Greenland survey stands in for Arctic resources more generally—a "prototype for the new . . . Circum-Arctic Resource Appraisal (CARA)" that USGS has since gone on to export to other zones of future exploitation across the Arctic. Greenland, it would appear, taught geologists to find fossil fuels all over the Arctic—to look through ice and see not water and rock but oil and gas.

This was the recent history that brought us to ask after a meeting with the minister of Fishing, Hunting, and Agriculture at the Inatsisartut, because the story of fossil-fueled futurity in Greenland criss-crosses so startlingly with the concerns of ice in a warming world. We didn't anticipate meeting with representatives of the fishing and hunting sector when we first landed in the capital, Nuuk, but our contacts at the Inuit Circumpolar Council (ICC) suggested the day before that the perspective we needed—if what we wanted to understand was that the many ways that ice *mattered* to Greenlanders—were those of the people fishing and hunting on, under, and amidst the ice. The idea was conveyed clearly enough to us: it isn't through climate change that concerns of ice figure most meaningfully here; it is through catch quotas. This wasn't to say that climate change doesn't matter to Greenlanders, who are over 90 percent Inuit and have been enormously vocal about the rapidly changing conditions of their home, but instead that climate change comes to mean hermeneutically not through the modality of looking at earth shared by NASA, the USGS, and their Danish counterparts at GEUS, but instead through what Lene Holm of the Greenland Climate Research Centre told us was an inherent multi-perspectivism animated by the crosscurrents of indigenous history, or what Rauna Kuokkanen calls "indigenous epistemes" (2017), and the uneven temporalities unleashed by home rule and state-led modernization programs. The standpoints convened at the terminus of the Greenland Ice Sheet *see*, *know*, and *think* ice through different sensibilities, ecological paradigms, and expectations. Lene's suggestion made a lot of sense.

Fishers and hunters of Greenland see ice through a particular set of concerns. The language of thinning ice is used to detail the rising danger of the industry, while the politics of quotas puts them directly at odds with the concerns of the nation-state whose economic priorities increasingly do not align with what elected leaders call the *traditional economy*. And since fish makes up 90 percent of exports in Greenland, you can see what was behind the suggestion to speak with their ministry reps: not only do fishers and hunters represent a powerful economic bloc, thinning sea ice and the increasing volatility of calving off the ice sheet also puts fishers and hunters in an epistemic position to make unique knowledge about the elemental forces unfolding at the moraine. Our intention was to have that conversation, but because our host at the front desk of the government offices in Nuuk heard "climate" and "the meaning of ice" during our introductions, we found ourselves instead in a meeting with the representative from the ministry of energy and industry, who spoke to us as potential investors. So we asked what had been on our mind in the first place: What exactly happened to the promise of hydrocarbons? What ever happened to the future promise of a fossil-fueled modernity mapped at the end of the last decade? And how from the

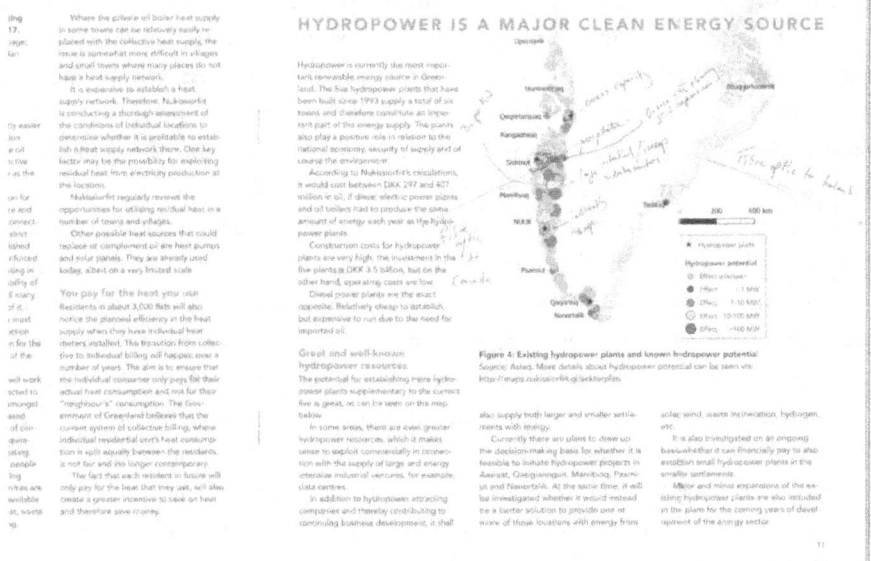

Figure 4.1 "Hydropower is a Major Clean Energy Source" research notes. Author research notes and photo.

standpoint of those this government is elected to represent does ice matter today? The answer was more than a little surprising. While the licenses issued earlier in the decade for hydrocarbon exploration had dried up during the extended glut between 2014 and 2018—a period when the barrel price of oil dipped far below the necessary profit window for new upstream investments to come online—the ministry had recognized a new resource accumulating at the edge of Greenland's terminal moraine. "Water," our minister rep told us, "will be the new oil" (see Figure 4.1).

The cost of current

Our hosts in the government offices started up a PowerPoint presentation and offered us two new pamphlets detailing the projected sites for hydroelectric potential at the moraine of the ice sheet, as well as a third collating extensive market research on bottled water for a thirsty world and the inexhaustible revenue potential for Greenlanders. As the young nation-state seeks to attract capital for much-needed development projects, employment sources and, by extension, a stable source for fiscal sovereignty from the Danish state, the landscape itself continues to animate various imaginaries of the future. But there is a key shift here in the way that the elemental profile of hydrocarbon resources differs from the political ecology of melt. The twenty-four licenses for oil exploration, fraught as they were with the tension between environmental, economic, colonial, and cultural pressures, precipitated from a conceptualization and visualization of the island as a standing reserve of hydrocarbons and rare earths: an industrial terminal between the geophysical dynamics of cryosphere and lithosphere, on the one hand, and the gaze of capital seeking future royalties and resources for the energy-intensive tempo of global trade, on the other. As oil prices plummeted to well below $40 a barrel in the fall of 2014, however, the ministers responsible for soliciting investment faced an infrastructural impasse: the standing reserve would have to remain locked under rock, sea, and ice so long as the intermediary apparatus of industrial power, refineries, storage farms, pipelines, and barge ports—in short, the terminal infrastructure needed to abstract resource into commodity—remained a future cost predicated on the mortgaging of upstream revenues. Without the infrastructure in place, materials, specialists, engineers, and laborers would need to be shipped in up the North Atlantic: Greenland's relative remoteness from the centers of capital materialized as a value relation instead of a geographical or cultural one, and an impediment to the localization of terminal infrastructures *in* Greenland upon which fossil-fueled capitalism futures worlds.

In Greenland, the capital investment required for large-scale industry of any kind has long been a massive hurdle that the ministries responsible for energy and industry have never been able to overcome. This, despite the impressive fact that nearly 70 percent of electricity in Greenland is generated by the country's five hydroelectric dams built between 1993 and the late 2000s (Bertelsen and Hansen 2015, 123). The island has no shortage of hydroelectric potential, especially when the rate of flow increases due to the rapid deterioration of the ice sheet that supplies the dams with their current.

And yet, despite the massive capacity of the country's hydropower, there is currently no way for the public utility company, Nukissiorfiit, to share load between the country's five completely independent grids. This is for a simple enough reason: between the seventeen cities and fifty-three settlements that dot the coastal areas of Greenland, there is virtually no infrastructure of *any* kind connecting them. In the words of Kåre Hendriksen, a civil engineer teaching at TU Denmark, "Greenland does not work as one, but as seventy-five independent islands. With a few exceptions, there are no settlements that ha[ve] roads or any other overland transportations connections with other settlements. All person- and goods transportation between the different settlements are by plane, helicopter, ships, dinghies or dogsleds" (Hendriksen 2016). Melting ice powered Greenland up precisely to the point of industrialization, while the geological and historical landscape between its built archipelagos prevents a spilling over into heavy industrial development or fossil-fueled sovereignty.

In the archive of Greenland's foray into industrialization, two recent cases stand out as common references justifying the new hydrological survey and the scaling-up of the grid to come. On the west coast, Alcoa proposed in 2007 to build an aluminum smelter powered by what the government promised would be two new dams in the area of the Tasersiaq Lake some 80 kilometers away. Aluminum smelters are famously energy-intensive because of the current required for the electrolytic processing of bauxite—so much so that the cost of energy represents around a quarter of the total cost, varying based on the price of labor and power (Sejersen 2015, 67). Electricity needs to be subsidized to somewhere around $0.029/kWh in order to make aluminum smelting profitable, at least when the price of ingot per tonne is around $1,300. So the promise of an inexhaustible and relatively clean source of energy meant that Greenland looked like an attractive alternative to China, where the bulk of aluminum is made today with coal power. During Danish colonialism, one of the world's first cryolite mines was operational in Ivittuut from 1854 to 1987. But the Alcoa plant promised upwards of 1,200 jobs to an economy of only 50,000 people hovering between seven and nine percent unemployment. After almost a decade of negotiations, the proposal collapsed because of a combination of contests over the cultural memory of the proposed dam site, including its proximity to the already-proposed UNESCO World Heritage Site around Sarfartoq, and archaeological archives at the Greenland National Museum and Archives suggesting the significance of the site to Inuit history (Sejersen 2015, 147). In Frank Sejersen's words, the archive corroborated a way of seeing an "undivided cultural landscape" at odds with the extractivist logic of a divisible landscape. Crucially, two of the largest dams in the country already operate to the north and south of Maniitsoq in Nuuk and Sisimiut. But no infrastructure connects these two dams, preventing anything like load sharing for the Alcoa project. Currents, as of yet, do not converge.

The second project still under contest is a proposed uranium and rare-earth elements mine in South Greenland. The prospect of uranium mining is nearly a century old in Greenland, ever since Niels Bohr in the 1950s famously turned the discovery of uranium near the southern city of Narsaq into the source of a grand vision of nuclear modernity in postwar Europe (Walsh 2017; Nielsen et al. 1999). Across Greenland there are a number of mining projects for gold, rubies, zinc, copper, and other metals, but uranium has long occupied a central position in the Danish imaginary of a post-oil modernity and Greenlandic independence (Nuttall 2013). Mining for the heavily toxic metal was banned in 1988 as Denmark moved to its zero-tolerance policy, but in 2013 it was repealed in Greenland as interest renewed in the energic and economic promise of its mining following first a 68-million-euro investment by Australian-owned firm, Greenland Minerals and Energy (now Greenland Minerals Ltd.) and more recently a partnership with China's largest rare-earth producer (see Plate 4). The problem from the 1950s onward was that the low concentration of uranium in the Kvanefjeld mountain plateau would require enormous amounts of energy to pressurize the material using wet oxidation on site, separating the uranium from the ore (Jastrup 2008); that and massively divisive sentiments in South Greenland about the environmental and social consequences of mining radioactive materials in the thick of the only agricultural enterprise in the country. Here in the only arable region of the country warm enough to support modest food production, Arctic food sovereignty and the promise of export revenue from rare earth elements collide as melt unleashes current in the resource gaze of late modernity.

The convergence of the coming deluge of meltwater at the southern tip of the Greenland Ice Sheet, the promise of food sovereignty in the nation's one percent of arable land, and the extractive potential of rare earths for twenty-first-century techno-utopianism unfold as possible and knotted worlds here, in this place, where the North Atlantic and Arctic waters interface colonial and oceanic currents. The Kvanefjeld plateau contains the second largest deposit of rare-earth elements on earth, and it is in the moraine of the southern tip of the Greenland Ice Sheet roughly 15 kilometers away. The closest hydroelectric dam in operation (of the island's five) is 70 kilometers away, but it only supplies the southern region with 7.6 MW of electricity. The mine has been assessed as needing nearly sixty. In the most recent plans, a "new 59 MW heavy fuel oil (HFO) combined heat and power plant" is planned beside the site to power the mining and refining processes (Mining Technology n.d.). In the hydrological survey of Greenland beginning this year, three sites with of a potential of 10 MW each have been identified in the triangle around the Kvanefjeld site and the ice sheet that you can see from the site on even the rainiest day.

As the ice sheet pulls back and the melt increases at speeds and volumes unanticipated until only a few years ago, the terminal landscape of southwest Greenland's moraine mixes materially, economically, politically, and culturally *with and as* the new concerns of ice (Williams, Gouremelen, and Nienow 2020, 2). At the crossroads of climate change, postcoloniality, indigenous knowledge, and the energyscape of late modern fossil capital, the turning of water into the new oil unfolds as an infrastructural promise of hydrological transition. At minimum, the structural force of ice at the moraine turns flow and rise into resource. So if water is the new oil, it is because it is, like oil, both energic force and commodity form.

We were thus at once taken aback and completely prepared to find in a draft leaflet lying on a table in the ministry office of Industry and Energy titled "Greenlandic ice cap water: Heading for the world market" that one of the main aims of the hydrological survey was to isolate and test key outlets of the melting ice cap in order to attract investors to export what would promise to be one of the most sought-after, if not troubling, sources of bottled water on the global market. An idiomatic shift from the promise of oil, concerns of climate and prospective mining, to be sure, what nevertheless sustains the various channels into the elemental currents of Greenland today is the unique voice of the salesperson distilling out the complexity of worlds in order to ventriloquize international investors into being. Outward facing, the very posture of the investor-speak turns Greenland inside out, carving the island's indigenous histories and ecological entanglements into an object of cartographic (and fiscal) clarity. The report identifies bottled water as an industry growing over 6 percent a year, with the vast majority of that coming from "Asian buyers," by whom nearly 34 percent of all bottled water is consumed. "If you combine the expectations of increasing demand worldwide for bottled water with Greenland's huge ice and water resources, the very first prerequisite for the future export of ice and water seems to have been achieved" (Naalakkersuisut 2018). And of course as the global mean temperature continues to creep up the thermometer year over year, the world will indeed find itself in search of hydration: two sides of the same dynamic focalized into the planet in and through Greenland's hydrological transition, except locked in a kind of feedback loop—global warming and bottled water—triangulated by the state-mediated politics of resource-driven decolonization. But this resource form of melting ice—bottled water for a thirsty world—is a secondary outcome to what we have noticed is the larger infrastructural promise underwriting successive waves of grid expansion as Greenland begins to tilt away from the poles and instead blur into the center of history. Both climate and capital temper the cartography of near and remote, center and periphery. The moraine is also a mine, and the mine needs a hell of a lot of current. As the imaginary of global climate discourse mourns the coming of water, the current Home Rule government waits for it. At the moraine, the hydrological gathers to a point where the glaciology, geology, and political economy of a warming world become a kind of infrastructure for seeing ice as a standing reserve—a terminal storage technology that yields commodity futures and modal abstractions: a kind of default apparatus for harvesting elemental flux. Increased current off land-terminating margins of southwest Greenland accelerates the prospect for uranium and other rare earth resources, at the same time that it conjures (and subsidizes) the large-scale infrastructures whose capital intensiveness in turn prefigures adjacent, complementary, and bundled industries—what economists call *path dependencies*. For the time being, Greenland's decentralized grid, and the ice sheet's topographical resistance to load sharing across the nation's autonomous hubs, paradoxically acts like a dam holding back the full flood of hydrological transitions. Water and ice remain poised at the moraine of the Holocene, but the ice itself is ever withdrawn in this elemental mapping that we began in 2018: beyond reference in all of the perspectives vying for institutional footing around the government offices in Nuuk. To get a feel for the ice sheet itself, we realized a different set of comparative tools would be needed—an analytic that in the next chapter I term *contrapuntal ice*.

5

Contrapuntal Ice

Sila

In Greenlandic, the word *sila* means the visible world, weather, and all the elements that are present to your vision.[1] By contrast, *silap aappaa* means the unseen or invisible world, which is both underneath but also amidst the expressions of *sila*. There is no word in Greenlandic or Inuktitut for "nature" because its rough equivalent would be a combination of *sila* and *silap aappaa*.[2] Their shared etymological root, however, suggests an interactive dynamic of becoming or unfolding. Greenlandic performance artist Jessie Kleemann calls this "co-creation" between the visible and invisible world; it makes no sense to say that nature is there (a place), or to say that "this is nature" (an object) (Kleemann, personal communication). Such a view would be a categorical mistake, like saying, "I are not am." As Janet Tamalik McGrath explains, *sila* "refers to many interconnected concepts, depending on context: outdoors, globe, Earth, atmosphere, weather, air, sky, intellect, intelligence, spirit, energy, cosmos, space, universe, and even life force" (McGrath 2019, 256). As both a materialist and spiritual concept, *sila* thus also captures the intermixing of forces that make up the feel of a place, and even an epoch. In this way it is conceptually resonant with the earth-bound poetics of Édouard Glissant's "relation," a mode of embodying material forces and flows against the colonial drive to territorialize the bodies and stuff of the world—a resonance that I mean to draw out in the final part of this chapter.

Standing at the extreme edge of the Greenland Ice Sheet's ablation zone, the relational blur between appearance and essence, visible and invisible, the elemental force of ice and the historicity of its animated and agitated state today, and what in Cymene Howe and Dominic Boyer's terms is the stochastic time of glacial response and the rapid rise of CO_2 (2018)—all appear to converge as the ground from which you both find and lose footing. As I will go on to develop in a moment, the ice places those who are drawn to it in contrapuntal relation to the colonial and capitalist duress that is currently tipping earth systems into unknowable and volatile terrain. The ice is *forced* into a reactive state—histories of emissions and conquest that are not just represented in Arctic cryosphere but materialize as a political ecology. To stand in front of the ice is also to stand in the wake of it—before and after become geo- and cryophysically intimate and coterminous. Rethinking category mistakes reproduced by the dominant regimes tasked with representing ice by way of adjustments in and through Greenlandic language, culture, and perspective is precisely the stake of a site-specific workshop entitled "At the Moraine: Envisioning the Concerns of Ice" that took place over a week-long period in Ilulissat, Greenland in June 2019. Me and my co-organizer Amanda Boetzkes, a theorist of art and environmental culture from Toronto, Canada, had the ambition of assembling a group that would, in Bruno Latour's terms, help us untie and retie the "Gordian knot" that binds and separates science and politics as both grapple with the planetary realities of climate change (Latour 1993, 3). We focused our efforts on the gaps and overlaps between glaciology and the politics of resource development in Greenland, and we called on artists to help us with this complex undertaking—a collaborative and open desire to envision glacier melt and a warming world at these interstices.

This chapter introduces our approach to interdisciplinary thinking and aesthetic praxes by way of that workshop. Our starting point was to site the workshop in Ilulissat as a way to define materialist parameters by which to approach climate change. The Ilulissat Icefjord marks the extreme edge of the ablation zone where the Greenland Ice Sheet shrinks and swells seasonally. It was designated a UNESCO World Heritage Site in 2004 because of its exemplary status as one of the fastest-moving ice streams in the world and "an outstanding example of a stage in the Earth's history, the last ice age of the Quaternary Period" (UNESCO World Heritage List n.d.). But it was not enough to simply site our workshop in Ilulissat; we developed a guiding planetary heuristic to govern our knowledge exchange: the moraine. A moraine is an accumulation of geological debris shaped and deposited by glaciers as they recede. To stand in front of the fastest-melting ice sheet on earth is to stand at its moraine. As I will discuss, moraine is both the index of glacier melt that located our inquiry specifically in a time of rapid warming and also a vibrant material that propelled our thoughts toward Greenlandic sovereignty, its presence in a global political ecology, and an aesthetic sensibility informed by the intractability of a people and a place that are co-creating a planetary future in and through climate change. From this heuristic, I here consider how melting ice acts as a "contrapuntal," to use Edward

Said's term. I suggest that glacier melt is an ecosystemic pivot by which to conceptualize the reciprocal geopolitical dynamics between the cryosphere and the hydrosphere. I conclude by offering an interpretive mode of engaging elementally with contrapuntal ice—one able to hold the important difference between melting ice and rising CO_2, as well as the varied ecologies drawn conjointly into the deluge of tipping points promised by anthropogenic climate change. I offer "enjambment" as an analytic response to what Édouard Glissant terms the "*chaos-monde*" (1997 [1990], 139) of dispossessed territory, and I read for the edges across which enjambment works across scales, scenes, and solidarities amidst the genres of representation vying for Greenland's ice.

Mixed signals

The morning never really starts in the Arctic summer because night never really concludes in Ilulissat in the middle of June. But this morning of the summer solstice, June 21, feels exactly like a morning because it is Greenland's National Day. Celebrating Greenland's Home Rule Referendum (1979) and this year the ten-year anniversary of the Self-Government Act (2009), which instantiated Greenland's independence from Danish colonialism, National Day draws out a plethora of political affects, economic challenges and optimism, and ecological concerns related to Greenlandic sovereignty. The old regime has been enveloped into the brave new world. But there is more than one idea about what the newness signals.

Over the past decade, Ilulissat has transformed from a fishing village of under 5,000 inhabitants to the epicenter of Arctic tourism and scientific study of the melting Greenland Ice Sheet. Breakfast at the Hotel Arctic elicits a strange convergence of guests: scientists, scholars, political figures, culture workers, and tourists from Europe, Asia, and North America all linger over coffee in the dining room, marveling at the icebergs that drift along the Ilulissat Icefjord. The dining room is a veritable traffic jam of intentionalities stemming from the diverse channels that have brought everyone here, whether National Geographic's ecotour, resource prospecting and geological surveying, scientific monitoring, fishers and hunters who have come to sell their catch, or our group: a micropolitical ecology seeking to articulate the concerns of ice. The different motivations of the varied groups of visitors to the city create troubling collisions of understanding about what it is we are all looking at and how to interpret what we are seeing.

The mixed signals in the dining room light up a casual conversation over the coffee station near the buffet. We are late for an interview with Mel Chin, a conceptual artist responsible for the film project *The Arctic Is Paris*, begun in 2015. A major component of that work was to bring the subsistence hunter from northwest Greenland, Jens Danielsen, to Paris for COP 21, the UN Climate Change Conference, to deliver a message about the Inuit perspective of global warming. In the film, Jens Danielsen's uncanny appearance in the boulevards of Paris, coupled with his direct address, scatters the hysteria of climate chatter that otherwise animates UN assembly. But before we can talk to Mel about the terms of this project and Jens' message, we need coffee. Amanda, Mel, and I line up at the coffee station with a retired American. "Are you here to save Greenland?" she asks innocently. Her question dispels the train of thought we've already started building in anticipation of the interview. It is shot through with colonial paternalism and we react in concert to ward off this apparent attempt to short-circuit the rigor of our thinking. We answer, in quick sequence: "No," says Amanda, irritated with the presumption. "Greenland doesn't need saving," follows Mel heatedly. "Are you?" I retort.

The workshop aimed to produce a situated perspective of glacier melt, to enrich both scientific and humanities-based knowledge through contact with the place and the people of Ilulissat. But it also needs to thread itself into existing infrastructures of knowledge production supporting scientific and economic attention to ice. These infrastructures are material and discursive—airports, military helicopters, conference rooms, granting bodies—and they are also part of what the workshop is studying. This means thinking intimately about how these infrastructures reproduce certain kinds of knowledge and prevent others from circulating. As might be clear already, the ambit of the workshop was not to "save Greenland" but was instead a procedure of jamming up and altering ("enjambment") the dominant channels of discourse that render Greenland into both a bearer of anthropogenic climate change and a mediated image coordinated between a satellite view, remote sensing instruments, geological surveys, laboratory samples, and the scenes of scientific study.

To jam and reroute the dominant channels of envisioning ice by first learning from and listening to how they work is part of a larger ecological methodology that draws from theories of animate materialities, decolonization, and environmental entanglement. Indigenous concepts and relations with ice in the circumpolar region have long been ignored or delegitimated by the thick ethnographic lens developed over centuries of resource extraction from Western imperial and colonial powers. These histories are fraught politically, ecologically, and epistemologically, but they continue to weigh on the study of ice in Greenland. Sometimes this history makes a seemingly benevolent appearance, as in the conservationist affect of environmental tourism. Other times it strikes malevolently as in the longstanding presence of the US military and the US Geological Survey's investment in sub-ice and deep-sea hydrocarbons exposed by the receding sea ice and ice sheet (see Nuttall 2008).

It is at the cross-section of these infrastructural channels that a contrapuntal frame for thinking with ice becomes both politically and ecologically necessary. The contrapuntal is postcolonial theorist Edward Said's way in *Culture and Imperialism* (1993) of describing the double vision required to see something like wealth extracted from the Caribbean plantation economy textured into (though not explicitly referenced in) a Jane Austen novel. In musical terms, the contrapuntal involves multiple melody lines that, while distinct and at times verging on interference, begin to create a new environment without the absorption of any one voice into the other or that new environment itself. The point is to attune the interpretive apparatus to the entangled voices, histories, forces, and desires that condition an image, scene, or object—a way in other words of being affected by polyphony in the cultural imaginary.

In the case of the Greenland Ice Sheet, the contrapuntal is an enormously complex and distributed object uniquely responsive to the *longue durée* of industrial capitalism. This required thinking across disciplines and histories whose modes of seeing, interpreting, placing, and practicing a relation to ice are varied and variably accorded meaning. Contrapuntal ice is a way of phrasing the simultaneously ecological, political, and historical significance of melting ice in this particular landscape. It is a way to situate myself bio- and geophysically in relation to the elemental materiality of ice itself in order to include the ethology of its dynamics in a larger mapping of how ice is envisioned at the moraine. The ice, in other words, is *included* in the assembly of expressive actors convened at the moraine—a body that responds to its milieu and in turn demands attention, but not in any communicative code or logic to which I am used to attending. I am not used to listening to ice, to being weathered by it, but sensing with many of my colleagues and friends that it is becoming incumbent upon researchers to become subjects of ecology—to listen a little differently. Or, at minimum, it entails a commitment to finding creative, collaborative, and sensitive ways to do this. Contrapuntal ice, then, is both descriptive and analytic. Melting ice brings to a focal point the larger climatic dynamics pulling the planet toward what the Intergovernmental Panel on Climate Change calls tipping points, beyond which any probable anticipation of planetary dynamics will get scrambled.[3]

If you are a meteorologist or glaciologist, the earth is a signaling body of dynamic processes. Your instruments observe and monitor those signals, recording the sensibility of the instruments which in turn are sensing the planet's multiply sensory currents of force and phase changes. The models computed into an image of space and time of a given region "are not real"—this is how Brice Noël, a glaciologist from the University of Utrecht, phrases the situation on the second day of the workshop. Models are "forced" with observation and run through million-dollar supercomputers in Milan and Reading. It takes a month to generate a model forced by forty years of observation, at one axis, and the global model run through computers in Colorado on the other. "The more sophisticated our models become, the more uncertain we are." Planetarity withholds itself from the global model. There is a kind of humility to the epistemic distinction made in the atmospheric sciences between the planet and its computationally rendered image. The global model is self-consciously forced into a virtual terrain that makes no claims on the real because its primary object of study is not a thing in the world but a thing to come: melting ice in the future tense, anticipated from the sedimented layers of the present. Modeling certainly strives toward a kind of verisimilitude, but its mimesis is less oriented toward the materiality of the planet and more toward the futurity of the globe: "It is about bringing *the future* into higher resolution," but the dynamics get more complex as you refine your model in response to more material complexity. Complexity means uncertainty at higher and higher resolution, not opacity at low resolution. Herein lies the demand for a contrapuntal view of ice: the closer you get to its planetarity, the more it recedes from view as such, and the complexity of its entanglements comes forward.

Likewise, reading the cultural imaginary of ice as a colonial archive requires a contrapuntal lens. But how does the weirdness of our historical present rewire the contrapuntal, where deep ecological time and cascading crises from the future sediment into our very mode of looking at the earth through microscopes, satellites, and virtual modeling? Anthropologist Ann Stoler's attention in *Duress* (2016) to the temporality of colonial duress knotted internally to bodies and archives and practices that carry it—a temporality that is not past, present or future, that is not sequential but rather simultaneous—is useful here for ecologizing the contrapuntal in the service of ice, because ice is always thought in a strict temporal logic of melt-to-come, even if what is being looked at is the sediment or residue of a buried and frozen past. Taken as an ecological agent, and not merely a postcolonial frame, the contrapuntal considers how colonial forces are embedded in the cryosphere, in the very layers of ice. To ecologize the contrapuntal is to account for the weird temporality of a tipping point when time speeds up and positive feedback loops accelerate. The dynamics animating the Greenland Ice Sheet are historical, ongoing, and prefigurative of a future rushing into the present, a phase change not just in the textual economy of colonial and capitalist structures but in the creative and critical modes solicited by a warming world.

A National Geographic tourist out to save Greenland is a symptom, cause, and consequence of disparate but interweaving signals that inform and form one another in Ilulissat. UNESCO protects the Icefjord as an object of conservation, as a site of world cultural heritage, and as an aesthetic object of desire for international ecotourism. But the posture of the ecotourist carries an orientation towards "the natural landscape" underwritten by a warming affect always coupled with the cold, colonial gaze that imagines space as empty. The kind of thing that could go either way: a frontier of the human at the so-called ends of the earth, or a territory of investment, like when Trump tweets about his bid to buy Greenland. In this idiom, the ice is an endangered object in need of saving, and Greenland (including whoever might live there) stands to fall without that saving.

The Dead Glacier

Including the helicopter pilots from Air Greenland there are thirteen of us standing about forty kilometers from the town of Ilulissat on the western coast of Greenland. For the most part it is impossible not to be "on the coast" in Greenland because the inland ice sheet covers over 80 percent of the island. But here we are inland, at the face of what is technically, and temptingly, termed a "dead glacier" (see Plate 5). The Dead Glacier was once connected to the famous Sermeq Kujalleq—known as Jakobshavn Glacier in Danish—from which 10 percent of all icebergs from the Greenland Ice Sheet calve and drift down through Baffin Bay towards the east coast of Canada. Sermeq Kujalleq is the glacier most famous for its credited collision with the *Titanic* in 1912. But this particular tentacle of the receding ice, called Sermeq Avannarleq, has been grounded in the bank of the Icefjord and so no longer calves into the sea quite so dramatically as its parent glacier twenty kilometers south. Melting here looks and sounds less like a crash and more like a thin leak. Water trickles in rivulets through the sand underfoot and through crevices that run along the wall face. It sits at the extreme edge of the rapidly thinning and retreating ice sheet, marking an important ecotone between the cryosphere, hydrosphere, and atmosphere—a site where worlds divide and conflict in more ways than one. This site encapsulates and embodies the moraine. Calving glaciers are metonymic stand-ins for the drama and trauma of anthropogenic climate change. The Dead Glacier does not express in this schematic way. Its embankment is a soft substance called glacier rock flour that is produced by the crushing weight of colliding ice against rock. The dramatic clash of geological forces—ice against rock—is imperceptible at this quiet and picturesque place. The moraine is manifest, but planetary activity seems to have receded long into a geological prehistory.

Still, it is difficult not to feel a little conflicted about the weather. For most of us who come from climates far south of the Arctic, it feels like a nice day. It is June 20, 2019, less than a month before wildfires would begin to rip through western Greenland and the largest single day of melt from the ice sheet would be recorded. The glacier is dead only from the perspective of what makes a glacier a glacier. Glaciers calve, and they do so in seasonal rhythms: in the long Arctic winter, they tongue out over moving water whose lapping force brings warmth to the underbelly of ice, which in turn pushes it into recession during summer months, only to have it accumulate and extend back out to sea once again.

This glacier has been grounded back into rock at the terminal point of the ice sheet. This is where moraine accumulates to form a rocky beach that skirts the fjord. It is a dead glacier, but it is still melting, loudly enough that it makes walking within feet of its face feel precarious. Pieces the size of buildings routinely crack and collapse into the deep blue lake that once connected this valley to the Arctic Ocean. But what is unique about this terminus, where we explore the complexity of the moraine, is the particular quality of the sediment dragged out from the bottom of the fjord (see Plate 6). Walking through this ecotone means walking in a fine dust that tastes faintly like chalk, rich in inorganic compounds like magnesium, potassium, and phosphorous. Of the cocktail of minerals sedimented here into dust, phosphorus is today the most noteworthy for its potential value for international agribusiness creeping steadily towards what the Global Phosphorus Research Institute in Sweden calls "peak phosphorus"—a specter that promises something of a global food crisis because, unlike nitrogen, you cannot synthetically produce phosphorus, and without both you cannot make industrial-grade fertilizer for global food production using the Haber–Bosch Process invented in 1909. Minik Rosing, geologist with the National Geological Survey of Denmark and Greenland (GEUS)—who, incidentally, also collaborates with Olafur Eliasson on a number of art projects involving the transport of ecological media from the Arctic into the centers of European culture, which I take up in the next chapter—believes the minerals ground up here will help replenish exhausted soil in South America. The same soils exhausted by the most advanced and hazardous applications of petrochemical fertilizers in the twentieth century (Bennike et al. 2019). The contrapuntal relation between industrial agriculture in one hemisphere and the resource logics soliciting investment and attention in another is dizzying. The dust both expresses and materializes the common ground where wires cross between space and place, capital and climate, globalization and global warming.

Mel Chin walks out on the moraine toward the surface of the Dead Glacier. Hailing from Houston, Texas, he looks as though he is about to get crushed under the weight of an enormous arch whose low-frequency moans signal to our guide that its shape is about to buckle. His assistant takes a picture of him like this, situated precariously against this uncanny backdrop. Mel tells us later that he has been inspired to write a second part to his film *The Arctic Is* (2015). The first part of this project was to bring Jens Danielsen to Paris for the COP 21 meetings in 2015. The second will be to bring the world back to Greenland. Chin spans the contrapuntal distance between Arctic settlements and capitals of globalization, but not just by bringing Jens Danielsen to Paris to be one voice in a chorus of competing voices. There is an uncanny quality to the contrapuntal collapse. The image of Danielsen pulled by a team of poodles through the Luxembourg Gardens (see Plate 7), or standing on the banks of the Seine donning furs and hunting gear in a city that routinely spikes over 40 degrees Celsius in the summer, is positively surreal. Shrinking the space between Paris and northern Greenland happens not through the focal object of ice but rather in producing *a perspective* of ice, an aesthetic form of knowledge made available through equivocations between the Arctic and the city—the Arctic is Paris, Berlin, Beijing, and so on—disorienting though this equivocation may be. Danielsen's voice and bodily presence are intimately bound to the rapid recession of sea ice. The aesthetics of glacier ice are unsettling not only for their scale jumps in time and space, but also because the dynamics animating glacier ice are of a magnitude embedded in the tectonics of planetarity. There is a reason Walter Benjamin calls the cosmic thud of wartime bombing an "immense wooing of the cosmos," because the scale of its "nights of annihilation" (Benjamin 2021) can only be figured as proximate to the theater of planetarity, a rough and provisional allegory pointing more to their difference then their identity.

Most of us standing in front of this Dead Glacier do not live with, on, or in ice in quite the same way as Jens Danielsen, except perhaps Mark Nuttall, an anthropologist who has spent thirty years in northwest Greenland. Nor do we pretend to. But the specificity of glacier ice begins to formulate in new ways here amidst the multiple channels of envisioning that mediate the ice in place. We do not construct it merely as an object, but in and through its flows through the perceiving subjects drawn to it in the first place. We begin to sense the glacier "coiling over" the edge of the ice sheet. This is the way Tim Ingold describes it in *Lines* (2007), borrowing Merleau-Ponty's phenomenology of perception: the ways in which the perceiver is weathered by the perceived, a perceived that is not an inert object but an expressive element of what places you *here* (see Figure 5.1). It has been designated a "dead" glacier, yet we see it as vital, multiply active, and enlivened, even if its glaciological status is morose.

We depart the Dead Glacier in the helicopter and travel 1,000 meters inland. As we approach the outer reaches of inland ice, we see patches of *rotting* ice. From the air, deep shades of pink and red caused by algae blooms pop into focus, which spring up in the million cryoconite holes in the ice sheet. Cryoconite holes are cylindrical spaces caused by concentrations of eolian dust carried from the Asian deserts and the Sahara that collect on the ice, absorb the sun's radiation, and drive through the ice's mass (Nagatsuka et al. 2016). The remaining air pockets create the conditions for algae to bloom on the surface.

The form and palette of the ice both indexes and is materially entangled with planetary flows—not just the flows of greenhouse gases that increase

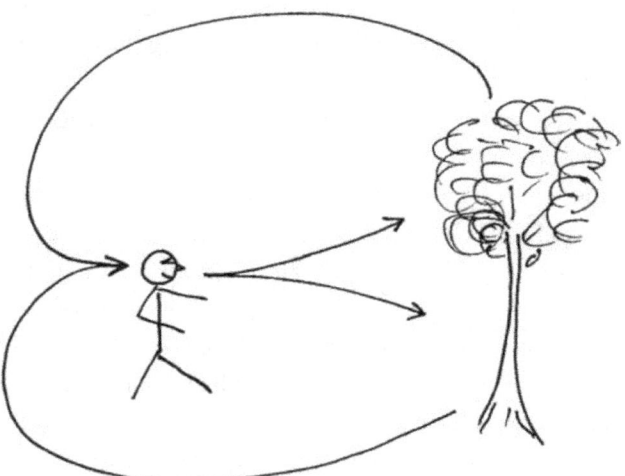

Figure 17.1 My being with the tree and the tree's being with me.
In this sketch, I observe the tree with eyes that have already absorbed its presence into their ways of looking. By way of these eyes of mine, the tree coils over and sees itself.

Figure 5.1 My being with the tree and the tree's being with me. Tim Ingold, *The Life of Lines* (London: Routledge, 2015), 86.

temperatures, but the atmospheric and hydrological dynamics that churn and animate the planet. These planetary flows are not just flows of organic material. Earlier in the week, Brice Noël told us about microplastics found floating down with snow across the ice. The concentration of microplastics *on and in* the Greenland Ice Sheet amplifies the intersections most of us worry about but have a hard time grasping: air masses mix with oceanic flows, which collect carbon and heat, circling back into feedback loop with the nearly three million cubic kilometers of ice melting before all our eyes. The ice is textured not just by the rising temperature but the petrochemical and petrocultural detritus that burgeons out from a fossil-fueled present, carrying from our reflection about the deep geological history of the Dead Glacier into an awareness of an immanent future in which glacier ice is alive, rotten, and shot through with plastic. The reality of microplastics redefines the designation of "remote" typically assigned to Greenland. If we are in a time after ice, it is not because glacier ice has disappeared, but rather because its elemental bond has constitutively transformed.

It is difficult not to read every crevice and circular hole as an allegory for anthropogenic climate change in the way ecocritic Elizabeth DeLoughry does in *Allegories of the Anthropocene* (2019). But that temptation is matched by an incommensurate realization: that the dynamics atop the cryosphere where inland ice meets atmosphere do not accommodate scales familiar to the human. The scales distributed here need mediation, some kind of instrument of measure to clarify the scale at which sensing can begin to translate into a sense of things.

Qivittoq: mediating contrapuntal ecology

In Figure 5.5, Jessie Kleemann, a Greenlandic performance artist from the small town of Upernavik in western Greenland is midway through a performance of what she titles *Arkhticós Doloros*. She performs on top of the ice sheet, in an area known as the Blue Lake. This is why we've flown here. Jessie wants to show us something. Dressed in black, starkly contrasting with the blinding white and blue of the place we've sought out, Jessie transforms silently and pensively into a presence and persona that quiets everything except the torrent of wind sweeping across the surface of the ice and the sounds of waterfalls from surrounding basins. She moves with the wind and then against it, letting the fabric of her dress billow out into a parachute that looks for a moment like it will flutter off and become weather, taking Jessie along with it. She is becoming what in Greenlandic oral tradition is called a *qivittoq*, a stranger whose strangeness is acquired at a distance from their home, wandering in the wilderness either by choice or force—an alienating and alienated persona that bears a relation to home but is not homely (see Plate 9). Janna Flora explains in her ethnography of *qivittoq* that "when the suicide rate in Greenland exploded in the 1970s, Greenlandic poets and writers at the time located suicide within a combined discourse of modernization, colonialism, and Danish political supremacy, on the one hand, and *qivittoq*, on the other" (Flora 2019, 72). This is Jessie's description of the core that links together her performance:

> A *qivittoq* is a person who has left their settlement or village and the community of the family. There are many myths concerning a person's becoming a *qivittoq* when that person has gone away, so far into his natural surroundings that he is regarded as having acquired supernatural strength and powers. In the North Greenland of my childhood the worst thing that could happen to you was to run into a *qivittoq*, be visited by a *qivittoq* or even become one.
>
> Kleemann 2012, 11

The figure she takes on is painful to watch as she bends, her bare feet freezing to ice that is both melting and impossibly cold. Yet she has embodied this figure many times in performances, in Amsterdam, Copenhagen, Nuuk, and now in this space on June 20, 2019 at the vanishing point of global perspectives of ice—a space that feels a little more like a place now, but not like any place (or concept of place) many of us have been invited to before. The place is becoming something else again, an interpreted and felt place with a knotting of conditions that animate the cultural meaning of ice in Greenland, from postcolonial memory, gender violence, and indigenous cosmology. Later, we learn from Jessie that there is a tension between those who live so-called "traditional" forms of life on remote settlements across Greenland and "new Greenlanders," who have an urbanized lifestyle in Nuuk, the capital.

Jessie is being photographed here by Chelsea Reid, an Ojibwe documentarian and scholar from Northern Ontario in Canada. The camera both records the performance and draws our engagement further into it, affecting its mood and our focus. Chelsea mediates between the place and the performance with an intimacy that is both site-specific and also technologically and medium-specific. I can't take my eyes off her camera, and I compare it critically to the litany of instruments that measure and monitor Greenland from both above and below. Is this performance, and this camera's measure of the performance, acting as a kind of instrument, by which we can begin to sense a fundamentally different order of things?

We have to take off soon, returning to the regional airport, to the conference room to gather ideas about what we have just seen and done, to compare notes from the different disciplinary perspectives drawn to the ice sheet—anthropology, glaciology, art history, cultural analysis, comparative literature, performance art, and conceptual art. But before we leave, we take some final moments to drink this site in one last time, quite literally. Some of us sip from the blue lake or from the cryoconite holes. Some of us press our hands into the surface of the ice to take in the exquisite cold. This surface is the interface between the hydrosphere, atmosphere, and cryosphere. We walk gently, trying to find a focal point at which to see the landscape in a familiar frame. It isn't possible. We take a lot of pictures. In about an hour, Jessie will tell us about *sila* and *silap aappaa*. But she has already given us a sense of their meaning.

The ends of the terminal: enjambment as reciprocity

The two most influential accounts to traverse the fields of study in the humanities most concerned with letting climate change our conceptual constellation have been Dipesh Chakrabarty's historicist distinction between climate and capital (and with that distinction the scaled-up correlates of globe and planet, which co-create worlds without ever becoming isomorphic) and Gayatri Spivak's great untranslatable: planetarity. Chakrabarty's is perhaps more straightforward, though no less critical to linger with: it would make no sense to return to the older Viconian or Stalinist distinction between human and natural history because we are now in the thick of cascading tipping points that remember industrial civilization in the idiom of a volatile climate (Chakrabarty 2009). The background to human history has now become foreground. Yet, the recognition of that entanglement of capitalism's energic output of carbon dioxide with a climate that is both animated by that output and outside the reach of capital's calculus does not mean that they have become isomorphic categories of cause and effect. That is Chakrabarty's point: they remain other to one another, though in an asymmetrical relation of reciprocity (unfolding conjointly, but at different scales and genres of historicity, and in accord with radically different forms of agency). When Spivak says that "the globe is on our computers. Nobody lives there" (2004, 291), she is making an important distinction between how the representational apparatus of climate figures a planet that is otherwise in what she calls "a species of alterity"—an Other to the categories of knowledge as they are logically treated in a Kantian epistemology.

This is how the Martiniquan poet and critical theorist Édouard Glissant counters colonialist and capitalist systems of cultural and ecological domination: not just an upgrading or weaponization of "the thought of the Other" as might be true of Edward Said's postcolonial critique—a retention of cultural difference against Occidental universals but more difficult still—"the other of Thought" (Glissant 1997 [1990], 154). The other of Thought is in Glissant's poetics internal to lives lived on land, to an "aesthetics of the earth" too dynamic for containment in sustainability or conservationist discourse because it is "an aesthetics of variable continuum, of an invariant discontinuum," of "rupture and connection" logically and materially hostile to the aesthetics of territory. The terms are deliberately tense and dialectical because he is not making a case for fixed essence somehow misrecognized by a Eurocentric colonial frame. Territory and bucolic love for landscape work in the mode of aesthetic reduction into a monolithic plane, so to pose them as counter to colonial domination would be to extend their poetics of identity (instead of relation). So, what Glissant has in mind is certainly not a return to a peasant practice of subsistence farming against global agribusiness in the Antilles. For Glissant, this other of Thought consists of a poetic relation or rendition of "*chaos-monde*" (139), not to pause or fix it, much less understand it in the realm of knowledge, but to fold into its vibration as a practice of writing and living relationality without symmetry or normative reciprocity (mutual benefit between two parties termed in the same sovereign idiom of Enlightenment subjectivity). Animate materiality is not a sovereign subject. Nor, if we take Chakrabarty, Spivak, and Glissant seriously, is a sovereign subject a sovereign subject. It is porous to its environment, at the same time that it is embedded actively in that environment. In short, the subject is variably ecological, whether it wants to be or not, and at scales that are both ready to hand and extended out through infrastructures, regimes, logics, and counter-logics.

A poetics of relation is necessary for Glissant to explain the actuality of historical division and domination in the postcolonial Caribbean with the planetary whole that is both internal to that division and domination, but also never reducible to it. A whole that is not a singular and static object of knowledge, like the globe, but a multitude of disjunctive scales, forces, and flows. While my focus in this chapter has been on the planetary dynamics of ice focalized through the moraine of the Greenland Ice Sheet, Glissant's uniquely planetary poetics of relation helps jam up the colonial channels dragging Greenland and its polities into ready-to-hand genres of representation and concern. Greenland is only in need of "saving" if we understand melt as a trauma or a loss of what it is that brings the ecotourist and its concept of ice to Greenland in the first place. The notion that Greenland and its ice is endangered by climate change is resolutely false: the planetary expression of animate materiality I have been tracking with my friends at the moraine means something altogether unintelligible from within the non-indigenous interpretive and affective frames attracted to the ice sheet. I myself am barely able to measure the difference between perspectives, but thinking with Jessie and the expressivity of the ice itself has made a difference. In part because it has helped me better grasp the stakes of what in Glissant's postcolonial context I was laboring to draw up from the earth in the language of poetry. Greenland and the Caribbean are connected intimately through the Atlantic Meridional Overturning Circulation (AMOC), which swirls warm waters from the Gulf up the eastern coast of the US and eventually east across the Arctic and Baltic seas, concluding its voyage in the relatively temperate (and moist) atmosphere of western Europe. This vast circulatory system is interactive and historical and is also rapidly slowing due to the changing chemistry of the Arctic. European colonization of North America and the slave trade, after all, were both entirely dependent on the seasonality and tempo of these trade winds. On this side of modernity, at the so-called ends of the world, the poetics of postcolonial planetarity demands a contrapuntal posture that Glissant's thinking helps bring into relief.

And as Arctic waters attenuate thermal relations between places far off, such as the Caribbean, a material sense of planetarity is also cascading into colonial geographies with heterogenous cultural histories. Relation, put differently, is changing as rapidly as the climate. It matters that Glissant's poetics are a major source of materialist critique for a wide range of thinkers researching the knotted history of colonialism, capitalism, and climate, including Achille Mbembe in postcolonial studies, Kathryn Yusoff in human geography, and Sylvia Wynter in Caribbean and Black Studies. If the poetics of relation carries the violence and terror of history without collapsing into despair, without becoming identical to that violence and terror, it does so by shifting punctuation around at the threshold of subject and object, like in a prose poem carried by enjambment—carried by the piling on of clauses and qualifiers and disjunctive jumps from place and pronoun while at the same time generating modes of being in place that are intimate to that place.

Much work in the environmental humanities inflected by feminist and indigenous epistemologies takes the poetics of relation seriously as a description of how bodies are situated at concentric spheres of historical and material channels and flows. The cultural theorist Stacy Alaimo terms this relationality an ongoing process of "transcorporeality" signaling the porosity of bodies that are immersed in ecological and historical milieus—the environs that are both the medium in which the body exchanges nutrients, energy, and toxins—and in symbiotic community of ecological relations with other kinds of bodies (Alaimo 2010).

To put my position in more methodological terms, I am arguing that enjambment is an answer to the question about how to practice a form of ecological thought without fixing either the object or subject of inquiry. I am mobilizing a descriptive technique adequate to the ways in which things relate materially in concrete environs. It certainly does not entail fetishizing the organic or the material over and above the synthetic or abstract forms of domination that capital curates for its ongoing reproducibility. Critically, enjambment is an interpretive approach to carrying thought and experience through the scales that channel through a planetary entity like the Greenland Ice Sheet, somewhere between the concerns of climate and the colonial gaze of capital. The prospector brings an aesthetic, a way of seeing ice, and that way of seeing is a channel that runs through the futurity that melting ice exposes. And so does National Geographic, UNESCO, the Greenlandic nation-state, Jessie Kleemann's forwarding of a conflicted cultural memory, the polar bear that wanders 1,000 kilometers across inland ice, an anthropologist drawing out the cultural meaning and function of ice, and the fishers and hunters that live with and on ice as the grounds of *sila*.

As the era of melting ice and rising seas turns the Greenland Ice Sheet into the vanishing point of a global visual culture eager to measure the causes and effects of climate change, the aesthetics of ice become both the subject and object of ecological reciprocity. An ethology of the Greenland Ice Sheet entails a contrapuntal enframing of multiple channels and grammatical tenses, but writing its entanglement with climate and capital involves a poetics of enjambment that I have been exercising in this chapter. The ice sheet is an animate concentration of forces, but also a convergence of scales and viewpoints, from deep geological time to the fast fumes of postindustrial energy cultures. Questions of social and ecological justice jam up the channels that draw the scramble for resources and territory toward the terminal moraine of the ice sheet, as I detailed in the previous chapter. This jamming up is part of the analytic and critical import of enjambment; it is a formal category. It simply names the carrying of a clause or concept or image across line breaks in verse or prose poetry, where the break both matters to the clause or concept but also does not define it. But it stretches out the carrying capacity of a concept because it frees the contents of a clause to drift around new scenes and moments of those scenes, as in Robert Frost's "Fire and Ice," whose terminal speculation—a world ended in fire and a world ended in ice—ends on three lines of enjambment, carrying the conditional tense of the world dying twice through the reciprocity of an icy destruction to the emotive intensity of hate.

> Some say the world will end in fire,
> Some say in ice.
> From what I've tasted of desire
> I hold with those who favor fire.
> But if it had to perish twice,
> I think I know enough of hate
> To say that for destruction ice
> Is also great
> And would suffice.
>
> Frost [1920] 1923

Enjambment has long been important for how literary critics have identified what is specific to ecopoetics. In their recent book *Ecopoetics*, Angela Hume and Gillian Osborne describe it as the "unceasing, deliberate movement" of different bodies through lively environments (Hume and Osborne 2018, 114). The distinction between the serene republic of nature poetry calmed into repose and an ecopoetics that jams up the timbre of oil prices, a general strike, air molecules, and dust fallout from 9/11 is crucial to understanding how aesthetic mediation brings the world into an encounter that differs from the modes of measure deployed by the scientific apparatus.[4]

Glissant's aesthetics of earth shifts the operations of enjambment in order to hold the multiple channels of memory and determination that give presence to place in time without resolving into a foundationalism. The aesthetics of earth also provide a bridging between the terminal concept and an emergent concept of ecological reciprocity not defined by mutual benefit but instead by entanglements that cross scales, and hence also the frames of measure available to the laboratory. If the terminal marks the multiple ends that converge discursively and materially in climate change, from tipping points across the earth system to what world-systems theorists and political economists called the terminal crisis of capitalism, then ecological reciprocity expresses the continuation of a world in the wake of so many ends. National Geographic tourists are out to save Greenland. Trump wants to buy it. This study of ice situates it at an angle from the frames of knowledge drawn to it in the first place. I picture this thinking as a measure of that oblique angle—the angle that converges multiple channels of concern and calculation—not because it pauses their positions for study, but because the ice acts as a kind of reverse exposure, blurring out the hardened lines of photographic form, epistemological confidence, and economic opportunity. It isn't that we bring a poetics of relation to the ice. The point is that a planetary vision of ice flees out of focus in the manner of an enjambment and asks for a different, and perhaps impossibly strange, kind of reciprocity from a world that is just beginning to tilt into focus.

6

Heliotropism at the Terminal Beach of Critique

The heliotropism of sunflowers should make psychologists see what Wolfgang Köhler meant when he refused to let behavior be parceled out between inherited and acquired components. No inherited mechanism, transmitted by the genes, makes the flower turn to the sun, nor has anybody taught it to do so. Rather, an inherent tendency toward a balanced distribution of energy moves the flower's head into the one position that guarantees the symmetry of solar justice to all its parts.

Rudolf Arnheim, *Parables of Sun Light*

So far, *Climate and Capital* has been tracking the recursive ecology of social, physical, and economic environments drawn into the worlding of postindustrial capital. I call these zones of convergence "terminal landscapes" in order to capture the ways in which energy terminals (physical infrastructure spaces that gather fossil fuels in place, like in ports and storage facilities) are now materially and logically related to the physical landscapes forced into irreversible transformation from climate change, such as the Greenland Ice Sheet, and are related by way of the economic environment through which energy gets distributed into the world both as commodities and as physical substance. By shifting over the past two chapters to an elemental analytic, I have been emphasizing the challenge and promise of thinking with the animate materiality and autochthonous forms of relation co-expressing terminalia otherwise to the settler-colonial forms of hydrocarbon modernity. But here I want to circle back to the beginning of *Climate and Capital* and consider how the elemental force of these embedded terminals—both the logistical and geophysical—press on some of the core concepts and ambitions of critical theory in the Western tradition I relied upon in Part 1 of this book. I'm after both a bridge and a breach between the historical and new materialist frames I have brought to the elements interacting between the terminals (oil, water, and ice), by which I mean a kind of boundary zone where planetary forces unnerve the stable ground from which either a historical or new materialist approach could be simply chosen as appropriate or adequate ways to make sense. The boundary zone in question, I argue, is the beach, and it is a boundary because it is both an ecotone—a meeting place where two ecosystems touch and blur, tides ever taking and silting back—and because it is the genre of place all over the planet where rising seas will erode the stable ground from which those subjected to global warming feel that subjection at its most visceral. But the energetic and rhythmic coordination of this meeting point between aquatic and terrestrial environments comes from the rotational and interactive force of solar and lunar pull. An interaction that is as much thermal as it is gravitational.

Hence, my interest in this chapter is in returning to a primary figure of climate discourse which, while primary, has been under-regarded as a source of critical and creative thinking about climate: the sun, or rather modes of relating to the physical and conceptual force of the sun by way of what, building on Rudolf Arnheim and Elizabeth DeLoughrey, I term "heliotropism." It's not that the sun—or solar power—has not figured at all in climate discourse. That is what I mean by a *primary* figure: photovoltaic power generation is, next to wind energy, the most immediate technology that comes to mind when you think of sustainable energy transition. So, technologically, the sun figures as a kind of key to something like an environmentally conscious capitalism, a sustainable techno-fix to a world broken by fossil fuels. What I am interested in is not necessarily the political economy of solar power, but the ways in which the sun figures itself into cultural forms of imagining a different relation we might have to the world, to other people, but also to nonhuman animals and to objects, and more critically, how such gestures of necessity (as I'll argue) brush us up awfully close to the threshold of critique as such. It is for this reason that I claim heliotropism is an under-regarded source of creative and critical thinking about climate: because while solar power has become a kind of *dispositif* of the discourse of climate, Foucault in his reading of the "solar hollow" (a term scaffolding his extended reading of the early-twentieth-century novels of Raymond Roussel) names a relation to the sun that is both material and symbolic, but with an asymmetry that cannot be captured or stalled. The hollow in his concept refers to the blinding core of the sun's illuminating force over both the planet and our mythologies, an emptiness that Derrida too notes in his extended deconstruction of logocentrism in Western philosophy (1967). Foucault stumbles upon the term after leaving a thought unfinished, about whether "there is not, solidly buried, an experience where sun and language..." (1986, 161, ellipses in original). The experience he is after is one of this symbolic and material origin, since the "visible and the invisible are of the same material and of the same indivisible substance. Light and shadow are from the same sun" (104–105). He grasps at a formulation, putting it this way and that, always using though the language of light and shadow, opening and closing, life and death, so that the solar hollow becomes a compendium of heliotropisms that draw us back to a persistent though uneven relation between materiality and the symbolic, or what he'll eventually term the "insolvency of words" (167). These heliotropisms ask us to consider gestures toward the sun in the abridged archive I offer here in the terms of an impossible promise of reciprocity that is both symbolic and material. At stake is whether an impossible promise is the same as a broken promise. I'll argue no.

That words are insolvent is Foucault's way of making good on the claim of *The Order of Things* about the recursive logic between objects of knowledge and discourses that generate them, but it is also, I think, an early gesture towards what Rosi Braidotti has noticed in her reading of that same book as a latent posthumanism in Foucault's cryptic gestures toward the ends of man, figured as a face washed over by the sea (Braidotti 2017). The so-called ends of man, for both Foucault and Braidotti, are situated on the beach. Hence what draws me to these gestures and the aesthetic economy of various genres of heliotropism are the means with which they give form to the problem of turning the body into an environmental concept before and after it is a liberal concept. It would seem that more than renewable energy is at stake in our increasing sensitivity to solarity.

It is for this reason that I claim heliotropism is an under-regarded source of creative and critical thinking about climate: because while solar power has become what Foucault would call a *dispositif* of the discourse of climate, gestures toward the sun (a relation to solarity, as authors of a recent journal collection term it) points to a radically different structure of feeling and relation to environment (Barney, Szeman, and Simpson 2021). In order to draw out the critical import of heliotropism, I think with three cultural interventions that turn coastal beaches into a terminal landscape upon which multiple futures—carbon, aquatic, and psychosocial—wash up against the habits of critical thinking today, and the sun as the elemental force upending the self-certain entrapment of late-liberal subjectivity.

Leviathan's mood

Ben, the male subject who speaks throughout the opening episode of Shezad Dawood's ten-part video cycle *Leviathan* (2017), does not fare so well. He meets

Yasmine, it's true, promising some semblance of heteronormative continuation past the point of what the film suggests is a kind of civilizational meltdown, but her attachment to him seems at most an extension of "really need[ing] to fuck" as opposed to some romantic attachment, and while he seems to have a pretty good time in the Venetian orgy in episode three, he is beaten up on a beach in Morocco in episode four, and finally raped repeatedly by the captain of a cargo ship in episode five. But one of the peculiar features of Dawood's *Leviathan* cycle is that the question of how Ben fares turns out not to be much of a question, which is to say a concern, at all. He figures in a plot, but what I will argue here is that *Leviathan* turns plot into a kind of scene, and that the mood of its multiple scenes (or landscapes) is what is at stake in its bifocal commitment to figures of the nonhuman alongside human discourse. Ben not faring well is, if I can put it this way, beside the point.

This bifocal commitment is established in the opening sequence of *Leviathan*, as the camera is drawn closer and closer to the sun. Ben is talking, and he is here half blaming the sun for the social crisis that precedes his present; but, in half blaming the sun (see Plate 10), he also half points to an incongruous relationship between the human, climate, and solarity, by which I mean he also appears to rationalize the apocalypse that the film takes as its starting point by emphasizing the insignificance of the human in relation to earth systems that dwarf the centrality of human affairs. In setting up the whole cycle through the figure of a sun that is both hostile and indifferent to the human subject, *Leviathan* turns the very paradox of dominant discourses on climate change into a narrative contradiction: the human is the agent of climate change, at the same moment that the very distinction between nature and human history folds in on itself, and with it the edifice of Liberal Reason responsible for our concept of the human to begin with. To be clear, this is a foundational problem for all manner of post-anthropocentric social and environmental theory in the humanities and social sciences over the past two decades: the double bind that comes with our collective coming to consciousness of our own agency *as a planetary force* named by climate change, at the same time that the multiplicity of agents distributed across the nonhuman world appear as the solution (either ethically, conceptually, or politically) to the problem of climate change. And, importantly, in the post-anthropocentric move that seeks to relegate the human to its biophysical place in the world, there typically comes a certain resistance to narrative, since narrative brings with it a set of genealogies and drives that are (usually) resolutely human. This double bind goes by many names, including the Anthropocene, the becoming geological of the human, the geontological turn, and, more broadly, the posthuman. So how does such a contradiction possibly get stretched out into a narrative like

Leviathan's, when narrative seems always and everywhere to demand a human set of drives, if not a human center, to begin with?

Each episode of *Leviathan* in turn is focalized through a new character, though the means of that focalization varies along at least two axes that will come to matter, in my account, for the dethroning of the subject that the climate of *Leviathan* helps figure. Ben, Yasmine, Arturo, Jamila, and Ismael take up the narrative discourse of each episode—they speak in different languages, and with different proximities to what it is we see in these films—but they are not responsible, strictly speaking, for the mood of each episode. Mood and voice in narratology are distinct categories because, in Mieke Bal's classic account (1985), a story can be narrated from one or many perspectives, while the focal point of that narrative can be a person or thing that never speaks (the golden bowl in Henry James' novel of that name, or Heathcliff in *Wuthering Heights*, who speaks but doesn't narrate, and whose character is predominantly responsible for the mood or affective atmosphere of the book). The distinction between mood and voice is important in the study of narrative because it helps name the distance between discourse, or what is said, and what is felt—those shifting centers of gravity that concern the cultural object as a whole, or what make a cultural object irreducible to characters or narrators who speak. Mood, in other words, need not (indeed, often is not) an effect of voice. More typically, and indeed more strangely, mood is just as much a quality of objects as it is of subjects.

What I want to do in this chapter is offer a reading of three recent cultural objects that help figure a new way of thinking about how climate changes theory, which is to say how critical theory has imagined, and might yet imagine, the relationship between the physical environment and the unfolding relationship between first nature and second nature in a context of planetary global warming—a context, in other words, in which what had been previously figured as the background to human history (the environment) suddenly turns (in Bruno Latour's phrasing) into the foreground of global affairs (Latour 2014, 13). Multiple concepts of the nature of the subject and the vitality of the material world have already made inroads into upending what looked like hardened and fixed categories of theory, namely the subjects and objects of history, but what I want to do here is draw out some of the concepts and aesthetic modes of perception made available by a set of cultural objects that in some ways already prefigure a new climate of critique in their very structure: *Leviathan*, which makes plot horizontal with landscape; a recent photography project that lets the sun burn holes through the negative; and a canonical installation at the Tate Modern in London that recreates the scene of a sunny day in order to make an experience of collective pleasure available to a viewership increasingly nervous about a warming world.

We are ten minutes into Ben's narration of *Leviathan*'s present—our foreshortened future—when he tells us in the past tense of the planetary attunement that marked the collapse of civilization. As the sun begins to "squeeze" and "amplify pressure," triggering a speculative terminus to earth's human subjects, and as the fires roar, the floods rush in, and that most Shakespearian melodrama of all, *The Tempest*, turns the environment strange, Ben notes, at precisely the moment that we finally have Ben the character before us in the frame, that "The weather seemed to parallel the mood of earth's remaining inhabitants. Sorry, monkeys!" At this, we return from Ben's past tense analepsis—a past tense that is our present today—and take up *Leviathan*'s own present tense, but with a new relationship in narrative voice and character. Ben, the character in the frame, spills something on his pants while the narrator refers to the spill in the present tense (see Plate 11). For the rest of the episode, the narrative voice will speak in the present tense of the frame, speaking from the viewpoint of Ben. But rather than tie narrative voice to mood, as is more typical of this diegetic attunement (where a character is also a narrator, though speaking from outside the frame of the camera), we get the opposite. The effect here is paradoxical: precisely because Ben's narrative voice is *not* the voice of Ben the character, since Ben the character doesn't speak to the camera as we follow him through an abandoned house, the distinction between mood and voice has now been exposed precisely as *distinguishable* at the moment that it looks as though they've become synchronized. For the minute or so that they share space, Ben and Ben's voice are only tenuously shared, and we know it is tenuous because when they break apart once again in what will be the final scene of episode one, we land on the terminal beach, anchored now to the mood of a whale's corpse—a whale that doesn't speak but doesn't need to (see Plate 12). This will matter for the conclusion of my argument in this chapter, where I suggest that the mode of perception that *Leviathan* makes available is one that is distributed between landscapes, characters and matter.

By episode four we return once again to the beach, except this time it is a Moroccan beach. Life under water and life above water are in this landscape at their most proximate so far in *Leviathan*, sharing both the frame (featuring constant jump cuts from underwater to the beach) and what Jamila calls "old shit, new shit, brown shit, dead shit" or, put differently, the shared relation to, and as, detritus. We see shit on the beach, are told that these nomads built homes out of the shit of the past, and watch living bodies turn back to decaying matter as Ben and Yasmine are saved in turn on the beach. But if our shared materiality is a temporal one (we came from and will return to raw materiality over time) then it is the concluding split between what Jamila says and what Jamila sees that signals *Leviathan*'s commitment to something like bifocalization, able to distribute mood across landscape, character and matter. "How am I recalling this?" Jamila asks, self-reflexively, "for on the beach I can see myself running, my heart pounding out of rhythm with this new imported beat, running for self-preservation." Jamila sees herself running and is more than a little troubled by this split in voice and body. Narrative discourse has once again been made *distinguishable* from the body to whom it is assigned, at precisely the moment that the body to whom it is assigned is running for self-preservation—which is to say, running for her life. It will turn out that the camera has not been scanning the landscape to set the scene, so to speak, but that the scene of each landscape is already a way of seeing. The film's visuality is distributed, never fully reducible to the attempts by any of its narrators to monopolize its point of view (see Plate 13). The terminal beach, I have been arguing so far, is the scene for what *Leviathan* prefigures as an aesthetic of perception able to dethrone the subject of late liberalism.

But what I want to say next is that this dethroned subject of late liberalism is *not* the same subject that—as we'll see in a moment—helped harden the core concepts of critical theory in the postwar era, around which so many critiques of culture, of capital, of ideology, of sex, and indeed of climate have since flowed. In short, the genealogy of critical theory carries forward in its core concepts a way of conceiving social emancipation not yet alert to the theoretical pressures that come with global warming. What *Leviathan* is imagining for us is the erasure of that originary subject of capital and critical theory alike. For this subject, on this beach, has already been unplugged in *Leviathan* from what we'll see was in the 1960s an ideological and embodied relation to environment coded by capital. But in returning to canonical positions to twentieth-century critical theory, we can also begin to tease out the *social* environment through which fossil-fueled modernity implied a kind of tragic dissociation of the subject from an experience of physical environment.

Adorno's tan lines and the scene of modern boredom

Recall that for Adorno, the scene of modern boredom is a sunny day, and its landscape is a beach. We do not need to imagine the scene, because it is imagined for us. For him, sunbathing is not just "physically unpleasant" but, more profoundly, "illustrates how free time has become a matter of boredom" (Adorno 1991, 191). By 1969, when the essay is first written, boring weather for Adorno is boring because its leisurely draw is no longer heliotropic, as we might say of the flowers that dramatize Monet's fair weather or Arnheim's sunflowers, but pathological. These bodies turned toward the sun do not occur to the critical theorist as a floral metaphor, much less a kind of aesthetic mimesis wherein the worker desires not just to behold the picturesque but *to be* picturesque. In order to read it this way we would have to imagine a different kind of aesthetic analysis on Adorno's part, much closer, that is, to Lukács' much earlier distinction between "first" and "second nature"—a distinction that proves not to be a difference but a process whereby an idea of first nature (unmediated, or immediate nature) reappears on the other side of second nature as its constitution (where desiring a direct experience of nature comes to verify one's own distance from the natural—a symptom, in other words, of one's socialization into second nature). Here, the mediations of the picturesque (or in our example, the desire for an experience outside of history, the terminal beach) appear from within the historicity of second nature (an aesthetic sensibility on the one hand, and a subjective drive to escape the domination of second nature over all experience on the other). But that is not what Adorno is after here: these people, he insists, are not after the appearance of first nature at all.

Adorno has something else in mind. The scene sits at the heart of the penultimate chapter of *The Culture Industry* entitled "Free Time." The purpose of that chapter more generally is to historicize the dialectic of labor productivity in twentieth-century capitalism and the free time it generates outside the work environment. "Free time," Adorno states at the outset, "has already expanded enormously in our day and age. And this expansion should increase still further, due to inventions in the fields of automation and atomic power, which have not yet been anywhere like fully exploited" (Adorno 1991, 188). He is being both descriptive (noticing a postwar upsurge in energic power put to use in the factory) and anticipating the paradox of labor productivity in the postindustrial era we'd call our own today: namely, that the calculus of work begins to structure the subject's creative, personal, and intimate desires so that the time of work will begin to resemble what Jonathan Crary (2014) has called the 24/7 work schedule. Free time becomes a form of unfreedom in Adorno's account, because it turns mimetically towards a productive impulse: whether through self-cultivation on a campsite (he is just as grumpy about camping as he is about sunbathing) or passive rejuvenation before the next day at work in front of the mass cultural object *par excellence*, the television set. It is this unfreedom which Adorno thus encounters on the beach, where the great unfree turn to the sun out of compulsion.

What Adorno's scene of boredom imagines for us is a commodity fetishism that has become fully embodied in the subject of the commodity itself—the body of mass culture, and the mass market, now treated *as a unified body* instead of some conflicted or split subject, the other to capital's domination. Laid out, precisely not like a flower, these bodies "who grill themselves brown in the sun merely for the sake of a sun-tan" express so literally the reach of this pathology: "In the sun-tan, which can be quite fetching, the fetish character of the commodity lays claim to actual people; they themselves become fetishes" (Adorno 1991, 191).

What I want to suggest here is that Adorno's lines about tanning give us a rather remarkable insight into something like an internal limit to mid-century critique. It is a threshold because it is to the frame of the weather on the one hand and the "damaged life" on the other that this scene gets played out at a conceptual register, and not the frame to which I will suggest next has come to unnerve the former: namely, the frame of climate and planetary life so central to recent work responsive to global warming in the humanities, as well as the social and physical sciences. The mass cultural body is heliotropic, to be sure, but solarity is paradoxically incidental to the scene, if by solarity we mean a social relation and rhythm somehow calibrated or attuned to solar energy. We are at the very cusp of a threshold to thought, here, on this beach: a threshold that Adorno, Benjamin, and so many others in the tradition that traces its roots back to Hegel will call, time and time again, the dialectic of nature and history. And it is a threshold for at least two reasons that I want to explore from the vantage of today's still nascent but increasingly historicist experience of what Andrew Ross (1991) calls "strange weather" and Amitav Ghosh (2016) has so provocatively termed "uncanny weather"—adjectives that in both accounts describe first the becoming climate of weather and second the supremely unhomely quality that it wreaks on our shared sense of habitat.

This is another way of asking the question this book has been tracking throughout, regarding how climate changes critical theory: namely, what happens to social theory when climate change bids farewell to boring weather on the side of the object—when the weather turns strange, uncanny? For one, the heliotropic pleasure of a nice day becomes relative to the heatwave, to the violence of late fossil capital, and to the surge in atmospheric volatility, occasioning in turn an ecopoetics of climate, *and an emergent climate of critique.*

Sunburn

In what I think I'd like to call this new heliotropism, the stress is on the climate of critique—tropism as a towardness that exceeds the figurative or allegorical since it is material. In Chris McCaw's recent photography series titled *Sunburn*, for instance, photography's innate tropism to light—a towardness that is part of its very ontology as a medium—is followed through to its terminal limit, where the photons from the sun are allowed to hit the photograph for long enough to burn a hole in the image, mixing any reasonable distinction you might make here between burn and image. The image is a burn, and the burn is an image, but it is an image in excess of its reference point on the film—that is, it is neither a representation nor an enigma on the film—since the duration of what McCaw calls "solarization" in fact saturates the tonality of the photograph as a whole, or, using my terms from earlier, provides the whole image with its mood. If Lucio Fontana's slashes broke through the medium, McCaw's burns here saturate it. Hence you get what looks like an inversion of tonality—a negative of a positive—returned finally to the black and white palette we see in the gallery thanks to the vintage fiber gelatin and black and white paper McCaw used after years of experimenting with different films. Unable to use a negative, McCaw's large-format photographs become unreproducible, in turn redefining *both* the tropism of photography and the ontology of the "punctum"—that element of the photograph that so famously reached out and pricked or bruised Roland Barthes and made it, and the experience of it, unique—since the cut here is literal and aesthetic. The sun doesn't merely figure itself into the image; it saturates the image as such. In McCaw's words, "the sun has become an active participant in part of the printmaking" (McCaw n.d.).

The various cuts made by the sun are indexical, then, of the flipped relationship between the subject and object of photography that takes shape in these enormously long-exposure sequences. In more recent iterations of the series, McCaw leaves the aperture open for nearly twenty-four hours in order to give the sun space and time to work on the paper (see Plate 14). They also become geolocated as a consequence of their horizon lines relative to planetary axis, so that for instance you can read the Arctic out from the sun's formal intervention. Here then is a kind of heliotropic realism, both because the materiality of the sun's radiation breaks through the barrier of representation and begins to reconstitute the medium of photography and because, to capture the relative position of the earth and the sun during a daily rotation, the photo paper must track in real time the horizon lines of the sun's daily arch.

Sunburn in my account so far is interesting less for its investment in climate change as a topic than for its commitment to letting something like planetarity overtake the medium of representation as such. It is precisely not a series of tropes about the subject's relation to the sun, much less a discourse of sustainable solar power driving us through to a kind of eco-capitalism, that is conceptualized in these photos. Instead, I am arguing that *Sunburn* is a turning of the sun into the subject and object of representation. And it is this turn to the materiality of the sun as the primary source of energy for life on earth that seems so crucial to let back into our critical compass of the present, amidst what so many have from different angles called the new conceptual terrain flooding the disciplines in the wake of our shared coming to consciousness of anthropogenic climate change. For Elizabeth Povinelli, this new terrain "put[s us] on the edge" of new genres of "antagonism": namely, "the clash between human beings and nature, between societies and natures, and between entangled species and the geological, ecological, and meteorological systems that support them" (Povinelli 2017, 294). The stakes here of course are multiple and exist at multiple scales of reference (from the animal to the meteorological), but the focal point of this "edge" is the category of the human in what Povinelli calls the "gerontology" of the present, and the late-liberal discourses and figures of reference that seek to inoculate the human against a world that appears to have a mind of its own. "The simplest way of sketching the difference between geontopower and biopower," Povinelli explains, "is that the former does not operate through the governance of life and the tactics of death"— as was true of what Foucault earlier termed the biopolitical— "but is rather a set of discourses, affects, and tactics used in late liberalism to maintain or shape the coming relationship of the distinction between Life and Nonlife" (Povinelli 2016, 4). In this contemporary form of power, "Nonlife" is not a description but an effect of being governed over as non-sovereign stock—from plants and animals to minerals and hydrocarbons. Life (or *bios*) becomes metabolic, reproductive, while Nonlife is merely the biophysical means for life. But geontologies also names an anxiety and a threshold to reason: no longer is the governance of Life and Nonlife merely an originary premise of settler liberalisms but a reaction against its fault lines, its real material limits—the sometimes slow and sometimes rapid erosion of its "backdrop to reason" (Povinelli 2016). So, if I can put this more simply, late liberalism is no longer operative merely along the difference between the Western subject and its Orientalization of the other who can be put to death by the state (the colonial other, the racial other, the gendered other), so not just an "us" and an "other" but now too an *otherwise* beyond even the other, which gets disfigured into Nonlife. Climate change in this way of thinking is the erosion to this backdrop.

What a weird idea, no? That the backdrop to late-liberal reason is an anxiety about the distinction between Life and Nonlife. Perhaps this is why *Leviathan* reduces Ben's plot, and plot more generally, to a feature of the landscape: the landscape, like McCaw's sun, is rushing into the frame.

Povinelli's periodization of late-liberal reason works to update Foucault's genealogy of power for the present, but the expressions of this new threshold to reason are for Amitav Ghosh even more pressing on the limits of cultural form. Ghosh's sustained critique in *The Great Derangement* (2016) is of what he sees as a resistance to climate change in contemporary literary realism. His worry is that contemporary fiction does not have the formal or historical capacity to engage fully with the strangeness of climate change. Strange and sudden weather events fit uneasily within the probabilistic disposition of contemporary realism, Ghosh maintains: it simply refuses to turn to uncanny weather events, for historical reasons pertaining to the institution of literature and the bourgeois sensibility attached in the nineteenth century to different genres of gradualisms, but also for reasons that bring us back to the subject and objects of climate change. Ghosh is looking in cultural form for an anagnorisis of climate change and a peripeteia in keeping with it, referring to the recognition of the true nature of events in Aristotle's *Poetics*, and the panning out of the narrative following that recognition. But here are the stakes of this anxiety: the uncanny is what precedes anagnorisis or recognition of the true nature of things in the classic theory of tragedy—since the uncanny *defamiliarizes* the protagonist's sense of homeliness, a planetary home turned strange. You can see why Ghosh wants to think about climate change in these terms: it is the inexorable rise of the past 200 years of industrial civilization now expressing itself in all manner of natural phenomena that we *understand* as bound together but lack cultural means of *recognition*, of cultural re-attunement. The tragedy of anthropogenic climate change, in this account of contemporary realist literature, is that it cannot yet figure the double bind of uncanny weather: on the one hand the "nonhuman forces and beings" that animate climate change and, on the other, the manner in which "they are the mysterious work of our own hands returning to haunt us in unthinkable shapes and forms" (Ghosh 2016, 32).

Haunted in the uncanny character of strange weather, the human and nonhuman get mutually figured and disfigured, and the "edge" of reason Povinelli claims for the anxiety of late-liberal geontopower returns us to the scene of the sun bearing down on the terminal beach. Except that the beach in this reading has now been doubled, so that there is one produced from within the bored subject of capital, and one that marks the "edge" of late-liberal reason. One feels awfully tempted to call them in turn the beach of first nature and second nature, but is this not already the distinction that is under erasure in the new climate of critique? We are not here after an antihumanism latent in in so many eco-fascisms or fascism as such, around which flows any number of romanticisms of *the natural*. Instead, it is an extended critique of bourgeois humanism in the face of its uncanny reappearance as strange weather that leads us back to the beach, looking for a heliotropism that breaks with the pathology of unfree time.

The weather as social form

In Olafur Eliasson's 2003 *The Weather Project*, this split exists on the same beach, a beach laid out beneath an artificial sun that holds the viewer in its gaze (see Plate 15). Bathing beneath an enormous assemblage of monofrequency lights resembling the sun, in the Turbine Hall of London's Tate Modern, this beach returns the terminal landscape to the institution of art and imagines a version of the heliotropic that is self-consciously infrastructural. Certainly, we are on the brink here of something like the participatory turn in art, if not the full-blown relational aesthetics so troubling to Claire Bishop (2004). But it is the material specificity of the encounter with other bodies here that I want to end on, since it is not for a normative investment in the relational as such (in short, Bishop's beef with the erasure of friction and antagonism in the relational turn) but an experience instead of a being together *in infrastructure* that *The Weather Project* helps make available. But it is a cheeky kind of togetherness whose cheekiness is part of the re-attunement that this heliotropism helps trigger, because the ease, pleasure, and drives that come with an infrastructural modernity that feels *precisely* like second nature is what is here being indexed by the sun. The Turbine Hall figures in *The Weather Project* not behind the backs of the viewer as a backdrop or frame but as the condition of its encounter. It is not for an illusion of modernity's control over the sun, over a solar economy re-harmonized with the meteorological, that the project invites its viewer in for heliotropic pleasure. The "weather" in *The Weather Project* is an expression of an electrified culture that experiences weather as, and as an effect of, the built environment—of a landscape that is coextensive with mood. We are returned to Adorno's tan lines then, the scene of modern boredom: a beach that is not a beach, in front of a sun that serves the subject of capital.

Well, almost—because remember that this was never at stake on Adorno's beach to begin with, and so treating Eliasson's installation as a betrayal or deviation from the experience of first nature would seem to presuppose the capacity (or desire) for such an experience in the first place. For Louise Hornby, Eliasson's installation and his more recent engagement with ice in *Ice Watch* "undermines notions of nativity and the natural environment" by turning the experience of the subject into the focal point of environment, in turn alienating environment from itself (Hornby 2017, 62). For the optics of towing melting ice from Greenland and Iceland to Western Europe, I find Hornby's objection compelling and worth pursuing amidst the larger trend in recent ecological aesthetics to bring climate to the subject, as it were. It matters, though, that viewers in both projects are invited into a collective and focused experience, even though the materialization of melt and the geographies of ecological time in *Ice Watch* work quite differently in *The Weather Project*. So the critique of *The Weather Project* on the shared grounds of *Ice Watch*, namely that they determine the conditions for an experience of weather first by simulating an environment in the mode of a soft militarization of climate, misses what in my reading is the character of *collective* experience that for Hornby does nothing more than "(justify) the human domination of the engineered environment" (64). Climate change is inextricably bound to resource-intensive infrastructures that turn daily life in a place like London into a feeling awfully hard to distinguish from first nature, precisely because infrastructure is the material grounds through which habitus hardens into the given. To my mind, it is the defamiliarization of this infrastructural condition of modern habitus that needs drawing out, rather than an aesthetic project that would naturalize a site-specific fantasy of second nature's supposed other.

Hence, my argument here runs against the grain of the normative discourse of the environmental humanities, which prefers an unmediated or *immediate* relation to the biophysical, since for me (finally) weather in *The Weather Project* gets turned into a source of *social form* that surges through the subject as much as it does London's grid, and by extension the energy apparatus that binds the polis to fossil-fueled planetarity. Another way to put this would be to say that the weather of *The Weather Project* is the opposite of a Romantic concept of nature, since it is here knotted to the built environment. We might term this instead man-made weather, not in order to promote the hubris of a modern discourse that plans to geoengineer its way out of climate change, but instead to underscore the lived experience of attaching oneself to the social, to a provisional collectivity, *amidst* infrastructure. This same code-switch of first and second nature is captured in the cute emblem of a little sun in Eliasson's startup work with the Little Sun Foundation, which distributes solar-powered lamps to villages and communities in Ethiopia who lack gridded infrastructures coordinated by power plants. Obvious critiques aside, the point is that the specifically infrastructural mediations of proprioception captured in the constructed image of the sun asks for a theorization attentive to the infrastructural contingency of a shared aesthesis. In other words, Eliasson's work registers the historicity of climate, more obviously as one approaches its mechanical arrangement up close, where the last thing one sees before entering the interior of the Tate Modern is the work's interface of aesthetic experience and the infrastructure of modernity. Whether or not pleasure turns into pain here, the force of the project's intervention is to refuse any knee-jerk moralization of form and instead expose the necessary relation between social form and the materialities with which it is entangled. The future tense of anthropogenic climate change might not yet depend on a simple opposition between techno-capitalism on the one hand and a kind of technophobia on the other. Modernity might yet resolve into a collective project of social and ecological justice that puts infrastructure to work in the service of a radically unimaginable future. The critique of the weather on the grounds of its (re)production from the assemblage of second nature seems to miss the whole point about both the weather and what its relation to climate unsettles. It unsettles the scene of modern boredom, and asks us to bid farewell to boring weather.

So how, finally, is the sun with which we open into the world of *Leviathan* different from the electric sun of *The Weather Project* or the subject and object of McCaw's *Sunburn* series? In the account I have offered here, heliotropism always draws us back to the terminal landscape of critique, not because it offers a vista onto sublime nature as such (that is, this is a terminal landscape of critique not because it is the *outside* of critique), but because the *historicity* of the gesture is what is made available as an aesthetic experience in each of these works. On Adorno's beach, it is an experience of modern capital in the form of a fully fetishized body. In McCaw and Eliasson, on the other hand, heliotropism is a means towards reconfiguring the medium of experience, via solarization of the photograph on the one hand and the infrastructuralization of pleasure on the other. In *Leviathan*, finally, the conditions have been imagined for us to bifocalize the materialities of landscape and character coequal with plot, but this bifocalization is also coextensive with how Dawood's films figure a historicity that is a future tense of our own today—that is, only because *where we are* in *Leviathan* is in the wake of the nation-state, the global economy, the pathologies of late-liberal reason, and, finally, the originary conditions of boring weather from which critical theory first emerged. But nobody ever said the post-anthropocentric turn would be easy, or that it would of necessity feel very good. And part of my argument has been that it will not feel very good, at least not until some new social form (or perhaps what Kathryn Yusoff has called a geosocial politics) emerges to care for us in the wake of which *Leviathan* re-attunes our aesthetic faculties, which is to say a radical social form capable for the first time in human history of caring for an "us" that is human in voice but not necessarily in mood (Clark and Yusoff 2017). Anything short of that is going to continue to feel really, really bad.

Conclusion: "Hail Horrors"

When I was a first-year student at the University of Toronto in the early 2000s, I remember learning a rumor from the teaching assistant responsible for my section of Major British Writers that the Robarts Library, famously designed to resemble a turkey when seen from a particular angle on Harbord and St. George, was sinking into the soil that held it up. Robarts' hulking hull, made of densely cooked concrete and steel rebar, is a menacing volume of nearly 100,000 m² bloating out into one of the oldest and most revered campuses in the settler-colonial state of Canada. It was sinking, the rumor maintained, because the engineers forgot to include the weight of the books in their rendering of the building's design. At the southeast corner of Robarts' main stacks sits the Thomas Fisher Rare Book Library, a gloriously lit, angular column lined with the largest collection of rare books in Canada (and by some counts, outsized across North America only by Harvard's). As a new student of English literature, I loved the idea of basking in the delicate and quiet aura of the Fisher collection. The space demanded absolute silence and attentiveness to the delicate pulp, leather, and ink. Their provisional form on and as the page, the binding, the book—all required climate-controlled protection from ultraviolet rays, moisture, and excessive handling. The glow and aroma of books penned and printed half a millennium ago proved alluring to any student bent on studying literature for, among other things, the texture (and textuality) of historicity. Here, Bakhtin's conceptualization of time taking on flesh, and space bending to time, plot, and history in *The Dialogic Imagination* made embodied sense. One of my assignments included an extended analysis of Satan in John Milton's *Paradise Lost* and the TA for my seminar encouraged me to visit the rare books collection, since they had one of the oldest surviving copies of Milton's text—a particular copy that circulated throughout England during Milton's last years of life in the 1670s. The prompt asked for a close reading of Satan's famous speech from Book I in which the rendering of Satan's sovereign soil flips the axis of the ascending metaphor and instead turns the bowels of the earth into a kind of heroic heaven for the fallen:

> Farewell happy fields
> Where joy for ever dwells: hail horrors, hail
> Infernal world, and thou profoundest Hell
> Receive thy new possessor: one who brings
> A mind not to be changed by place or time.
> The mind is its own place, and in itself
> Can make a Heav'n of Hell, a Hell of Heav'n.
>
> I. 249–255

Satan's self-certain stance as a bringer of worlds independent of "place or time," and the Red Angels' ambition to newly possess the subterranean caverns and cracks of the earth as modal agents "since he / Who now is sovereign can dispose and bid / What shall be right" (I. 246–248), troubles more than the narrative structure of ascension and salvation so central to the biblical tradition. Here Satan's conviction that "the mind ... Can make a Heav'n of Hell, a Hell of Heav'n" is another way of laying claim to territory as sovereign domain: a carving out and a displacement of any prior claimant to "this the soil, the clime" (I. 242) in order to focalize the earth as a place to "reign" over from below, as it were.

I had not yet read my John Locke and (what I now read as) the metaphysical extension of one's own property into land as the founding figuration for sovereign liberal subjectivity (and territorial command over an expanding colonial map). But I do remember smelling the discolored and fibrous pulp of the second edition in the Fisher during that first fall semester, well below the forty-ninth parallel of Canada where the tree line turns orange, yellow, and red amidst the full shift of seasons. And I remember thinking the question of Satan's heroic function in *Paradise Lost* must have something to do with his ability to turn a bad situation good. To make a heaven out of hell and to lay claim to the locus of character amidst the less-than-ideal conditions of a torrid inferno. "Hail horrors" sounded to me like a premonition of a punk rock attitude. The library sinks down into the dirt, dragged back into a geosphere from which its rebar and blocks first came. I said something about Satan's industrious voice in that first essay I wrote in my undergrad. I think the paper scored me an A, and suddenly I felt like I could make a go of literary and cultural analysis. I can see now, reading Milton's Satan in what is both literally and figuratively the sinking ship of the Western canon—the very archive in which the aura of modernity's prophetic origins remain climate controlled but exposed to the forcing agency of geological time, buckling down into a terrestrial ground that *can neither bear the weight of its archive, nor signal as a load-bearing agent to its authors*—that the heroic bringing of horrors is the call of the sovereign subject of capital, of the settler colonialist, and of the freedom-loving habitus of late-liberal reason. Not the clarion call of the dispossessed. Satan sounds more like the property developer than the destroyer of worlds. "You might see a soggy mangrove forest," I can hear him saying, "but hell is a state of mind, and heaven is a plantation, a five-star hotel, waste turned to wealth!"

That rumor of the sinking library stayed with me long after I left Canada for a teaching and research post in the Netherlands. Most of the buildings that surround my home and the University were built in the same years that Milton penned *Paradise Lost*, and they are sinking into the sodden mud all the time. Not because of a miscalculation on the part of the engineers, nor because they are full of books, but because Amsterdam is built on marshland. In this city, where the first stock exchange opened in 1602 not 500 meters from my office, the early modern enterprise of Satan's possessive sovereignty takes the shape of a colonial emplotment of wealth imbibed into the antinomy of financial abstraction and concrete, sinking capital. The whole city is raised on stilts and the material horrors of slavery, sunk very literally into the fixed capital that UNESCO protects as heritage, as the canal belt, and as cultural memory remembered as secularization and modernization: the origins of our times, as Giovanni Arrighi (1994) would put it. The dramatic hero of capitalism's financial turn is figured here in these streets and in these infrastructures as a refusal to be at the mercy of environmental conditions—to keep the fixed forms of capital afloat with labor extracted from a cacophony of bodies and ecologies spread out across the republic's map of influence. A refusal of the ecological given—to submerge, get mossed over, and loosen back into the force of the elemental—even as that ecology breathes beneath the city, soliciting ever more capital and fortification. Like Robarts, Amsterdam is an archive of the Western canon, and they are both at the mercy of landscape ecologies to which yielding would mean obliteration: a tragic disaggregation of meaning, since without the archive of modernity's call to "hail horrors" there would be mere fragments held together as so much Holocene terminalia.

The terminal is as much a condition of the Greenland Ice Sheet as it is of the Port of Amsterdam, where this book began, and it thrums as much in the ground beneath Robarts as it does in the mud upon which capital's accumulated wealth in Amsterdam floats with rotted beams and buckled bridges. Coming to terms with the conceptual apparatus, material histories, and contorted categories of sovereign and non-sovereign being is what the fossil- and capital-fueled crisis of the present heaves up on critical inquiry today as a necessity. What is profoundly unnerving about critique today is that it can and should begin with the immediate situation of its encounter, because without too much work the whole cascade of horrors hailed by white, liberal forms of self-determination comes crashing into focus. You can do this through the battery in your phone, the energy costs of a Netflix film, the land theft wedged into rare-earth elements catalyzing global transmission of data, or the planation economies literalized in the food you buy at the grocery store or the lumber lining an Ikea cabinet. The Western archive weighing down on the grounds beneath Robarts is mostly a financial misfortune for the board of directors at the University—a bit less dramatic, perhaps, than I am insinuating. But its sinking into the lithosphere also portends the cunning of an ecological outside to the same disposition of the early modern period, negotiated as it was through poetry, political tracts, philosophy, and plantations of the early modern period. The story of learning literature in a sinking library is a story about how the situation of interpretation has always *mattered* but is increasingly *mattering* in strange and troubling ways.

To matter at the end of the Holocene is to carry the noise and texture of a background into the foreground of comprehension, but not as more content for cognition. *Mattering* in the Black and feminist traditions that are today bridging the gap between historical and new materialisms troubles the deracination of both the subject of understanding and the categories and concepts He brings to earthly concerns. This is the opposite of both Satan and Kant's prolegomena for a metaphysics of presence, where the mind makes sense of the stuff of the world—makes a heaven of hell and a hell of heaven—on the condition that the stuff of the world holds still: on the condition that matter not matter. The ground of thought in western metaphysics matters, but only insofar as it provides the materiality for forms. We are learning that there is no stable or neutral ground, not even for the Kantian mind without properties. On this point, Denise Ferreira da Silva argues, "repeating Descartes's assertion that the mind can only know with certainty that which is akin to it—that is, the abstract or the formal—Kant consolidates modern thought when he elevates the formal (as the pure or transcendental) to that moment that is before and beyond what is accessible to the senses" (da Silva 2017, 5). In the Black and feminist materialisms of da Silva, Kathryn Yusoff, Tiffany Lethabo King, Sylvia Wynter, Achille Mbembe, and Édouard Glissant, this hard distinction between matter and form is a distinction from which racialization (and hence the premise of inhuman exploitation) unfolds as a historical marker of difference. A marker that in contemporary modes of extractive value creation persists as a geologic of life and nonlife, or mattering and not mattering. Distinct from the forms of modern cognition, matter marks the untrained thinker as non-modern, and as such gets leveraged in what Elizabeth Povinelli calls the governance of late liberalisms threshold of reason (2016, 168). What prevents this man without properties extending to all *men* is the *matter* it abstracts into formal reason, and with it all the racial and gendered categories that figure as more material, and thus less modern, in the larger project from which capitalism would emerge as an organizing, modal logic of the present.

What I have not being arguing in this book is that the terminal is thus ahistorical—a constant ecological threat posed to the fiction of fixed and ever-accumulating capital. Capital's world-building logic is premised on an abstract excision of value precisely from the bio- and geophysical restraints posed by bodies, brooks, and biotic entanglements. The terminal is not, in my account, the gnostic specter of dark materiality waiting in the wings to drag the modern back into the abyss. Though I am tempted to resolve my argument on the poetics of Bataille's general economy or Glissant's poetics of relation as I explored in Chapter 5, I have been insisting instead that the *interactive* threshold of capital's indifference to the bio- and geophysical on the one hand, and the enormously unpredictable and profound power of elemental forces on the other, is where the historical specificity of the terminal as condition, as process, and as chronic impasse is at its most tangible. Modal abstractions and geophysical forcing converge in and as the terminal. This book has been an extended effort to read and write together with a version of the world that comes into focus at this interface.

Why insist that neither capitalism nor the political ecologies it has unleashed are *ending* in an eschatologically and environmentally meaningful sense, as so many others concerned with climate and capital seem to maintain? My reason is more political than it is theoretical. Insisting that "nature" will ultimately trump capitalism's reproducibility out into the uncharted waters of the post-Holocene earth strikes me as bad politics. On that account, capital will have nevertheless dug its own grave (as it were), so time is on our side, even if we fail as socialists, communists, anarchists, and even certain (though only a handful of) liberals. What nonsense. The archive, assets, and shorelines of capital might be sinking (or submerging) but it is a category error to imagine that the concrete or infrastructural *real* of capital is where its modal logic gets unveiled as a kind of simulation. The abstractions are as real as the pipelines. What if the ongoing extraction of surplus value from laboring bodies situated in concrete (and increasingly toxic) ecologies, compounded as they both are by the fossil-fueled forms of productivity, does not suddenly cease but instead *increases* in intensity over the next century? The argument that capital will run out of energy, resources, or an amenable climate is somewhat comforting, but its logical response begs for a moralism instead of a critical praxis situated immanently to and against capitalism's power and modality.

The moral argument is passivist—either we win or we wait, but good sense will eventually find an alibi in natural systems—and imagines that a better, more sustainable form of capitalism is on the other side of the moral campaign. We would have to fight hard to win hearts and minds, but we would still be up against the terminal, ecological crisis—at least in this way of treating the concept of the maximal edge or ending—because the *natural forms* that inform capitalist commodity production will have finally triumphed over the fictions of unabated growth. This is a critical environmentalism completely emptied of the critique of political economy. Remember that strangely non-materialist axiom in *Capital*, that "not an atom of matter enters into the objectivity of commodities as value" (Marx (1867) 1976, 128)? Marx claims there that the appearance of value in commodities is independent of what he goes on to call their "coarsely sensuous objectivity ... as physical objects" (128). The exchangeability of commodities, as opposed to their usefulness for a potential buyer, portends a *value* relation between other commodities measured in the metric of their value-bearing function. Value, then, is neither hydrocarbons *as such* nor the particular use for which a buyer recognizes a solution: "We may twist and turn a single commodity as we wish; it remains impossible to grasp it as a thing possessing value" (128). Then what is this substance that pertains as a condition of exchangeability but is nowhere to be seen in the thing ready to hand?

In this exposition of the non-materiality of exchange value, we are still very early in the dialectical unfolding of capital's logic. It would take another 800 pages of commentary in the first volume of Capital to track the relation between simple exchangeability and the capitalist system of world building more generally (including the introduction of abstract labor, which comes next), though that narrative would get us usefully back to the persistence of land dispossession and the territorial violence of capital's ground clearances under the heading of "primitive accumulation." What matters here for the difference between a moral argument *for* the terminal, on the one hand, and an ecological materialism invested in *critiquing* and thus strategically situating political ecology *at* the terminal, on the other, is the simultaneous intimacy and antinomy of sensuous objectivity (the physical character of the thing at hand and its use value) and the modal abstractions of value production writ large (the systematization of exchange value). They come coupled, presupposing one another, but they also come from different planets. And in this book I have been insisting that the places where those two worlds come into closest proximity are in the recesses of fossil capital's terminal landscapes. New and historical materialists alike ought to find common cause here at the interface of climate and capital.

That is because the energic affordances that fossil fuels have provided capitalism since the nineteenth century have altered the recursive (though asymmetrical) relation between the *matter* of value production and the social relations animated by hydrocarbon modernity. Postindustrial capital, as I tried to show in Part 1 of this book, precipitates the intensified expressions of anthropogenic climate change as a general, planetary condition, as opposed to a localized effect of terraforming. The postindustrialization of labor, culture, energy production, and philosophy itself, at least as witnessed in the Western centers of capital, *appears* as a drift away from hydrocarbon modernity. But only crudely so. The period of secular stagnation that followed the 1970s oil crises in the West was underwritten by successive waves of both financialization and energy deepening across all sectors of the economy. The offshoring, digitization, and geographic distribution of energy's crude forms expanded the contrapuntal lineaments of capital's energy profile, but it did nothing to unnerve the now centuries-long intimacy of capital and fossil fuels for the productivity of everyday life. Maybe no atom of matter enters into the objectivity of the commodity as value, but a whole lot of energy and accumulated social knowledge does.

So too then must the opposite be true: not a bit of exchange value enters into the animate materiality of a planet teetering out of focus amidst multiply interactive scales of dynamic warming, rising, acidification, and in some cases die-off. No matter how you twist and turn the Greenland Ice Sheet, its viscous manifestation of hydrocarbon modernity cannot be fully figured from within the logic of political economy or even its critique. Sure, new financial instruments are already able to *recognize* and bet on climate change. And geologists are scrambling to territorialize the new ground exposed in the recessive path of the ice sheet. The moraine is a terrain where two poles of the terminal converge once again, and over which multiple claims are contested: by Chinese and Australian mining consultants; geologists on hire for dozens of oil and natural gas companies; wildlife; Western NGOs; National Geographic tourists; Inuit hunters, farmers, and businesspeople; anthropologists and archaeologists; and artists and the like. But that is not the same as saying that planetary dynamics are internally configured by capital.

What do the two poles of the terminal mean for a left politics historically attentive to the violence of capital's world-making facility with real subsumption, and by extension the tyranny of the value form? There will be and could be no real subsumption of ecology under capital. This is a terminal landscape in recursive relation to the ports, plants, and factories of late modernity, but *fundamentally* other to the modal logics that hold the logistical infrastructure of capitalism expanding, deepening, and sinking. That's why Part 2 of this book deliberately shifted focus and idiom in order to sense out and help narrate an elemental ethnography of animate materiality at the so-called ends of the world. Because if the political posture in Part 1 asked for comrades to take more seriously the interventions solicited by the uniquely sensitive function of the energy terminal, the form of socialism I see as a coming into focus at the terminus in Greenland is one where human and nonhuman entanglements are attenuated through a situated and hotly contested commitment to decolonization.

Autochthonous forms of governance and sociality have long been silenced in Greenland due to the centuries-long Danish occupation and extractive regime. Even as the Inuit peoples of Greenland have achieved successive waves of independent governance since the 1970s, the Inuit Circumpolar Council (ICC) has positioned itself agonistically toward the new nation-state and its settler forms of governance. So decolonization is split at least three ways, between the new grid of the state, the transnational governance of the ICC, and the knotting of fiscal progress to the exploitation of mineral reserves as I explored in Chapter 4. Thinking with non-settler forms of ecological and political knowledge involves each of these positions, as well as the planetary forcing at the moraine—at least to the extent that a multi-modal and militantly *eco*-socialism can foster non-settler epistemic cultures. The planetary stakes of recent efforts to resist hydrocarbon and rare-earth extractivism in Greenland are high because reserves in both mining sectors promise to keep global fossil capital expanding well into the next century. This involves a triangulation of decolonization with a politics of decarbonization and decapitalization of the future (Diamanti and Szeman 2020). More than rising sea levels sourced from Greenland's shores, the geological stuff from under its rock will soon circulate through capital's terminals too. The prolepsis of terminal flows intimates more horror, more digging, and more sinking.

Temporality is proprioceptive. In Chapter 5, as well as in recent writing with Amanda Boetzkes (Boetzkes and Diamanti 2020), I narrated how Jessie Kleemann drew out this bounded complexity of prehension in her performance near the blue lake atop the Greenland Ice Sheet. We also learned this from twentieth-century physics. As Mark Rifkin notes, "there is no inherently privileged or mutual 'now' (or sense of time's passage more broadly) shared by disparate frames of reference" (Rifkin 2017, ix). Temporality at the terminal is paradoxical because it situates origins and ends *in medias res*. Just because the terminal situates, and therefore demands a situated attention and analytic, however, does not mean that temporality is personal. It might be that too. But it is also infrastructural, shared, and contested through the socially mediated logics that press in on the body and the body politic. This is Brian Larkin's point about the shared aesthesis indexed to an infrastructural relation (Larkin 2013). The coming of the rail; Pound's faces in a station of the metro; the hydrocarbon mobilities of postwar city building; the fast and deep time of anthropogenic climate change witnessed as a late coming of winter in the Arctic or month-long megafires ripping across New South Wales, California, Siberia, and Western Greenland too: these are moments of witnessing the configuration of terminal time. But if temporality is proprioceptive, and if the terminal crisis of capital is chronic since it knows no internal material limit as such—indeed, if one wants to be a good Marxist about it, it knows no materiality *at all*, and if we want to be thoroughly anti-racist, as da Silva shows us, then the equation of value turns capital's mystery of materiality back always to the category of blackness (da Silva, 2017)—then how might our concept of and politics at the terminal take on the temporalities sensed out by the nonhuman (indeed non-"living") proprioception? What concept of time is made thinkable by the reticulation of the vanishing cryosphere and the expansion of energy terminals in Amsterdam, Fujairah, Tianjin, and everywhere else on earth? When climate and capital beseech the antinomies of the terminal? There are horrors aplenty drenching the present in the sovereign remains of settler capitalism's pride of enterprise. Not least of which is the fantasy that capitalism will *naturally* transition to some better social form, armed with a militia of accountants insisting on the internalization of social goods, natural capital, and just futures (Büscher and Fletcher 2020, 43). That would be neat. But that future asks for more suffering, violence, exploitation, and domination than any good socialist, anti-racist, or environmentalist ought to stomach. Fossil-fueled capitalism got us into this catastrophe. My argument in this book has been that the reproduction of that catastrophe out into the future is contingent on what happens at the terminal. And that we might therefore situate the struggle there.

Notes

Introduction: To the Terminal!

1. Geologist Minik Rosing has been exploring the nutritional capacity of rock flour for agricultural purposes with the Natural History Museum of Denmark, the Department of Plant and Environmental Sciences at the University of Copenhagen, The University of Greenland, The National Geological Survey of Denmark and Greenland, and the logistics company Usisaat in Nuuk (University of Copenhagen n.d.). Rosing has also explored the aesthetic and ecological economy of glacial rock flour with Danish artist Olafur Eliasson, to whom I turn in Chapter 6.
2. See Hayes and Diamanti (2020), where Megan Hayes and I expand on this occlusion in Sekula through what we term the "intermodal aesthetics" focalized by the shipping container.
3. For a more sustained investigation into the history of the closure of Hemweg 8, see Roy and Diamanti (2020).
4. In an interview with officials at the Port of Amsterdam (since removed from their website) Rijkswaterstaat spokesperson Wouter Bulthuis explained, "Each time one of the IJmuiden locks is used, a volume of sea water flows into the Canal. Using the new sea lock, however, involves a much larger volume than using the North Lock. Converting the extra volume into weight, it means that roughly 40 extra truckloads of road salt are brought into the Canal. That is a lot. There is also another factor playing a role in the background. That factor is sea level rise as a result of climate change. It means that more seawater—and more salt—is expected to be entering the North Sea Canal in the future. Also, due to the hydrostatic pressure of sea water, more seepage water will enter the low-lying polders. This is called salinization and especially in dry periods it can be detrimental to nature, agriculture, horticulture and the supply of drinking water in the vicinity of the North Sea Canal." Countering salinization requires the installation of a "zoutvang" filtration system, which at the time of writing has not been contracted out.

Chapter 1: Our Future is Still the Future of 1973

1. A case in point is Jörg Friedrichs' *The Future Is Not What It Used to Be* (2013), which begins with the false premise that fossil fuels form an external limit to continued

capitalist expansion—both because they are apparently in "terminal decline" and because the environmental costs associated with their emissions will exceed "carrying capacity" in the near future (Friedrichs 2013, 3). While I am sympathetic to the environmental concern animating the thesis that capitalism has an external limit, the danger with the thesis is in its normative assumption that 1) fossil fuels are past peak supply, and 2) capital has built into it an ecological consciousness in the form of a natural limit, or carrying capacity. Neither of these things is true. First, proven reserves of oil have long been recursive to the economic and technical apparatus of the geologist's gaze, so that for instance the largest single discovery of oil occurred in the past decade in the Wolfcamp Shale formation at 46.3 billion barrels of oil (U.S. Geological Survey 2018); well over 100 billion barrels have been estimated offshore and underneath the Greenland Ice Sheet (Gautier 2007) and the EIA estimates 332 years left of Demonstrated Reserve Base coal (U.S. Energy Information Administration 2019), not to mention the natural gas revolution all over the world. Second, capital does not have an external relationship to energy. On the contrary, capital's historical dynamics and contradictions are a feature of its internalization of energy in the process of value production, which practically speaking means that capital has no concept of external matter to rationalize into a limit, much less worry over as a latent ethic. Capital's ecology is dynamic and dialectical, which unfortunately means there is neither a reason to wait around for it to hit the proverbial wall (something like an eco-accelerationism) nor an effective ground from which to wage normative claims about its exogenous limits.

2   The most extensive and critical study of the postwar boom and long downturn signalled by 1973 is by Brenner (1998).
3   See Szeman and Boyer (2017b); Wilson, Carlson, and Szeman (2017).
4   This is Patricia Yaeger's (2011) watershed claim for the study of energy culture.
5   For a theoretical overview of energy materialism, see Bellamy and Diamanti (2018).
6   For more on the oil barrel as a medium of exchange, see Diamanti and Cetinić (forthcoming).
7   The phrase appears in the title of Wack's second installment of the *Harvard Business Review* series on Shell scenarios (Wack 1985b), but serves as an organizing metaphor since it does not appear directly in the text. In the first installment (Wack 1985a), we encounter it directly: "Shell was like a canoeist who hears white water around the bend and must prepare to negotiate the rapids."
8   For the strongest version of the social-constructivist account of the postindustrial energy sector, see Zalik (2010).

Chapter 2: The Cultural Work of Architecture

1. Maurizio Lazzarato's influential essay on "Immaterial Labor" (1996) usually stands in as the most developed expression of the theory, but I have in mind the even more recent collection on *Crisis in the Global Economy* put out by the UniNomade network on *Semiotext(e)* in which "financialization," "biopower," "cognitive capitalism," "the becoming-rent of profit" and the "new affective enclosures" are all deployed diagnostically to describe, in no uncertain terms, what in Carlo Vercellone's contribution (2010) is called "the crisis of the law of labour time-value." The position I am favouring in this chapter is not one that understands Post-Fordist capitalism as a break in the long view of capitalism's internal laws, as in the case of the UniNomade position, which is not to say that their work (and Vercellone's in particular) is not endlessly insightful and indispensable to political organizing after 2008.
2. The two best examples of recent architectural criticism to isolate building craftsmanship and critical regionalism are the chapter "Light Modernity" in Foster (2011, 52–70) and Frampton (1983).
3. Aureli's (2011) recent analysis of Cedric Price's 1966 plans for the Potteries Thinkbelt in North Straffordshire, England suggests one such predecessor to the architecture of intangible assets.
4. Tronti ([1963] 1973) is a translated reprint from the original chapter in *Operai e capitale*, 1966, which first appeared separately in the Marxist journal *Quaderni Rossi* in 1963. Future reference will be to the online version.

Chapter 3: Energyscapes, Architecture, and the Expanded Field of Postindustrial Philosophy

1. My preference for the word "setting" here, over and above the ecocritical nomenclature of place and space, is meant 1) to flag my sense that energy and capital modulate experiences of and ideas about setting (coded as environments) and the rhythms and scales that texture it; 2) to underscore the cultural history of what is typically understood as the environment, though what I am saying has been setting all along; and 3) to mark my debt to Leerom Medovoi's claim (2010) (and Michael Rubenstein's sharp interpretation of it, which he was so kind to share with me). Medovoi's eco-Marxism stakes its position in a revision to the metaphysical binary at the heart of much ecocriticism in which, despite rigorous efforts to avoid such a schema, man and environment are figured as forever separate. "The historicizing alternative to such metaphysics," Medovoi argues,

> would be an ecocritical inquiry into the materially specific (and recent) invention of the "population/environment/capital" triad, a systemic exercise of political power that only some two hundred years ago began to develop strategies for pacifying, harnessing, and reorganizing the mutual relationships of human and nonhuman life toward the end of optimal capital accumulation.
>
> Medovoi 2010, 131

This "historicizing alternative" reads setting as both responsive to and the result of capital's dependence on, but ideological re-presentation of, the environment. Thus,

> the key contribution of a Marxist ecocriticism, or an ecocritical Marxism, would be to focus attention on the recodings of setting as a mechanism through which the biopolitical environmentalization of actual spaces (as governable milieus for life) might pass into the literary
>
> Medovoi 2010, 133

to which I will add here the capitalization and spatialization of energy.
2. My thinking about the singularity of infrastructural circuits across distinct geographies of extraction and circulation is heavily informed by Keller Easterling's reading of "infrastructure space" in *Extrastatecraft* (2014).
3. Timothy Mitchell's account of the economization of fossil fuels (Mitchell 1998; 2011; and elsewhere), has been formative to my understanding of where and how to isolate energy in the critique of political economy. Especially inspiring have been Mitchell's insights about the function of fossil fuels in the conceptual history and composition of terms such as "the economy" and "the globe" (Mitchell 2011, 109). In Mitchell's account, it is oil's saturation of "currency systems" in the postwar era in particular that has created the conditions for national accounts, macroeconomic management, and a concept of boundless growth (139). This latter sense of a variegated relationship between spatiality and temporality driven by the industrialization of fossil fuels is what I am tracking in this chapter.
4. In Bryant's account, what distinguishes these speculative positions is their hostility to what routinely gets called "correlationism," which assigns a determinant role to the subject that discovers an object in the world. Critical theory, very broadly understood, is in Bryant's account opposed to speculative theory.
5. It is precisely these qualities of Blur that make Cary Wolfe (2010) enthusiastic for the project's implications for a specifically posthuman architecture and that alarm Mark Dorrian (2007).
6. My use of the term "setting" is meant to be distinguished from Jeff Malpas and Ursula Heise's return to Heidegger's thoughts on place—which is to say, a sense of place. I'm not concerned with Heidegger, which is why I use the term here. Thinking about the effect of fossil-fueled economic growth on the physical and social

cartographies is consistent with the argument that Andreas Malm makes about the production of an 'abstract spatio-temporality' for capital:

> the necessary material substratum for this spatio-temporality—long hidden from the view of most Marxists, however sharp their eyes have otherwise been—is fossil fuels. They represent the geological compression of the time and space required for photosynthesis hundreds of millions of years ago, when no humans roamed the planet; *sui generis*, their dense energy permits capital to produce its own abstract spatio-temporality for the production of surplus-value. They are incorporated into capital *as its own motive force*.
> Malm 2013, 56

7 In Robert Ayres and Benjamin Warr's groundbreaking analysis in ecological economics, upwards of twelve percent of growth in the twentieth century remains unexplained so long as energy is considered an independent variable in economic growth. When they internalize energy in their measures of growth, on the other hand, continued global growth is fully explained despite lowering labour inputs (due mainly to automation) at the macroeconomic scale (Ayres and Warr 2005, 196).

8 In *The Human Motor* (1990) Anson Rabinbach traces the conceptual and theoretical overlap between the emergent theory of the conservation of energy in the 1840s and Marx's turn to the concept of labour power, a transformation that Brent Bellamy and I elaborate on in *Materialism and the Critique of Energy* (2018).

Chapter 4: Elemental Ethnography Between Hydrocarbons and Hydrology

1 For more on the project and our treatment of "moraine" for twenty-first-century environmental theory, see Boetzkes and Diamanti (2020) and Chapter 5 of the present book.

Chapter 5: Contrapuntal Ice

1 I am grateful to Amanda Boetzkes and Jessie Kleemann for their generous engagement on this chapter. I also thank the participants of "At the Moraine" for helping scramble academic voice, and Megan Hayes for expert research assistance on the concept of "ecological reciprocity."

2 For more on the etymology and cosmology of *sila*, see Nuttall 2010.

3 Tipping points on the horizon of climate discourse suggest to the historian Dipesh Chakrabarty (2014) that the critique of capital and the concerns of climate are entangled but also epistemologically distinct as sites of analysis.
4 I have here in mind Juliana Spahr's *That Winter the Wolf Came* (2015) as a preeminent example of the radical potential of ecopoetics.

References

Adorno, Theodor W. 1991. *The Culture Industry: Selected Essays on Mass Culture.* London: Routledge.

Alaimo, Stacy. 2010. *Bodily Natures: Science, Environment, and the Material Self.* Bloomington, IN: Indiana University Press.

Arboleda, Martín. 2020. *Planetary Mine.* London: Verso.

Arrighi, Giovanni. 1994. *The Long Twentieth Century.* London: Verso.

Aureli, Pier Vittorio. 2011. "Labor and Architecture: Revisiting Cedric Price's Potteries Thinkbelt." *Log* 23: 97–118.

Ayres, Robert, and Benjamin Warr. 2005. "Accounting for Growth: The Role of Physical Work." *Structural Change and Economic Dynamics* 16, no. 2: 181–209. https://doi.org/10.1016/j.strueco.2003.10.003

Bal, Mieke. 1985. *Narratology.* Toronto: University of Toronto Press.

Banham, Reyner. 1960. *Theory and Design in the First Machine Age.* New York: Praeger.

Barney, Darin, Imre Szeman, and Mark Simpson, eds. 2021. Special Issue of *South Atlantic Quarterly* 120, no. 1.

Barthes, Rolande. (1957) 1972. *Mythologies*, translated by Annette Lavers. New York: Hill and Wang.

Bellamy, Brent Ryan, and Jeff Diamanti. 2018. *Materialism and the Critique of Energy.* Chicago and Edmonton: MCM Prime Press.

Benjamin, Walter. 1968 [1955]. *Illuminations.* New York: Harcourt Brace Jovanovich, Inc.

Benjamin, Walter. 2021. *One-Way Street and Other Writings.* London: Verso

Bennike, Ole, Jørn Bo Jensen, Frederik Næsby Sukstorf, and Minik T. Rosing. 2019. "Mapping Glacial Rock Flour Deposits in Tasersuaq, Southern West Greenland." *GEUS Bulletin* 43: e2019430206. https://doi.org/10.34194/GEUSB-201943-02-06

Bertelsen, Rasmus Gjedssø, and Klaus Georg Hansen. 2015. "From Energy to Knowledge? Building Domestic Knowledge-Based Sectors around Hydro Energy in Iceland and Greenland." In *Diplomacy on Ice: Energy and Environment in the Arctic and Antarctic*, edited by Rebecca Pincus and Saleem H. Ali, 113–127. London: Yale University Press.

Bhaskar, Roy. 2009 [1986]. *Scientific Realism and Human Emancipation.* London: Routledge.

Bishop, Claire. 2004. "Antagonism and Relational Aesthetics." *October* 110 (Fall): 51–79. DOI: 10.1162/0162287042379810

Boetzkes, Amanda, and Jeff Diamanti. 2020. "At the Moraine." *e-flux* "Accumulation", September 14. https://www.e-flux.com/architecture/accumulation/341644/at-the-moraine/

Boetzkes, Amanda, and Andrew Pendakis. 2013. "Visions of Eternity: Plastic and the Ontology of Oil." *e-flux* 47 (September). https://www.e-flux.com/journal/47/60052/visions-of-eternity-plastic-and-the-ontology-of-oil/

Blum, Jordan. 2018. "USGS: Permian's Wolfcamp is Largest Potential Oil and Gas Resource Ever Assessed." *Houston Chronicle*, December 6, 2018. https://www.houstonchronicle.com/business/energy/article/USGS-Permian-s-Wolfcamp-is-largest-potential-oil-13447556.php

Braidotti, Rosi. 2017. "Posthuman Critical Theory." *Journal of Posthuman Studies* 1, no. 1: 9–25.

Brenner, Robert. 1998. *The Long Downturn*. London: Verso.

Bryant, Levi. 2011. *The Democracy of Objects*. Ann Arbor: Open Humanities Press.

Bryant, Levi. 2014. "Energy, work and thermopolitics". *Laral Subjects*, January 17. http://larvalsubjects.wordpress.com/2014/01/17/energy-work-and-thermopolitics/

Bryant, Levi, Nick Srnicek, and Graham Harman. 2012. "Towards a Speculative Philosophy." In *The Speculative Turn*, edited by Levi R. Bryant, Nick Srnicek, and Graham Harman, 1–17. Melbourne: re.press.

Buchanan, Peter. 1993. *Renzo Piano Building Workshop: Complete Works, Volume One*. London: Phaidon.

Buchanan, Peter. 1995. *Renzo Piano Building Workshop: Complete Works, Volume Two*. London: Phaidon.

Buchanan, Peter. 1996. "Reviving Lingotto." *Architectural Review* 200, no. 1197: 62–67.

Burrington, Ingrid. 2015. "The Environmental Toll of a Netflix Binge." *The Atlantic*.

Büscher, Bram and Robert Fletcher. 2020. *The Conservation Revolution*. London: Verso.

Carruth, Allison. 2014. "The Digital Cloud and the Micropolitics of Energy." *Public Culture* 26, no. 2: 339–364. https://doi.org/10.1215/08992363-2392093

Chakrabarty, Dipesh. 2009. "The Climate of History: Four Theses." *Critical Inquiry* 35, no. 2 (Winiter): 197–222. DOI: 10.1086/596640

Chakrabarty, Dipesh. 2014. "Climate and Capital: On Conjoined Histories." *Critical Inquiry* 41, no. 1 (Autumn): 1–23. DOI: 10.1086/678154

Ciferri, Luca. "Agnelli—The Uncrowned Monarch of the Italian Motor Industry." *Automotive New Europe*. http://www.autonews.com/files/euroauto/inductees/agnelli.htm

Clark, Nigel, and Kathryn Yusoff. 2017. "Geosocial Formations and the Anthropocene." *Theory, Culture and Society* 34, nos. 2–3: 3–23. https://doi.org/10.1177/0263276416688946

Code, Lorraine. 2006. *Ecological Thinking*. London: Oxford University Press.

Cooper, Melinda. 2016. "Secular Stagnation: Fear of a Non-Reproductive Future." *Postmodern Culture* 27, no. 1 (September 2016). doi: 10.1353/pmc.2016.0023

Corner, James. 1999. *Recovering Landscape*. Princeton, NJ: Princeton Architectural Press.

Corner, James. 2006. "Terra Fluxus." In *The Landscape Urbanism Reader*, edited by Charles Waldheim, 21–34. New York: Princeton Architectural Press.
Crary, Jonathan. 2014. *24/7*. London: Verso.
Daggett, Cara New. 2019. *The Birth of Energy*. Durham, NC: Duke University Press.
Danish Parliament. 2009. "Act on Greenland Self-Government." Act no. 423 of June 12, 2009, Section 8.1–2. https://naalakkersuisut.gl/~/media/Nanoq/Files/Attached%20Files/Engelske-tekster/Act%20on%20Greenland.pdf
Danowski, Deborah and Eduardo Viverios de Castro. 2016. *The Ends of the World*. Cambridge, UK: Polity Press.
Dawood, Shezad, dir. 2017. *Leviathan*. https://leviathan-cycle.com/information
Day, Gail. 2012. *Dialectical Passions*. New York: Columbia University Press.
Deleuze, Gilles. 2006. *Nietzsche and Philosophy*. New York: Columbia University Press.
Delforge, Pierre. 2015. "America's Data Centers Consuming and Wasting Growing Amounts of Energy." *NRDC*. https://www.nrdc.org/resources/americas-data-centers-consuming-and-wasting-growing-amounts-energy
DeLoughry, Elizabeth. 2019. *Allegories of the Anthropocene*. Durham, NC: Duke University Press.
Derrida, Jacques. 1967. *De la grammatologie*. Paris: Les Éditions de Minuit.
Diamanti, Jeff. 2018. "Extractivism." *Krisis* 3 (July): 54–57.
Diamanti, Jeff and Marija Cetinić. Forthcoming. "The Abstract and the Concrete in Jeanne-Claude and Christo's Oil Barrels." In *Saturation*, edited by Rafico Ruiz and Melody Jue. Durham, NC: Duke University Press.
Diamanti, Jeff and Imre Szeman. 2020. "Nine Principles for a Critical Theory of Energy." *Polygraph* 28.
Diller, Elizabeth, Ricardo Scofidio, and Charles Renfro. n.d. "Blur Building." *Diller Scofidio + Renfro*. Accessed April 12, 2015. https://dsrny.com/project/blur-building
Dorrian, Mark. 2007. "Clouds of Architecture." *Radical Philosophy* 144: 26–32.
Easterling, Keller. 2014. *Extrastatecraft: The Power of Infrastructure Space*. London: Verso.
Energy Information Administration. 2016. International Energy Outlook 2016. https://www.eia.gov/outlooks/ieo/pdf/0484(2016).pdf
European Environment Agency. 2017. "Global and European Sea Level." https://www.eea.europa.eu/data-and-maps/indicators/sea-level-rise-5/assessment
Federici, Silvia. 2006. "Precarious Labor: A Feminist Viewpoint." https://inthemiddleofthewhirlwind.wordpress.com/precarious-labor-a-feminist-viewpoint/
Flora, Janne. 2019. *Wandering Spirits*. Chicago: University of Chicago Press.
Foster, Hal. 2011. *The Art-Architecture Complex*. London: Verso.
Foucault, Michel. 1986. *Death and the Labyrinth*. London: Continuum.
Frampton, Kenneth. 1983. "Towards a Critical Regionalism: Six Points for an Architecture of Resistance." In *The Anti-Aesthetic: Essays on Postmodern Culture*, edited by Hal Foster, 16–30. Port Townsend, WA: Bay Press.

Fredericks, Murray. "End of the Earth." *National Geographic*, March 2015. https://www.nationalgeographic.com/magazine/2015/03/greenland-ice-sheet/

Friedrichs, Jörg. 2013. *The Future Is Not What It Used to Be*. Cambridge, MA: MIT Press.

Frost, Robert. (1920) 1923 "Fire and Ice." *New Hampshire*. New York: Henry Holt.

Gabrys, Jennifer. 2018. "Becoming Planetary." *E-flux*, "Accumulation" series. https://www.e-flux.com/architecture/accumulation/217051/becoming-planetary/

Galloway, Alexander. 2013. "The Poverty of Philosophy: Realism and Post-Fordism." *Critical Inquiry* 39, no. 2 (Winter): 347–366. DOI:10.1086/668529

Gautier, Donald L. 2007. "Assessment of undiscovered oil and gas resources of the East Greenland Rift Basins Province [U.S. Geological Survey Fact Sheet 2007-3077]". *U.S. Geological Survey*. https://pubs.usgs.gov/fs/2007/3077/

Gearheard, Shari Fox, Lene Kielsen Holm, Henry Huntington, Joe Mello Leavitt, Andrew R. Mahoney, Margaret Opie, Toku Oshima, and Joelie Sanguya. 2013. *The Meaning of Ice*. New Hampshire: International Polar Institute Press.

Ghosh, Amitav. 2016. *The Great Derangement*. Chicago: University of Chicago Press.

Gissen, David. 2011. "The Architectural Reconstruction of Geography." In *Coupling: Strategies for Infrastructural Opportunism*, edited by Becca Casbon. Pamphlet Architecture 30, 42–45.

Glanz, James. 2012. "Power, Pollution, and the Internet." *New York Times*, September 22, 2012. https://www.nytimes.com/2012/09/23/technology/data-centers-waste-vast-amounts-of-energy-belying-industry-image.html

Glissant, Édouard. 1997 [1990]. *Poetics of Relation*. Ann Arbor: University of Michigan Press.

Gretner, Jon. 2019. *The Ice at the End of the World*. New York: Random House.

Grusin, Richard. 2010. *Premediation*. London: Palgrave Macmillan.

Guattari, Félix. 2000 [1989]. *The Three Ecologies*. London: The Athlone Press.

Hallward, Peter. 2006. *Out of this World: Deleuze and the Philosophy of Creation*. London: Verso.

Hayek, Friedrich August. 1943. "A Commodity Reserve Currency." *The Economic Journal* 53 (210/211): 176–184. DOI: 10.2307/2226314

Hayes, Megan and Jeff Diamanti. 2020. "Intermodal Aesthetics and the Otherwise of Cargo." In *Transportation and the Culture of Climate Change*, edited by Tatiana Prorokova, 173–190. Morgantown: West Virginia University Press.

Hendriksen, Kåre. 2016. "Greenland island infrastructure: Energy challenges to the fishing industry." Paper presented at Arctic Circle Conference, Reykjavik, Iceland, 2016. https://backend.orbit.dtu.dk/ws/portalfiles/portal/126612139/160805_Article_Greenland_infrastructure_Master.pdf

Hornby, Louise. 2017. "Appropriating the Weather: Olafur Eliasson and Climate Control." *Environmental Humanities* 9, no. 1: 60–83. https://doi.org/10.1215/22011919-3829136

Howe, Cymene and Dominic Boyer. 2018. "Redistributions: From Atmospheric Carbon to Melting Cryospheres to the World Ocean." *e-flux* "Accumulation," September 21. https://www.e-flux.com/architecture/accumulation/212496/redistributions/

Hume, Angela, and Gillian Osborne. 2018. *Ecopoetics: Essays in the Field*. Iowa City, IA: University of Iowa Press.

Ingold, Tim. 2007. *Lines*. London: Routledge.

Ingold, Tim. 2015. *The Life of Lines*. London: Routledge.

Intergovernmental Panel on Climate Change. 2018. *Global Warming of 1.5°C. An IPCC Special Report on the impacts of global warming of 1.5°C above pre-industrial levels and related global greenhouse gas emission pathways, in the context of strengthening the global response to the threat of climate change, sustainable development, and efforts to eradicate poverty*. https://www.ipcc.ch/sr15/chapter/spm/

International Energy Agency. 2008. *World Energy Outlook*. Paris: OECD. https://doi.org/10.1787/weo-2008-en

Jameson, Fredric. 1981. *The Political Unconscious*. Ithaca, NY: Cornell University Press.

Jameson, Fredric. 2003. "The End of Temporality." *Critical Inquiry* 29, no. 4: 695–718. DOI: 10.1086/377726

Jastrup, Morten, ed. 2008. "Energy for the future: with Risø from nuclear power to sustainable energy." Risø National Laboratory for Sustainable Energy. https://backend.orbit.dtu.dk/ws/portalfiles/portal/151577373/ris_jubilee_50_uk.pdf

Jorgenson, Dale W. 1984. "The Role of Energy in Productivity Growth." *The American Economic Review* 74, no. 2 (May): 26–30.

Khalili, Laleh. 2020. *Sinews of War and Trade*. London: Verso.

Kleemann, Jessie. 2012. *Qivittoq*. Vejby, Denmark: Hurricane Publishing.

Krauss, Rosalind. 1979. "Sculpture in the Expanded Field" *October* 8 (Spring): 30–44. DOI: 10.2307/778224

Krauss, Rosalind. 2000. *A Voyage on the North Sea: Art in the Age of the Post-Medium Condition*. London: Thames & Hudson.

Kuokkanen, Rauna. 2017. "Indigenous Epistemes." In *A Companion to Critical and Cultural Theory*, edited by Imre Szeman, Sarah Blacker, and Justin Sully, 313–326. London: Routledge.

Labban, Mazen. 2010. "Oil in Parallax: Scarcity, Markets, and the Financialization of Accumulation." *Geoforum* 41, no. 4: 541–552. DOI: 10.1016/j.geoforum.2009.12.002

La Berge, Leigh Claire. 2015. "How to Make Money with Words: Finance, Performativity, Language." *Journal of Cultural Economy* 9, no. 1: 43–62. https://doi.org/10.1080/17530350.2015.1040435

Lanteigne, Marc. 2018. "Greenland's Airports: A Balance between China and Denmark?" https://overthecircle.com/2018/06/15/greenlands-airports-a-balance-between-china-and-denmark/

Larkin, Brian. 2013. "The Poetics and Politics of Infrastructure." *The Annual Review of Anthropology* 42: 327–343. https://doi.org/10.1146/annurev-anthro-092412-155522

Latour, Bruno. 1993. *We Have Never Been Modern*. Cambridge, MA.: Harvard University Press.

Latour, Bruno. 2014. "Agency at the Time of the Anthropocene." *New Literary History* 45: 1–18.

Lazzarato, Maurizio. (1996) 2014. "Immaterial Labor." In *Contemporary Marxist Theory: A Reader*, edited by Andrew Pendakis, Jeff Diamanti, Nicholas Brown, Josh Robinson, and Imre Szeman, 77–91. New York: Bloomsbury.

Le Corbusier. (1923) 2008. *Towards a New Architecture*, translated by Frederick Etchells. Hawthorne, CA: BN Publishing.

LeMenager, Stephanie. 2013. *Living Oil*. London: Oxford University Press.

LeMenager, Stephanie. 2014. *Living Oil*. Oxford: Oxford University Press.

Levinson, Marc. 2016. *An Extraordinary Time*. New York: Penguin.

Libbert, Natascha. 2018. *I Went Looking for a Ship*. Breda, Netherlands: The Eriskay Collection

Loder, Asjylyn. 2015. "The Oil Crash Has Caused a $1.3 Trillion Wipeout." *Bloomberg*, August 4, 2015. https://www.bloomberg.com/news/articles/2015-08-04/the-oil-crash-has-caused-a-1-3-trillion-wipeout

Malabou, Catherine. [1996] 2005. *The Future of Hegel: Plasticity, Temporality and Dialectic*. Translated by Lisabeth During. London: Routledge.

Malm, Andreas. 2013. "The Origins of Fossil Capital: From Water to Steam in the British Cotton Industry." *Historical Materialism* 21, no. 1: 15–68.

Malm, Andreas. 2016. *Fossil Capital*. London: Verso.

Malm, Andreas. 2018. *The Progress of this Storm*. London: Verso.

Marder, Michael. 2017. *Energy Dreams*. New York: Columbia University Press.

Marinetti, Filippo Tommaso. 1909. "Manifeste du Futurisme." *Le Figaro*, February 20, 1909.

Marx, Karl. 1845. *The German Ideology*. Marxists Internet Archive. http://www.marxists.org/archive/marx/works/1845/german-ideology/ch01a.htm

Marx, Karl. 1951. *Karl Marx and Frederick Engels: Selected Works in Two Volumes*, vol II. London: Lawrence & Wishart.

Marx, Karl. (1867) 1976. *Capital Volume 1*. London: Penguin.

McCaw, Chris. n.d. "About Sunburn." *Chris McCaw*. https://www.chrismccaw.com/about-sunburn

McGrath, Janet Tamalik. 2019. "Sila." In *An Ecotopian Lexcon*, edited by Matthew Schneider-Mayerson and Brent Ryan Bellamy, 256–265. Minneapolis: University of Minnesota Press.

Medovoi, Leerom. 2010. "The Biopolitical Unconscious: Toward an Eco-Marxist Literary Theory." *Mediations* 24, no. 2 (Spring): 122–139. https://doi.org/10.1057/9781137339959_5

Meyer, Gregory. 2017. "US Oil Futures Market Overtakes London." *Financial Times*, September 17, 2017. https://www.ft.com/content/2d644842-9a51-11e7-b83c-9588e51488a0

Mills, Mark P. 2013. *The Cloud Begins with Coal: Big Data, Big Networks, Big Infrastructure, and Big Power.* Amsterdam: Digital Power Group. https://www.tech-pundit.com/wp-content/uploads/2013/07/Cloud_Begins_With_Coal.pdf

Milton, John. (1674) 2003. *Paradise Lost.* London: Penguin.

Mining Technology. n.d. "Kvanefjeld Rare Earth—Uranium Project." Accessed April 2018. https://www.mining-technology.com/projects/kvanefjeld-rare-earth-uranium-project/

Mitchell, Timothy. 1998. "Fixing the Economy." *Cultural Studies* 12, no. 1: 82–101. https://doi.org/10.1080/095023898335627

Mitchell, Timothy. 2011. *Carbon Democracy.* London: Verso.

Mitchell, Timothy. 2011. *Carbon Democracy.* London: Verso.

Mitchell, W.J.T. 1994. *Landscape and Power.* Chicago: University of Chicago Press.

Mitchell, William J. 2013. "Against Program." In *Architecture Theories of the Environment: Posthuman Territory*, edited by Ariane Lourie Harrison, 154–162. New York: Routledge.

Moore, Jason. W. 2015. *Capitalism in the Web of Life.* London: Verso.

Mostafavi, Mohsen. 2010. "Why Ecological Urbanism? Why Now?" In *Ecological Urbanism* edited by Mohsen Mostafavi, and Gareth Doherty, 12–54. Zürich: Lars Müller Publishers.

Mouginot, Jérémie, Eric Rignot, Anders A. Bjørk, Michiel van den Broeke, Romain Millan, Mathieu Morlighem, Brice Noël, Bernd Scheuchl, and Michael Wood. 2019. "Forty-six years of Greenland Ice Sheet mass balance from 1972 to 2018." *Proceedings of the National Academy of Sciences of the United States of America* 116, no. 19: 9239–9244. https://doi.org/10.1073/pnas.1904242116

Naalakkersuisut. 2018. *Greenlandic Ice and Water for Export: A Legal Framework.* Nuuk: Greenland.

Nagatsuka, Naoko, Nozomu Takeuchi, Jun Uetake, Rigen Shimada, Yukihiko Onuma, Sota Tanaka, and Takanori Nakano. 2016. "Variations in Sr and Nd Isotopic Ratios of Mineral Particles in Cryoconite in Western Greenland." *Frontiers in Earth Science* 4 (November). https://doi.org/10.3389/feart.2016.00093

Neale, Timothy, Thao Phan, and Courtney Addison. 2019. "An Anthropogenic Table of Elements: An Introduction." *Cultural Anthropology*, June 27, "Theorizing the Contemporary."

Nielsen, Henry, Keld Nielsen, Flemming Petersen, and Hans Siggard. 1999. "Risø and the Attempts to Introduce Nuclear Power into Denmark." *Centaurus* 41: 64–92. https://doi.org/10.1111/j.1600-0498.1999.tb00275.x

Nietzsche, Friedrich. 1968. *The Will to Power.* New York: Vintage Books.

Noël, Brice, Willem Jan van de Berg, Stef Lhermitte, Bert Wouters, Horst Machguth, Ian Howat, Michele Citterio, Geir Moholdt, Jan Lenaerts, and Michiel van den Broeke. 2017. "A Tipping Point in Refreezing Accelerates Mass Loss of Greenland's Glaciers and Ice Caps." *Nature Communications* 8.

Nourse, Edwin. 1953. *Economics in Public Service.* New York: Harcourt, Brace.

Nuttall, Mark. 2008. "Self-Rule in Greenland: Towards the World's First Independent Inuit State?" *Indigenous Affairs* 3–4: 64–70. https://www.iwgia.org/images/publications/IA_3-08_Greenland.pdf

Nuttall, Mark. 2009. "Living in a World of Movement: Human Resilience to Human Instability in Greenland." In *Anthropology and Climate Change*, edited by Susan A. Crate, and Mark Nuttall. Walnut Creek, CA: Left Coast Press.

Nuttall, Mark. 2010. "Anticipation, climate change, and movement in Greenland." *Études Inuit. Inuit Studies* 34, no. 1: 21–37.

Nuttall, Mark. 2013. "Zero-tolerance, uranium and Greenland's mining future," *The Polar Journal* 3, no. 2: 368–383. https://doi.org/10.1080/2154896X.2013.868089

O'Brien, Sean. 2018. "The Aesthetics of Stagnation: Ashley McKenzie's *Werewolf* and *The Separated Society*." *Discourse* 40, no. 2: 208–230.

Piano, Renzo. 1982. *Pezzo per Pezzo*. Rome: Casa del Libro Editrice.

Pinkus, Karen. 2013. "Thinking Diverse Futures from a Carbon Present." *Symploke* 21: 1–2. DOI: 10.5250/symploke.21.1-2.0195

Planning Studies Centre. 2012. "Progetto '80: A Project for the Renewal of the Italian Society." *Planning Studies Centre*, April 8, 2012. http://www.planningstudies.org/research/progetto80/index.htm

Povinelli, Elizabeth A. 2016. *Geontologies*. Durham, NC: Duke University Press.

Povinelli, Elizabeth A. 2017. "The Ends of Humans: Anthropocene, Autonomism, Antagonism, and the Illusions of Our Epoch." *South Atlantic Quarterly* 116, no. 2: 293–310. https://doi.org/10.1215/00382876-3829412

Povinelli, Elizabeth, Mathew Coleman, and Kathryn Yusoff. 2017. "An Interview with Elizabeth Povinelli: Geontopower, Biopolitics and the Anthropocene." *Theory, Culture & Society* 34, nos. 2–3: 169–185. https://doi.org/10.1177/0263276417689900

Rabinbach, Anson. 1990. *The Human Motor*. Los Angeles: University of California Press.

Ragazzola, Laura. Nd. "Interview with Renzo Bianchi, partner RPBW." *Interni*. https://www.internimagazine.com/projects/kallithea/

Reiser, Jesse, and Nanako Umemoto. 2006. *Atlas of Novel Tectonics*. New York: Princeton Architectural Press.

Rifkin, Mark. 2017. *Beyond Settler Time*. Durham, NC: Duke University Press.

Ross, Andrew. 1991. *Strange Weather*. London: Verso.

Rossi, Aldo. 1981. *A Scientific Autobiography*. Cambridge, MA: MIT Press.

Roxburgh, Charles. 2009. "The Use and Abuse of Scenarios." *McKinsey & Company*, February 1, 2009. https://www.mckinsey.com/business-functions/strategy-and-corporate-finance/our-insights/the-use-and-abuse-of-scenarios#

Roy, Simon and Jeff Diamanti. 2020. "The Bifurcation of Amsterdam's Terminals and Tourists: Urgenda and Beyond." *FRAME* 33.1: 13–29.

Safety4Sea. 2017. "Berth Capacity in Amsterdam Terminal Expanded." https://safety4sea.com/berth-capacity-amsterdam-terminal-expanded

Said, Edward. 1993. *Culture and Imperialism*. London: Chatto & Windus.

Schurr, Sam. 1960. *Energy in the American Economy.* Baltimore, MD: Johns Hopkins University Press.
Scott, Felicity D. 2007. *Architecture or Techno-Utopia.* Cambridge, MA: MIT Press.
Sejersen, Frank. 2015. *Rethinking Greenland and the Arctic in the Era of Climate Change.* London: Routledge.
Sekula, Allan. 2018. *Fish Story.* London: MACK.
Shane, Grahame. 2006. "The Emergence of Landscape Urbanism." In *The Landscape Urbanism Reader*, edited by Charles Waldheim, 55–68. New York: Princeton Architectural Press.
Shannon, Kelly. 2006. "From Theory to Resistance: Landscape Urbanism in Europe." In *The Landscape Urbanism Reader*, edited by Charles Waldheim, 141–163. New York: Princeton Architectural Press.
Shell International BV. 2008. *Shell Energy Scenarios to 2050.* http://folk.ntnu.no/skoge/book-cep/more/shell_energy_scenarios_2050.pdf
Shell International BV. 2011. *Shell Energy Scenarios to 2050: Signals and Signposts.* http://www.proyectomilenio.org/documents/10156/43639/Shell+Energy+Scenarios+2050+-Signals+%26+Singposts-.pdf?version=1.0
da Silva, Denise Ferreira. 2017. "1 (life) ÷ 0 (blackness) = ∞ − ∞ or ∞ / ∞: On Matter Beyond the Equation of Value." *E-flux* 79 (February). https://www.e-flux.com/journal/79/94686/1-life-0-blackness-or-on-matter-beyond-the-equation-of-value/
Smil, Vaclav. 2010. *Energy Transitions.* Oxford: Prager.
Spahr, Juliana. 2015. *That Winter the Wolf Came.* Oakland, CA: Commune Editions.
Spivak, Gayatri. 2004. "Planetarity." In *Dictionary of Untranslatables*, edited by Barbara Cassin. Princeton, NJ: Princeton University Press.
Starosielski, Nicole. 2015. *The Undersea Network.* Durham: Duke University Press.
Stengers, Isabelle. 2010. *Cosmopolitics I.* Minneapolis: University of Minnesota Press.
Stern, Nicholas. 2007. *Stern Review: The Economics of Climate Change.* Cambridge: Cambridge University Press.
Stoler, Ann. 2016. *Duress: Imperial Durability in Our Times.* Durham, NC: Duke University Press.
Szeman, Imre. 2007. "System Failure: Oil, Futurity, and the Anticipation of Disaster." *South Atlantic Quarterly* 106, no. 4: 805–823. DOI: 10.1215/00382876-2007-047
Szeman, Imre and Dominic Boyer. 2017a. "Rise of the Energy Humanities." *University Affairs.*
Szeman, Imre. 2013. "How to Know about Oil: Energy Epistemologies and Political Futures." *Journal of Canadian Studies* 47.3.
Szeman, Imre and Dominic Boyer, eds. 2017b. *Energy Humanities: A Reader.* Baltimore: Johns Hopkins University Press.
Tafuri, Manfredo. 1976. *Architecture and Utopia*, translated from the Italian by Barbara Luigia La Penta. Cambridge, MA: MIT Press.
Tafuri, Manfredo. 1989. *History of Italian Architecture 1944-1985.* Cambridge, MA: MIT Press.

Tagliabue, John. 2003. "Giovanni Tagliabue, Fiat Patriarch and a Force in Italy, Dies at 81." *New York Times*, January 25, 2003. http://www.nytimes.com/2003/01/25/business/giovanni-agnelli-fiat-patriarch-and-a-force-in-italy-dies-at-81.html

Toscano, Alberto. 2015. "Plasticity, Capital, and the Dialectic." *Plastic Materialities*. Durham, NC: Duke University Press.

Toscano, Alberto, and Jeff Kinkle. 2015. *Cartographies of the Absolute*. Winchester, UK: Zero Books.

Tronti, Mario. (1963) 1973. "Social Capital." *Telos* 17: 98–121. http://www.zerowork.org/TrontiSocialCapital.htm

Tschumi, Bernard. 1994. *Architecture and Disjunction*. Cambridge, MA: MIT Press.

Tsing, Anna. 2015. *The Mushroom at the End of the World*. Princeton, NJ: Princeton University Press.

United Nations Environment Programme. 2016. "Global Material Flows and Resource Productivity: Assessment Report for the UNEP International Resource Panel." https://www.resourcepanel.org/reports/global-material-flows-and-resource-productivity-database-link

UNESCO World Heritage List. n.d. "Ilulissat Icefjord." https://whc.unesco.org/en/list/1149/. Accessed October 5, 2019.

U.S. Geological Survey. 2016. "USGS Estimates 20 Billion Barrels of Oil in Texas' Wolfcamp Shale Formation." *U.S. Geological Survey*, November 15, 2016. https://www.usgs.gov/news/usgs-estimates-20-billion-barrels-oil-texas-wolfcamp-shale-formation

U.S. Geological Survey. 2018. "USGS Announces Largest Continuous Oil Assessment in Texas and New Mexico." *U.S. Geological Survey*, November 28, 2018. https://www.usgs.gov/news/usgs-announces-largest-continuous-oil-assessment-texas-and-new-mexico

University of Copenhagen. n.d. "Theme Package, Glacial Rock Flour," Greenland Perspective. https://greenlandperspective.ku.dk/theme_packages/green_land/glacial-rock-dust/

Vercellone, Carlo. 2010 "The Crisis of the Law of Value and the Becoming-Rent of Profit: Notes on the Systemic Crisis of Cognitive Capitalism." In *Crisis in the Global Economy: Financial Markets, Social Struggles and New Political Scenarios*, edited byAndrea Fumagalli and Sandro Mezzadra, 85–118. Cambridge, MA: MIT Press.

Wack, Pierre. 1985a. "Scenarios: Uncharted Waters Ahead." *Harvard Business Review*, September 1985. https://hbr.org/1985/09/scenarios-uncharted-waters-ahead

Wack, Pierre. 1985b. "Scenarios: Shooting the Rapids." *Harvard Business Review*, November 1985. https://hbr.org/1985/11/scenarios-shooting-the-rapids

Waldheim, Charles. 2006. *The Landscape Urbanism Reader*. Princeton, NJ: Princeton University Press.

Walsh, Maurice. 2017. "You Can't Live in a Museum: The Battle for Greenland's Uranium." *The Guardian*, January 28, 2017. https://www.theguardian.com/environment/2017/jan/28/greenland-narsaq-uranium-mine-dividing-town

Watts, Michael J. 2015. "Securing Oil: Frontiers, Risk, and Spaces of Accumulated Insecurity." In *Subterranean Estates*, edited by Hannah Appel, Arthur Mason, and Michael Watts, 211–236. Ithica, NY: Cornell University Press.

Weller, Richard. 2006. "An Art of Instrumentality: Thinking Through Landscape Urbanism." In *The Landscape Urbanism Reader*, edited by Charles Waldheim, 68–86. New York: Princeton Architectural Press.

Wenzel, Jennifer. 2017. "Introduction." In *Fueling Culture*, edited by Imre Szeman, 1–16. New York: Fordham University Press.

Wenzel, Jennifer. 2020. *The Disposition of Nature*. New York: Fordham University Press.

Wilkinson, Angela, and Roland Kupers. 2014. *The Essence of Scenarios: Learning from the Shell Experience*. Amsterdam: University of Amsterdam Press.

Williams, Joshua J., Noel Gouremelen, and Peter Nienow. 2020. "Dynamic response of the Greenland ice sheet to recent cooling." *Scientific Reports* 10, no. 1647 (February). https://doi.org/10.1038/s41598-020-58355-2

Wilson, Sheena, Adam Carlson, and Imre Szeman, eds. 2017. *Petrocultures*. Montreal and Chicago: McGill-Queen's University Press.

Wolfe, Cary. 2010. *What is Posthumanism?* Minneapolis: University of Minnesota Press.

Yaeger, Patricia. 2011. "Editor's Column: Literature in the Ages of Wood, Tallow, Coal, Whale Oil, Gasoline, Atomic Power, and Other Energy Sources." *PMLA* 126, no. 2 (March): 305–326. DOI: 10.2307/41414106

Yergin, Daniel. 1990. *The Prize*. New York: Simon & Schuster.

Zalik, Anna. 2010. "Oil 'futures': Shell's Scenarios and the Social Constitution of the Global Oil Market." *Geoforum* 41, no. 4: 553–564. DOI: 10.1016/j.geoforum.2009.11.008

Index

abstraction, 4
accumulation, 10
    infrastructures of, 62–7
actor network theory, 66–7
Adorno, Theodor, 123–5
aesthetic economy
    heliotropism, 119
    infrastructures of accumulation, 63
    landscape infrastructures, 72–6
    philosophical tradition, 76–80
    postindustrial landscapes, 67–72, **71**
aesthetic interventions, 17
agency, 120
Agnelli, Giovanni, 43
Agnelli, V.G., 48
Alaimo, Stacey, 7, 113–4
Alcoa, 95–6
algae blooms, 108
Allen, Stan, 15–6
aluminum, 95–6
Ambasz, Emilio, 69
Amsterdam, 7, 7–8, 10, 11, 12–3, 83, 135, 143n4
analytic postures, 2–3
Anthropocene, the, 87, 120
nthropogenic climate change, 87–8
antihumanism, 129
architecture
    aesthetic, 50–1
    aesthetic economy, 61–80
    capitalist logic, 46
    cultural work, 43–59
    deconstructive, 70–2
    infrastructures of accumulation, 62–7
    landscape infrastructures, 72–6
    media ecology, 15–6
    philosophical tradition, 76–80
    postindustrial, 15, 15–6, 43–59
    postindustrial landscapes, 67–72, **71**
    social capital, 56–9
    Tafuri's critique, 45–6, 51
    Viennese urbanism, 45

Archizoom, 45
Aristotle, 128
Arnheim, Rudolf, 118
Arrighi, Giovanni, 23, 135
"At the Moraine' of the Greenland Ice Sheet" project, 90–4, 100, 102
Athens, Stavros Niarchos Cultural Center, 59
Atlantic Meridional Overturning Circulation, 113
atmospheric space, 73
austerity, 59
automobiles, hegemonic weight, 51
Ayres, Robert, 147n7

Bachelard, Gaston, 78
Bal, Mieke, 121
Banham, Reyner, 49
Barthes, Roland, 8–9, 126
bauxite, 95–6
beach, the, 118, 122–3, 124, 129–32
Benjamin, Walter, 77, 107, 125
Bentham, Jeremy, 40
Bhaskar, Roy, 80
binaries, 2–3
biogeochemistry, 88–9
biopolitical, the, 127
biopower, 145n1
Bishop, Claire, 129
Boetzkes, Amanda, 6, 65, 100, 140
Bordiga, Amadeo, 48
boredom, modern, 123–5
bottled water industry, 97–8
Boyer, Dominic, 99
BP, 33
Braidotti, Rosi, 119
Bretton Woods Agreement, 29–30, 35, 69
Bryant, Levi, 66–7, 146n4
Bulthuis, Walter, 143n4
Burrington, Ingrid, 61
business environment, 35

Cambridge Capital Controversy, 56
capital, 4, 137–8
  cycle of accumulation, 23
  hegemony, 23, 124–5
  infrastructures of accumulation, 62–7
  organic composition of, 57
  spatio-temporality, 147n6
  terminal crisis, 141
  valorization of, 58
  variable, 59
  world-building logics, 14
capital expansion, 40
capitalism, 137
  and climate change, 3
  growth categories, 56–7
  hegemony, 76
  infrastructure, 140
  limit, 144n1
  sustainable, 138
capitalist accumulation, 57
carbon futures, 27
carbon imaginary, the, 22
carbon-capital complex, 63, 74–5
Carruth, Allison, 64
Centre Pompidou, Paris, 51–2
Chakrabarty, Dipesh, 87–8, 111, 112, 148n3
Chin, Mel, 17, 102, 107
Circum-Arctic Resource Appraisal, 92
civilization, collapse of, 122
climate change, 3, 120, 127, 127–8
CO_2 emissions, 41, 99, 111
Code, Lorraine, 6
cognitive capitalism, 145n1
Cohen, Jeffrey Jerome, 91
colonial domination, 112
colonial forces, 104
colonialism, 85
commodities, value-bearing function, 138
Commodity Futures Modernization Act
    (2000) (US), 26
conservation, 105
contrapuntal, the, 103–5
contrapuntal ice, 98
  the dead glacier, 105–9
  definition, 103
  engagement with, 101–5
  interdisciplinary thinking, 100, 101–5
  sila, 99–101
Cooper, Melinda, 27

COP 21, 102
Corner, James, 70, 71–2, 74
correlationism, 146n4
COVID-19 health and economic crisis,
    40–1
Crary, Jonathan, 124
critical environmentalism, 138
critical inquiry, 135–6
critical realism, 78–80
critical theory, 17, 62, 67, 123, 125
Croner, James, 15–6
cryosphere, the, 109
cultural imaginary, ice, 104–5
cultural objects, reading, 121–2
culture, investment in, 44
cybernetic revolution, 46

da Silva, Denise Ferreira, 136, 141
damaged life, 125
Danielsen, Jens, 102, 107
Danowski, Deborah, 4
Dawood, Shezad, 17
  Leviathan (video cycle), 119–23, 131
Day, Gail, 51
De Stijl, 49
decision scenario, the, 23–4
decision theory, 46
decolonization, 98
deconstructive architecture, 70–2
deindustrialization, Italy, 15, 43–59
DeLanda, Manuel, 73–4
Deleuze, Gilles, 72, 77
Delforge, Pierre, 61
DeLoughrey, Elizabeth, 118
DeLoughry, Elizabeth, 109
dependency, on fossil fuels, 26–7
Derrida, Jacques, 70–2, 118
design, 72–3
developmentalism, 91
dialectical criticism, 51
dialectical thinking, indispensability
    of, 67
digital culture, 61–2, 64–5, 65–6
digital farms, 61
Diller, Elizabeth, 74
Diller, Scofidio + Renfro, 74
Direct Sphere of Variable Capital, 57
Dubai, 74
Dutch East India Company, 8

earth systems, 3
eco-apocalypse, 29
ecological catastrophe, 88
ecological economics, 147n7
ecological methodology, 102–3
ecological relation, 16–7
ecological theory, 89
ecological urbanism, 75–6, 76
eco-Marxism, 145–6n1
economic elasticity, 62, 65
economization, 146n3
economy, power of, 30–1
ecosophy, 75–6
ecotourism, 105
Elementarism, 49
Eliasson, Olafur, 17, 106–7
    The Weather Project, 129–32
Emscher Park, 70
ends of the earth, 85–6
energy crisis, 1970s, 15
energy culture, 5
energy deepening, 16, 37, 46, 58, 62–7, 68–9, 75, 76, 139
energy demand, 12
energy futures, 25–31
energy industry, 11
Energy Information Administration, 18
Energy Information Agency, 41
energy infrastructure, 11
energy production, 40
energy supply, growth, 64
energy systems, future scenarios, 22–4
energyscapes
    aesthetic economy, 61–80
    definition, 62–3
    landscape infrastructures, 72–6
    philosophical tradition, 76–80
    postindustrial landscapes, 67–72, **71**
enjambment, 114–6
Enron scandal, 23
environmental humanities, 113–4
environmental risk, 63–4
ethnography, 84, 85–6
Eurocentric colonial frame, 112
exchange value, 38, 138, 139
exploitation, 88
extracted materials, and traded goods, 9
extractive value, 136

Federici, Silvia, 44
feedback loops, 91, 98
feminist materialism, 7
Fiat
    Central Research Fiat, 55
    diversification, 54–5
    guided growth, 43–4
    investment in culture, 44
    layoffs, 55
    postindustrialization, 43–59
    restructuring scheme, 55
Fiat factory, Lingotto, Turin, 43–59
    closure, 55
    design, 48
    history, 47–56
    layoffs, 55
    notoriety, 47–8
    Piano's retrofit, 45, 50, 53–4, 58–9
    social capital, 56–9
    workflow, 49–50
financial abstraction, 11–2
financial system, 11
financial volatility, 41
financialization, 25–6, 30–1, 46, 139, 145n1
Flora, Janna, 110
food sovereignty, 96–7
Fordism, 47–56, 57
forecasting, 32
Foreign Office Architects, 72
fossil capital, 63
fossil fuels
    dependency on, 26–7
    economization, 146n3
fossil-fueled futurity, Greenland, 92
Foucault, M., 118–9, 127
Frampton, Kenneth, 70
Fredericks, Murray, 85
free time, 124
Friedrichs, Jörg, 143–4n1
Frost, Robert, 114–5
Fujairah, 7, 17–8
futures markets, 22–3
futures trading, 25–31
Futurism, 47–56

Gaswirth, Stephanie, 89
Gearheard, Shari Fox, 91
Geological Survey of Denmark and Greenland, 89, 91–2

geontopower, 9
geosocial politics, 132
Ghosh, Amitav, 125, 128
Gissen, David, 72–3
Glanz, James, 61
Glissant, Édouard, 16–7, 99, 112–3, 115, 137
Global Phosphorus Research Institute, 106
global warming, tipping points, 4
globality, 2–3
globalization, 4, 10, 107
governance, 73, 140
Graff, Werner, 49
Gramsci, Antonio, 48
greenhouse gases, 108–9
Greenland
    "At the Moraine' of the Greenland Ice Sheet" project, 90–4
    bottled water industry, 97–8
    decolonization, 140
    discourse of emptiness, 85–6
    ecology, 85
    ethnography, 85–6, 90–4
    food sovereignty, 96–7
    fossil-fueled futurity, 92
    GDP, 90
    hydrological survey, 91–2
    hydropower, **93**, 94, 94–5, 97–8
    industrialization, 95–6, **97**
    mining projects, 96–8, 98
    oil exploration licenses, 94–5
    path dependencies, 98
    petroleum resources, 89–90
    postcolonial condition, 16
    postcoloniality, 90
    sila, 99–101
    sovereignty, 16, 90, 91, 100, 101
    status, 85–6
    traditional economy, 93
    unemployment., 96
Greenland Ice Sheet, 1–2, 4–6, 7, 16, 84, 114, 117
    ablation zone, 86, 99–100
    contrapuntal understanding, 103
    the dead glacier, 105–9
    dimensions, 86
    historical dynamics, 105
    melt, 97, 105–9
    microplastics, 109
    terminal moraine, 17, 89, 97, 106
    UNESCO World Heritage Site, 100
Greenland Minerals and Energy, 96
Greenland Minerals Ltd., 96
Gretner, Jon, 86, 86–7
Gross, Peter, 63
growth, 9, 76
    energy supply, 64
    guided, 43–4
    technological recession, 33
    terminals, 12
growth rates, 36
Guattari, Félix, 75
guided growth

Hallward, Peter, 77
Hayek, Friedrich, 30
heliotropism, 117–34
    aesthetic economy, 119
    and boredom, 123–5
    and the collapse of civilization, 122
    importance of, 117–9
    Leviathan (video cycle), 119–23, 131
    and social crisis, 120
    the solar hollow, 118
    Sunburn, 125–9, 131
    and weather, 128
    The Weather Project, 129–32
Hendriksen, Kåre, 95
historical cost principle, 56
historical dynamics, 105
historicity, 131
Holm, Lene, 91, 92
Holocene, the, 88–9, 136
Home Rule Government of Greenland, 90
Hornby, Louise, 130
Howe, Cymene, 7, 99
human labor, intensification of, 57–8
Hume, Angela, 115
hydropower, **93**, 94, 94–5, 97–8

ice, 16–7
    cultural imaginary, 104–5
    cultural meaning, 110
    ethnography, 90–4
    thinning, 93
ice melt, 16, 86, 91, 97, 100–1, 103, 105–9
Iceberg Alley, 85

IEA, 41, 64
IJmuiden, 8, 10, 12
Ilulissat, 101, 105
immaterial culture, 64
immaterial labor theory, 44
immateriality, 65–6
    information, 61
immaterialization, 51
independence, 13
indigenous epistemes, 92–3
Indirect Sphere of Variable Capital, 57–8
industrialization, 31, 50
inequality, 88
information, immateriality, 61
Information and Communication Technology, energy use, 64
information sources, 15
infrastructure, 130–1
    of accumulation, 62–7
Ingold, Tim, 108, **108**
interdisciplinary thinking, 100, 101–5
Intergovernmental Panel on Climate Change, 5, 6, 18, 21, 41, 103
International Accounting Standards Committee, 56
International Petroleum Council, 29–30
internet, the, 61
Inuit Circumpolar Council, 92
Irigaray, Luce, 91
Italian Communist Party, 48
Italy
    deindustrialization, 15, 43–59
    operaismo, 47
    Progetto 80, 55–6
    valuation protocols in the Civil Code, 56

Jameson, Fredric, 22–3, 37, 51
Jorgenson, Dale, 37
justice, 131

Kahn, Herman, 32
Kangerlussuaq, 1–2
Keynes, John Maynard, 29–30
Khalili, Laleh, 6
Kinkle, Jeff, 62
Kleeman, Jessie, 99, 109–11, 140
knowledge production, 102

Koolhaas, Rem, 70, 72
Krauss, Rosalind, 68
Kupers, Roland, 34

La Berge, Leigh Claire, 26
La Tendenza, 45
Labban, Mazen, 30
labor, 4
labor productivity, 124
labor theory of value, 80
landscape, redefined, 72
landscape infrastructures, 72–6
landscapes
    infrastructures, 72–6
    logistical, 62
    mood across, 122
    philosophical tradition, 76–80
    postindustrial, 62, 67–72, **71**
Larkin, Brian, 141
late liberalism, 88, 123, 127–8, 137
Latour, Bruno, 100, 121
Lazzarato, Maurizio, 145n1
Le Corbusier, 49, 50
LeMenager, Stephanie, 26
Leviathan (video cycle), 131
Levinas, Emmanuel, 91
Levinson, Marc, 27
Libbert, Natascha, 5–6, 6
Life, 127–8
light and shadow, 119
Lingotto, Turin, Fiat factory, 43–59
Little Sun Foundation, 130–1
living oil, 26
Locke, John, 134
logistical landscapes, 62
Luxembourg Gardens, Paris, 107

McCaw, Chris, 17
    Sunburn, 125–9, 131
McGrath, Janet Tamalik, 99
macroeconomic trends, 21
Malabou, Catherine, 66
Malm, Andreas, 63, 147n6
Marder, Michael, 67
Marinetti, F.T., 48, 49
maritime transport enterprise, 6
market media, 15
Marx, Karl, 67, 80, 138
Marxism, 79–80

mass culture, 125
mass market, 125
material dynamics, 21–2
material entanglements, junctures, 2
materialism, 3
materiality, 112
mattering, 136–7
Mattè-Trucco, Giacomo, 48
Mbembe, Achille, 113
media ecology, 13, 16
    architecture, 15–6
mediation, 29
Medovoi, Leerom, 145–6n1
Meillassoux, Quentin, 74, 77
memory, 115
microplastics, 109
Milton, John, 133–5
Mitchell, Timothy, 26, 29–31, 146n3
Mitchell, W.J.T., 72, 74
models and modelling, 104
modernity, 39, 50, 117, 131, 139
    ends of, 14
    inertia, 83–4
MoMA, 69
Moore, Jason W., 22
moraines, 1, 4–5
Mostafavi, Mohsen, 16, 75–6
Mussolini, Benito, 48–9
MVRDV, 72

narratology, 121
NASA IceBridge program, 86
Negri, Antonio, 44
neoliberalism, 39, 40
neoliberalization, 24, 46
Netherlands, the, 135
New Climate Economy Commission, 40
New York Times, 61
Nietzsche, Friedrich, 77
Noël, Brice, 17, 104, 109
nonhuman animals, 118, 120
Nonlife, 127–8
nostalgia, 44
Nourse, Edwin, 30
Nukissiorfiit, 95
Nuttall, Mark, 107–8

object-oriented ontology, 66–7, 77
Odum, Howard, 69

oil embargo, 1973, 27, 32, 36–7, 68–9
oil futures, 25–31
oil prices, 15, 25–6, 27–8, 33, 36–7, 39, 65, 94
Organization for Economic Co-operation and Development, 41
Organization of Arab Petroleum Exporting Countries, oil embargo, 1973, 27, 36–7, 68–9
Osborne, Gillian, 115
other, the, 111–2
overaccumulation, 43–4

Parc de la Villette, Paris, 69–72, **71**
Paris
    Centre Pompidou, 51–2
    COP 21, 102
    Luxembourg Gardens, 107
    Parc de la Villette, 69–72, **71**
    Schlumberger factory, 52–3, 54
passivism, 138
paternalism, 102
path dependencies, 98
pattern recognition, 36
peak phosphorus, 106
Pendakis, Andrew, 65
perception, mode of, 122
Petersen, Emanuel A., 86
petrocultural criticism, 27, 28–9
petrocultural mediation, 15
petrocultural penumbra, the, 29, 41
petrocultural present, the, 13
petroleum industry, 15
philosophical tradition, 76–80
phosphorus, 106–7
photography, 125
Piano, Renzo, 15, 45, 50–4, 58, 58–9
picturesque, the, 124
Pinkus, Karen, 27
planetarity, 2–3, 111, 113
planetary dynamics, 89
planetary flows, 109
plasticity, 8–9, 65–7
    social, 62
pleasure, infrastructuralization of, 131
poetics, of relation, 112–6
political ecology, 11, 13, 21, 22, 100, 137
political economy, 16, 24–5, 37, 79
pop-up factories, 75–6

positivism, 80
post-1973 saturation, 25
post-Fordism, 44
posthumanism, 119
postindustrial architecture, 15, 15–6
postindustrial landscapes, 62, 67–72, **71**
postindustrial market setting, 15
postindustrial petroculture, 25
postindustrialization, 47, 58, 62, 75
post-medium condition, the, 68
postmodernism, 7, 68
Postone, Moishe, 28
Povinelli, Elizabeth, 7, 9, 22, 88, 127–8, 137
privatization, 57
processual character, 2
Progetto 80, 55–6
property, 134

qivittoq, 109–11

Rabinbach, Anson, 147n8
racialization, 136
radical antidesign, 46
RAND Corporation, 32, 35
rationalism, 73
raw material trade balance, 10
reciprocity, 112, 119
    relation of, 111
recursive ecology, 13
regionalism, 51
Reid, Chelsea, 110
Reiser, Jesse, 15–6, 73–4, 74
relation, poetics of, 112–6
relational aesthetics, 129
representation, problem of, 39
Rifkin, Mark, 140
Rijkswaterstaat, 12
risk, environmental, 63–4
rock flour, 1, 106, 143n1
Rogers, Richard, 51–2
Rosing, Minik, 106–7, 143n1
Ross, Andrew, 125
Rossi, Aldo, 73
Rotterdam, 8
Roxburgh, Charles, 22
Royal Dutch Shell, 21, 34–6, 83
    decision scenario, 23–4
    Energy Scenarios to 2050, 40
    scenarios department, 15, 32–8, **35**, 38–41
    scenarios thinking, 23
    social-constructivist account, 39
    theory of political economy, 37
Royal Vopak, 8
Ruffalo, Giorgio, 55

Said, Edward, 16–7, 100–1, 103, 112
salinization, 12
scenarios planning, 83
    anticipation, 24
    background, 21–5
    critique, 38–41
    energy futures, 25–31
    forecasting, 32
    narrative apparatus, 24–5
    Shell, 32–8, **35**, 38–41
Schlumberger factory, Paris, 52–3, 54
Schwartz, Peter, 32
Scott, Felicity D., 69
sea level rise, 12–3
secular stagnation, 27
seeing, politics of, 91
Sejersen, Frank, 96
Sekula, Allan, 6, 10
Sermeq Kujalleq, 105
Serres, Michel, 78
Shane, Grahame, 69–70
shipping industry, 5, 11
shooting the rapids metaphor, 32–3
sila, 99–101
social capital, 56–9
social crisis, and heliotropism, 120
social environment, 123
social form, weather as, 129–32
social plasticity, 62
socialism, 15, 140
sociality, 140
soft spaces, 74
solar hollow, the, 118–9
solar power, 118
sovereignty, 16
spatial modulations, 76
spatio-temporality, 147n6
species loss, 18
speculative realism, 66–7, 77
Spivak, Gayatri, 111, 112
stagflation, 27

Starosielski, Nicole, 63
Statoil, 33
Stavros Niarchos Cultural Center, Athens, 59
Steedman, Ian, 56
Stengers, Isabelle, 78–80
Stern, Nicholas, 40
Stoler, Ann, 104
strategic realism, 28–9
Summers, Larry, 27
Sun, the. *see* heliotropism
sunbathing, 124, 125, 125–9
Superstudio, 45
surplus value, 57
sustainability, 75
Sweezy, Paul, 56
systemic dynamics, 34
Szeman, Imre, 28–9

Tafuri, Manfredo, 45–6, 51
tank storage, 8
techno-fetishists, 33
technological recession, 33
techno-utopianism, 28–9
temperature rise, 109
temporality, 18, 73, 140–1
terminal beach, the, 17–8
terminal form, 8–9
terminal landscapes, 10–1, 13, 83, 117, 131, 138–9, 139–40
    definition, 2
    representations, 6–7
terminals, 2, 6
    growth, 12
    search for, 6–8
    thick of, 5
The Economist, 27
thermodynamic reason, critique of, 79–80
thermodynamics, laws of, 79
thermopolitics, 67
Thomas Fisher Rare Book Library, 133
time, 18, 73, 140–1
tipping points, 4, 5, 18
Toscano, Alberto, 62, 66
trade balance, raw material, 10
trade winds, 113
traded goods, and extracted materials, 9
transcorporeality, 113–4

Tronti, Mario, 44, 57–8
Tschumi, Bernard, 70–2, **71**
Tsing, Anna, 7, 14

Umemoto, Nanako, 15–6, 73–4, 74
unemployment., 96
UNESCO, 105, 135
UNESCO World Heritage Site, 100
unfreedom, 124
United Nations Environmental Program, 9, 9–10
United States of America, 26, 27, 28
universal convertibility, 79
Universitas Project, 69
uranium mining, 96
US Geological Survey, 5, 103

value, 80, 138
value controversy, the, 56
value creation, 47–56, 139
variable capital, 59
Viennese urbanism, 45
Viganò, Paola, 70
Viveiros de Castro, Eduardo, 4

Wack, Pierre, 25, 32–8, **35**, 38–41
Waldheim, Charles, 71–2
war, romanticization of, 48
Warr, Benjamin, 147n7
Watts, Michael, 26
weather, 124, 125, 128
    as social form, 129–32
Weller, Richard, 70
Wenzel, Jennifer, 28, 88
White, Harry Dexter, 29–30
Whitford, Josh, 43
Wilkinson, Angela, 34
wind energy, 118
World Bank, 64
world-building logic, 137
world-systems ecology framework, 22
worldviews, destroying, 34–5
Wynter, Sylvia, 113

Yergin, Daniel, 26
Yusoff, Kathryn, 113, 132

Zone of Uncertainty, 40

Plate 1 Moraine in Kangerlussuaq, Greenland (September 2018). Photo by author.

Plate 2 Hemweg 8 Coal Plant, Amsterdam (November 2018). Photo by author.

Plate 3 Fujairah, UAE. Photo by author.

Plate 4 Greenlandic rare-earth elements. © Kiliii Yuyan. Reproduced with permission of the photographer.

Plate 5 Sermeq Avannarleq, Greenland. Photo by author.

Plate 6 Glacial rock flour, Sermeq Avannarleq, Greenland. Photo by author.

Plate 7 Poodles in the Luxembourg Gardens from Mel Chin's *The Arctic is Paris* (2015).

Plate 8 *Arkhticós Doloros* by Jessie Kleeman 2019. Photo by author.

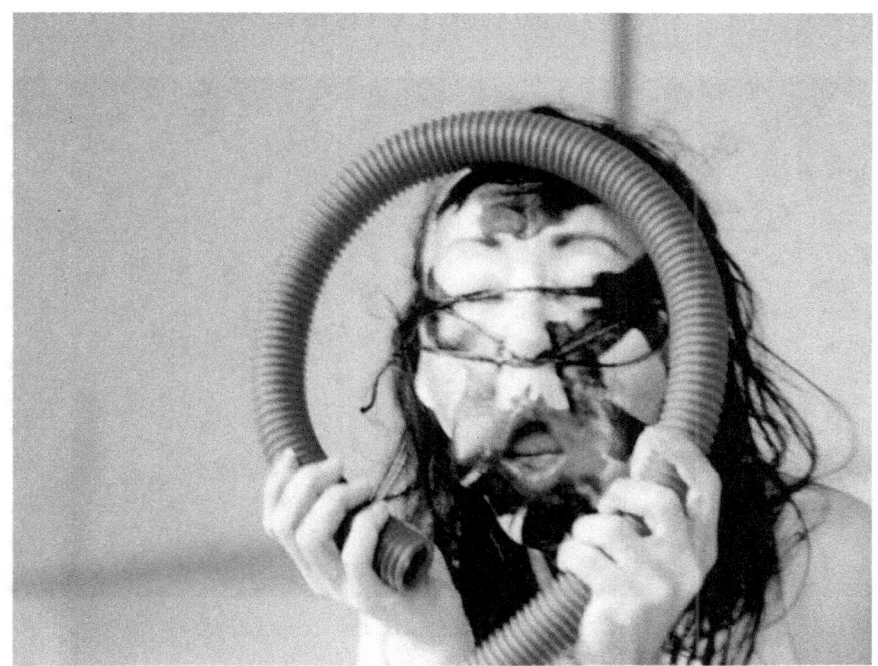

Plate 9 Jessie Kleeman as *Qivittoq*. © Allard Willemse.

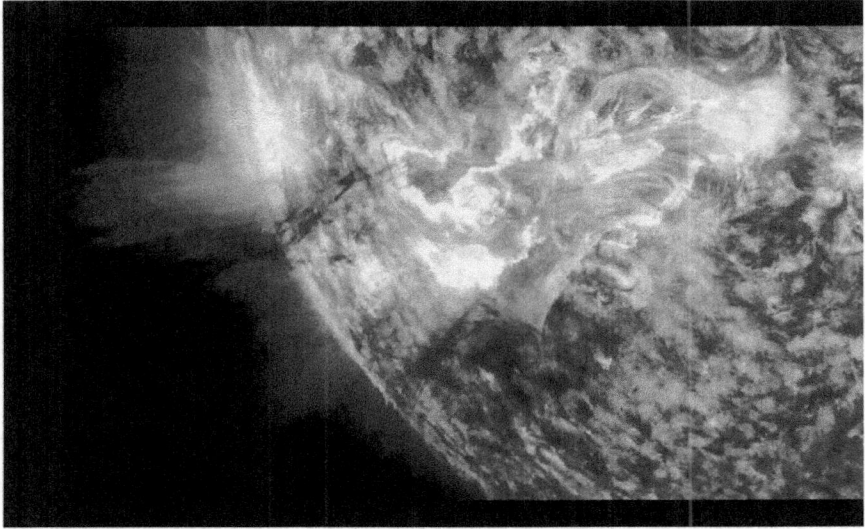

Plate 10 *Leviathan*, "Ben". Shezad Dawood, video installation 2016.

Plate 11 *Leviathan*, "Ben". Shezad Dawood, video installation 2016.

Plate 12 *Leviathan*, "Ben". Shezad Dawood, video installation 2016.

Plate 13 *Leviathan*, "Jamila". Shezad Dawood, video installation 2018.

Plate 14 Chris McCaw, *Sunburn* Gsp #428 (Sunset, Sunrise, Arctic Circle, Alaska). © Chris McCaw.

Plate 15 Olafur Eliasson, *The Weather Project*, 2003. Monofrequency lights, projection foil, haze machines, mirror foil, aluminum, and scaffolding, 26.7 m x 22.3 m x 155.4 m. Installation in Turbine Hall, Tate Modern, London. © Olafur Eliasson 2003.

www.ingramcontent.com/pod-product-compliance
Lightning Source LLC
Chambersburg PA
CBHW061835300426
44115CB00013B/2387